THE CORRECTIONAL OFFICER
INSIDE PRISONS

THE CORRECTIONAL OFFICER INSIDE PRISONS

Steven Herberts

Nova Science Publishers, Inc.

Commack, *New York*

Editorial Production: Susan Boriotti

Office Manager: Annette Hellinger

Graphics: Frank Grucci & John M. T'lustachowski

Information Editor: Tatiana Shohov

Book Production: Patric Davin, Donna Dennis and Tammy Sauter

Circulation: Cathy DeGregory, and Maryanne Schmidt

Library of Congress Cataloging-in-Publication Data

Herberts, Steven,

CORRECTION OFFICER: INSIDE PRISONS, Steven Herberts.

     p.   cm.

Includes bibliographical references.

Originally Published: 6-5. A Different Shade of Blue. New York, Kroshka books

ISBN 1-56072-586-9 (Alk. Paper)

1. Correctional personnel—United States. 2. Prisons—United States. 3. Prisons—United

States —Officials and employees. I. Title

HV9470.H47   1998   98-28662

365'.973—dc21 CIP

Copyright © 1998   by   Steven Herberts

                   Nova Science Publishers, Inc.

                   6080 Jericho Turnpike, Suite 207

                   Commack, New York 11725

                   Tele. 516-499-3103   Fax 516-499-3146

                   E-Mail: Novascience@earthlink.net

                   Web Site: http://www.nexusworld.com/nova

For my wife and partner Michelle and my son, Evan, with love. They know only too well the personal sacrifices made for the Department of Corrections.

CONTENTS

FOREWORD

Concealed behind tons of concrete, bricks and steel lies a truly bizarre world. A world neither known nor understood by most people. This world is called prison.

For Officer Robert Cabral, corrections, at the very least, was a strange calling within the law enforcement field. Unlike the police, whose duties and responsibilities are widely understood by the community they protect, the correction officer is seldom thought of. Both professions share many of the same problems, though the police are forever in the "public eye" keeping their community well-informed of the services they provide. Countless television programs and films, based on real-life police work, have allowed every interested citizen good insight into the experiences of the very romanticized, but often dangerous job, police officers perform. However, the same is not true in regards to the duties performed by a correction officer, who, for many years has contended with poor public relations, unfair media coverage and as in that old adage, the "Out of sight, Out of mind," feeling from the public. How unfortunate, as it is hard earned tax dollars that pay the salaries of the men and women who also provide similar services to the community, which in essence, is public protection.

Although Robby did wear a different shade of blue from that of a police officer, the duties, responsibilities and services provided were more comparable than imagined. Enclosed within the thick walls, Robby walked a distinctively different beat, but the job was no less dangerous, as the same risks to personal safety were taken.

Right from the beginning, each day had been tougher than the one before it. Robby found that the isolated and self-contained society functioning within those walls was often violent and unpredictable, primarily negative and depressing, but always dangerously fascinating. It had been his good fortune to have observed, at first-hand, the complete picture of modern prison life. For the most part, it was an abstract and dreary picture, painted by the most interesting people he had never wished to meet. These real-life characters included every convicted criminal from murderers to child molesters, with both the strong and the weak found within the general population.

Survival was the name of the game and only the strong did survive while the weak were preyed upon in a shark feeding frenzy. It was a place where horrors became reality and reality was continually changing. With the dominant emotions being fear and anger, any and all power was achieved through either deceit or intimidation and force. The good were few, and the bad, more than likely, would become worse. Within this sub-society, a completely unconventional culture was created, forming its own code of morals and values, or lack thereof. The law enforcers of this unique world were preferably referred to as correction officers.

After several years in the business, Robby Cabral was promoted to prison investigator. It was in that capacity, that he, along with the members of the Bravo Team, struggled to maintain order within the concrete jungle. Once he gained a closer look at the criminals, the crimes that convicted them and their place within the prison's pecking order, it was easier to think as they did. From there strong desire for drugs and weapons to their illicit businesses such as prostitution, loansharking and gambling, the games never ended. Robby and his partners encountered every con-artist imaginable, but with the assistance of many informants, they continually penetrated the prison's underworld. Somehow, no matter what the Bravo Team did, Robby found that violence was woven into everything.

Very often, a heinous crime was committed, such as rape or murder, forcing the Bravo Team to step in and sweep up the remains. Robby soon found that for many inmates, there were only two exits out of this world of monsters. There was suicide or escape, and quite often, one road or the other would be taken. Then, every once in a while, Robby would have to take a step back to observe the unbelievable. Completely bizarre incidents to include drug deals and forbidden sex between inmates and staff, along with the liberal programs offered to the inmates and the dangerous trips leading outside the wall.

Through the years, Robby struggled with his doubts about his chosen profession. The constant negativity and brutal effects of the job, brought conflict to his inner-spirit. As Robby searched for the answers, each day, nightmares were becoming reality behind the walls.

However, through all the trials and tribulations, Robby Cabral firmly believed that correction officers were the unsung heroes of the criminal justice system. The days of the unfamiliar "Prison Guard" had passed and a new breed of correction officer has arrived. Robby's only wish was that each person could see life inside those prison walls through his eyes, or the eyes of any correction officer. He knew in his heart that through understanding would come respect. Prison had been a dark and mysterious segment of society for many years, but what had been considered taboo for centuries, Officer Robert Cabral was prepared to reveal in every heart-wrenching detail!

ACKNOWLEDGMENTS

First and foremost, Jesus Christ-my Lord and Savior. With Him...all things are possible.

I would like to thank the following, for without them, this book would not have been a reality:

Nova Science/Kroshka Publishing for believing in the work, then allowing others to tour prison from their own homes.

My wife Michelle-for her endless support and encouragement.

Mom and Dad, my family-for everything.

Barry Michael McKee-for the challenge.

Nelson Julius and Bernard F. Brady-for the opportunity.

Manual 'Sonny' Raposa-for the inspiration.

In no particular order, I also wish to thank:

Lynn Stanton and Lisa Ahaesy, the copy-editors.
Robert M. Letendre and Arthur Leister, the software consultants.
Bob Dube, the cover artist.
Capt.'s Daniel Calis and Vincent Martin, Lt.'s Stephen P. Goldrick and Robert Eklund, Sgt. Robert Couture, C.O.'s Dennis Butler, Karl Anderson, Christopher Shaw, Russ Curran, as well as the remainder of the incredible staff whom I have had the pleasure to work alongside.

For reasons known only to them:

Gary Ouellette and Ken Weiss.

Last, but certainly not least...For any officer who has ever worn the correctional uniform. This book is not only about you, it was written for you!

INTRODUCTION

Many years ago, on death row, when the warden, chaplain and correction officers came for the inmate intended to face his death in the electric chair, a warning would be yelled down the tier. "Number six moving to five, number five moving to four.....with number one heading for the chair." With each inmate moving one step closer to his fate, this coded warning has been passed on through the ages and is still used today. Six moving to five or "six-five" is a general warning to all inmates that an officer has just entered the area, so beware!

"Six-five"...Warning: A correction officer is on site!

❶

The last day of October, set aside for ghouls and goblins, is believed by many to be the night that spirits roam the earth. This night, celebrated by children in costumes who beg treats and play pranks, is actually the eve of All Saint's Day. Ironically enough, on one particular Halloween, two evil spirits had decided to at least roam a rural, residential community after successfully escaping from a local medium security prison.

It was a late Sunday afternoon when the telephone rang twice before the young investigator, Officer Robby Cabral picked up the receiver. On the other end, Robby heard the distinctive voice belonging to his supervisor, a seasoned veteran named Lt. Stephen Redman. Redman, not wasting any time with small talk, explained the recent escape from the sister-institution and the call for mutual aid which had come down from headquarters. Although he did not have the details of the current situation, Lieutenant Redman disclosed, "The two inmates who have flown the coop were both doing life sentences for murder!"

Robby quickly asked, "Who are they?" As Redman named the men, Robby could feel the hair on the back of his neck stand on end. The conversation turned dead silent for a long moment. Robby knew there would be no routine area search, but that an all-out man-hunt would be conducted. Before hanging up the receiver, Lieutenant Redman offered some last words of warning, "Robby, whatever happens, keep in mind that both inmates are considered armed and dangerous. I don't expect either to return without a serious fight!"

Robby had returned home from work less than an hour before, but was back in uniform within five minutes flat. Grabbing his jacket from the hall closet, he kissed his disappointed wife. "Don't worry Babe, I'll be home in no time!" he said. She hugged him tight, knowing it could be hours before his return. This had not been the first emergency call from the prison, but the waiting and worrying never seemed to get any easier. Knowing she would be left alone on the scariest night of the year, she smiled brilliantly, yelling after him "Good luck!" Robby hurried out the door.

Robert had served as a correction officer for eight years. With blond hair, blue eyes and the facial features of a child, it had been difficult from the start. However, his perseverance had been the dominant trait which made him good at his profession. After five long years of working the prison's feared blocks and chaotic recreation rooms, Robby found himself promoted to prison investigator. From that moment on, he was on call twenty four hours a day. Robby investigated everything from prison rapes to brutal assaults and homicides. It seemed that every day, it was always one horrifying thing after another. However, it would be the Halloween escape which would make him take a step back in order to get a good look at his life. Unfortunately, Robby Cabral wouldn't like what he would see.

The ride back to the prison complex was driven at break-neck speed. As always, Robby was thinking of a thousand and one situations which he might encounter within the dark hours to follow. He arrived earlier than he had expected.

After drawing a set of handcuffs and a multi-channel portable radio from his own institution, Robby reported directly to the scene of the escape. His first thought was, "What organized chaos," as security staff rushed from one area to the next without accomplishing very much. The brand-new institution had not yet experienced a major escape since its opening, so a little confusion and finger pointing was to be expected. He took a brief glance at the crime scene from which the escapees had fled. There appeared to be a towel and one glove lying between two perimeter fences known as the 'Dead Man Zone.' Keeping this in mind, Robby curiously entered the prison in search of Lieutenant Redman.

Upon meeting with his supervisor, Robby was assigned to interview various inmates residing in the same block, or housing unit where the two escaped felons had so recently lived.

One hour had passed and at least fifteen inmates, the majority of them lifers, had been interviewed. The results were disappointing. It was becoming quite clear to Robby that the two inmates were either feared by many, or confided in no one. More than likely, it was a combination of the two. He began with exceptionally vague questioning during the interviews, so as not to give out more information than he was receiving. As the interviews progressed, the general frustration of getting nowhere had set in and the method of questioning had become more abrasive and abrupt. It led to the same results, "I don't know anything. I keep to myself." It was all bullshit. Robby thought, "No inmate completely keeps to himself in prison. He is at least aware of his surroundings and of what others are doing. It happens to be a survival technique which every inmate learns early."

Upon completing the interviews of all inmate's residing in that unique lifer's block, a meeting was called in order to compile all the information which had been gathered by officers involved in the escape investigation. Although the interviews had proven fruitless so far, other pieces to the puzzle were starting to fit together nicely.

It appeared that the escape, though seemingly quite daring, had been meticulously thought out and planned for some time. Intelligence data revealed that both inmates had been training for their autumn getaway for several years. The two, belonging to the runner's club, had run marathons in excess of twenty-five miles, in order to shed large amounts of weight. Both held jobs within the institution which enabled them access into areas other inmates were not allowed. Even with prior escapes on record, unsuspecting staff considered them cooperative and almost "trusted" inmates.

The lifer's block, which they called home, faced the front of the prison. From their own cells, they were easily able to monitor the general traffic and pedestrian flow from day-to-day. Also from that viewpoint, they could monitor staff response each time a 10-33, or emergency was called. It was a simple matter of counting how many officers ran to which location, from what location, the amount of time it took for the response, etc.. Located just outside their housing unit was a small grassy yard. It was left bare, with the exception of a couple of picnic-style benches. This yard was enclosed behind an eight foot brick wall, topped with razor wire.

The scheming inmates knew there would be a skeleton crew to work Halloween, a Sunday, and with no office personnel walking in and out of the front entrance, their timing would have to be perfect.

Earlier in the day there had been two fights in the main yard. The first involved two white inmates, previously known to be friends. They were found rolling around on the ground. As neither combatant was throwing any real punches or kicks, the fight was easily broken up with a stern verbal command from a responding officer. Neither sustained any injuries, which left several officers suspicious of the reason for the strange conflict. This small altercation, which required full emergency response, had definitely disrupted the normal running of the institution for better than fifteen minutes. It was enough time to distract everyone's attention away from the lifer's block. Hence, the diversion. It was later discovered that one of these combatants had been out walking in the yard with one of the escapees earlier that same morning.

The second altercation, which occurred only a half-hour after the first, involved fifteen to twenty black inmates. They had viciously "beat down" three white inmates. Due to the size of the altercation, the fact that a weapon (rock) was used, and the injuries sustained by the whites had proven quite extensive, this incident was deemed a major disturbance. A major lock-down was ordered. Once locked-down, a count was conducted and much to the surprise of the count officer, two murderers were unaccounted for. There had been an escape.

Both escapees had been well-aware that during the emergency, the block officer was required to forfeit his keys to the corridor officer. He would then respond to the fight which was now happening halfway across the prison. While the first fight transpired, the two inmates were left unsupervised inside that small, grassy yard. There were only three obstacles between them and freedom. There was the inside brick wall, then a quick dash to the two perimeter fences. Each fence was approximately eighteen feet high, topped with coiled razor wire and non-climbable mesh. Apparently, they had planned on a one hour head-start before anyone noticed their absence. The second fight, a spontaneous brawl, had cut that time in half.

Robby, along with other investigators, determined that one of the picnic benches had been propped up the long way against the eight foot brick wall. Therefore, the first obstacle was easily cleared. From there, it was a fast sprint to the innermost fence where they shimmied up to the top. Using a steel hook fashioned from a foot-locker handle, and later left at the scene, they pulled down the non-climbable mesh and pushed the razor wire aside just enough to get past it. Once again, good luck was to be theirs, because the tower officer located just to their left, had never turned toward their direction. Had he done that, he may have seen some movement along the fence line. Though, his vantage point was at best, fair. Over the first fence, they jumped into the 'Dead Man's Zone' where microwave motion detectors should have also ended their journey, but did not. As they knew, through previous surveillance, those detectors were only being turned on at night. Due to the heavy pedestrian traffic during the day, they were continually activated causing frequent interruptions and full emergency responses each time. Considered a disruptive security problem and losing their intents and purposes for being there, the administration opted to utilize the system only during the dark hours. Though this was rational and completely understandable reasoning, it afforded the men the luxury of avoiding a barrier which undoubtedly would have stopped them dead in their tracks.

Also left at the scene were a pair of padded gloves covered in blood indicating that one of the men had cut himself on the razor wire. The two felons maneuvered over the second fence as they had the first, only this time one of them got hooked up. This appeared to be their only hitch, then it was one easy jump into freedom. The bloody gloves were found lying alongside a towel which had also been used to brush the razor wire aside. It was figured that the entire escape, from start to finish, lasted no more than 10 minutes before both killers vanished into a nearby wooded area.

Through an anonymous telephone call, there was additional information that money had been dropped off for them in a nearby parking lot. The caller also claimed that they had followed a nearby power line directly out of the area. Neither claim could be confirmed.

What was known, was that it was late October and nightfall was now becoming an enormous factor. There was a serious and valid concern for the safety of the neighborhood children because it was Halloween. In a few short hours, those kids would be walking house-to-house collecting candy. Also, anyone found in disguise on this night would not draw very much attention to themselves. Last, but just as important, the weather was turning miserably cold and wet. It was another advantage for the escaped felons, who were, no doubt, running like the wind.

Robby soon found himself teamed up with his 'road-dog' friend and partner, Officer Keith Petrie. Keith was a street-smart officer with more than four years experience as an investigator. Standing 6'2" and weighing 240 lbs., he was slightly larger than Robby. With dark hair and eyes, Keith continually boasted about his Italian blood-line. He claimed that it was the reason for his mean-streak. The inmates believed it, but Robby knew that his friend was anything but mean. Keith was just a serious guy who could never find the humor in the things that Robby did. Understandably so, as Robby searched for humor in everything.

Keith had also assisted in interviewing some of the murderers and rapists who had lived with the two escapees. Unfortunately, he proved to be just as successful in getting answers. In any case, the partners now found themselves preparing for a more dangerous mission. An assignment that would take them into the wee hours of the next morning.

Firearms were issued and the two officers were stuffed into the rear compartment of an old beat-up station wagon. The tired vehicle barely transported them to a strategic location referred to as an escape post. Throughout the ride, other officers were dropped off to relieve their fellow officers who had been on site since the escape had been declared. Everyone inside the cramped vehicle kept repeating the same things, "What a perfect night for an escape," and "I hope those assholes don't fuck with any of the kids." Finally, the old wagon reached its outermost destination, post #33, assigned to Cabral and Petrie. Post #33 was known as "the boonies." Upon exiting the vehicle, both men stood back in awe, as the officers they relieved literally dove into the wagon, in search of heat. As the vehicle raced back to the prison, Robby and Keith looked at each other and laughed. They knew it would be a long night. It was then that the steam whistle, which was located at the power plant, let out an echoing shriek. Its intent was to warn area residents that a recent "break out" had occurred. This haunting sound, heard every half-hour, was figuratively loud enough to wake the dead.

Post #33, an observation and listening out-post, resembled an old dumping ground. There were truck tires and wooden planks strewn about. Once comfortably in place, the partners conducted a check of the entire area surrounding the post. Led in a circular fashion, the terrain consisted of heavily wooded areas to the right side and rear, with open fields to the left and front. Everything seemed normal and quiet, appearing as though no other people had been through the area for years. To Robby, the mission felt more like a military operation than any correctional duty. Issued equipment included communications and firearms. After insuring that all was in working order, both men sat back-to-back and listened to the silence for awhile. Sitting quietly would satisfy many state employees, however, there was a tension in that cold air, as there should have been. Any good officer knows that getting too comfortable, when at any moment the absolute worst could happen, is beyond stupid. It could prove fatal. There were two known murderers on the loose, possibly camped out near post #33. It was essential to stay alert to keep the senses keen.

Whispering, Robby and Keith talked about how each would react if faced with contact of the known murderers. Perhaps just to alleviate their fear in anticipation of such contact, both pledged they would presume the escapees were armed. They would shoot first, not allowing the felons any chance to shoot them. Going over their game plan, they talked in detail about potentials they may be forced to face. Then, it was time to rest again. The weather was getting colder and what had been a slight mist was turning into a heavier drizzle.

It was certainly not the best of scenes to choose for the filming of any coffee commercials, but during trying times such as this one, officers developed closer friendships and tightly bonded through the hardship.

With enough food and water to last a week in the woods, the only items they wished for were wet weather gear. Sometimes wishes do come true. Found buried inside an escape post bag was a poncho large enough to fit a medium size Girl Scout. Robby joked that the garment was probably donated from that same organization. With the drizzle turning to rain, Robby and Keith, still in good spirits, draped the plastic protector over both their heads. Despite the humor within this picture, both officers, too large to be completely covered from the rain, decided it was time to take more drastic measures. Like two possessed soldiers, the truck tires were stacked, so that the wooden planks could be laid across the top. Once this was done, Robby leaned more planks across the back. Then, the poncho was spread across the ground to create a dry floor. Within minutes, Robby and Keith had their own 'hooch' or shelter. Though they were somewhat wet, this improvised shelter made the remainder of that unusual night more bearable. Cold was livable, even acceptable, but the key was to stay dry.

Taking turns on watch, they continued to talk quietly, which not only passed the time, but kept both men awake and alive. At first, the conversation was mainly about the escape. They agreed the staff had done a good job within the prison, as well as out on patrols, posts, etc.. Several problems were evident, such as the picnic benches being left inside the yard and the motion detectors being shut off. However, these were easily remedied and probably already had been. The staff could not be blamed. The block officer and the tower officer both did their jobs. Robby grumbled, "The real shame is that the department's public relations people, who have probably never even worked behind prison walls, will release some generic, vague press release. Of course, it will explain nothing about the escape. The community, who are enraged because two more nuts are on the loose, will not understand how it happened. Inevitably, they will think the prison staff was not doing its jobs. Perhaps, we even opened the front door, allowing these murderers to leave. Unfortunately, where there are prisons, there are escapes. They go hand in hand!"

Occasionally, the conversation was interrupted with miscellaneous radio transmissions such as, "There's been a spotting on main street," followed by a short wait to find this claim unconfirmed. Another was a public announcement, "Keep your children indoors, Halloween has been postponed." This warning was taken lightly by many parents who allowed their children to continue trick-or-treating. Robby and Keith covered many topics of conversation on that rainy night, from personal prison experiences to plain, old gossip. At one point, Robby half-heartedly stated, "Someone should really write a book about this insane business we work in!" Keith shook his head, as Robby laughed at his friend's serious facial expressions. Then, the quiet night was again interrupted by that old steam whistle.

On two separate occasions, post #33 was approached by unidentified people. Immediately, the partners halted the silhouettes and ordered them to identify themselves. The moving shadows had both been officers on foot patrols. With adrenaline shooting hard through their veins, Robby and Keith re-holstered their weapons and continued talking as though they were unaffected. Both men had felt fear.

The major man-hunt lasted right into the following day. Hundreds of correctional personnel, including a multitude of K-9 units, local and state police had all been incredibly thorough. No stone was left unturned. Even the tactical response team, a riot squad, was sent knee-deep into a swamp where they probed the area with large sticks. Sparing no expense, the search resulted in negative findings and was finally called off.

Six hours into the watching, listening and waiting, Robby and Keith were looking forward to ending the mission. The novelty of the make-shift shelter had worn off. Indeed, their intentions had been good, but both men were left soaked to the bone and cold beyond explanation. Dry clothes and hot coffee were now a priority. That old wagon finally returned and the hooch was quickly destroyed. This time the cramped interior of the vehicle did not seem so bad. On the ride back, the officers shared a solemn mood. Each knew the mission was not complete. There were still two murderers on the run. Each one very capable of harming others who might get in their way. Eventually, most got caught, but that thought did not make anyone involved in the search feel any better. Breaking the thick silence, the driver asked, "How in the hell did we ever end up in this business? It's always something!" That innocent statement left each man gazing deeper into himself. Each officer contemplating exactly what being a correction officer meant to him personally. The silence droned on.

Robby and Keith were eventually dropped off at their own vehicles. Keith said, "See you back here in a few hours," then thought to himself for a second, adding "they'll get 'em." Perhaps the older officer was attempting to convince his less experienced partner that it wasn't over yet. Then again, maybe Keith was merely attempting to convince himself. Both friends said their good-bye's, then headed home for a few hours of restless sleep. As Robby drove past the power plant, the steam whistle let out one last faint warning. Somehow it had lost its haunting meaning in the long hours which had passed.

The search, however, did continue on a more investigative level:

As fate would have it, both escaped felons were captured barely forty miles north of the prison from which they had fled, almost three weeks earlier. When apprehended, there were two handguns found in their possession, along with ski-masks. It was strongly believed that the fugitives were preparing to "pull-off" an armored car heist in the very near future.

The media, in its infinite wisdom, credited the entire investigation, resulting in the capture of the two fugitives to the local and state police. Although these departments had assisted tremendously, the Department of Correction Fugitive Apprehension Team was not acknowledged. Yet, these were the key people who had located the escapees through an intense investigation. The efforts put forth by this team successfully landed both fugitives into maximum security before the November's end.

Robby and Keith had agreed that no other inmate could successfully escape from the same area the two murderers had. Hard lessons had been learned. Nevertheless, there would be more escapes from that institution, as there would be from hundreds of prisons nationwide. Escapes were one of the most misunderstood elements of the prison business. With thousands of inmates incarcerated within various facilities, one thing those prisoners did possess was time. Hours upon hours were spent studying ways and conspiring plans of gaining access to the outside world. There would always be the ingenuity and perseverance to gain freedom on behalf of the inmates, human errors made by prison staff, structure breaches, flaws in technological security systems and so on. Robby had snickered, "Yes, there will be others. It should be expected. It may very well be one unavoidable element in this business of housing convicted felons... for the time being, anyway!"

❷

For weeks after the escape, Robby Cabral tossed and turned each night. The same haunting question kept repeating in his mind. It was the question which had been innocently asked on that dismal, rainy night. "How in the hell did we ever end up in this business, corrections?" Night after night, Robby found himself leaving the warmth of his bed to sit in the darkness of the living room. Lighting one cigarette after another, he would stare off in deep thought. With the small orange glow of the cigarette being the only light in the house, Robby started to remember his earliest prison experiences. Right from the beginning, working behind the giant prison walls was tough. For one reason or another, after eight years, it never seemed to get any easier.

Most children do not grow up as aspiring young correction officers, but wish to become cowboys, astronauts, or cops. If the former were true, those same children should probably be considered a tad bit sadistic and in dire need of psychiatric help. Though Robby had the same dreams as most normal children, his life was destined to take a rough detour. It wasn't something that he wanted. It was something that just happened. Corrections was definitely a strange calling, perhaps more of an indirect calling. Either way, Robby had heard the call loud and clear.

Robby, like so many other correction officers, desired a career in law enforcement. His first choice was police work for two reasons: That honorable call to serve his public and the respect and prestige that the job carried. At 18-years-old, he was appointed a part-time position on his town's police department. It was an incredible start. He was working details on the weekends while attending college full-time. With his new partner, Mike Ferreira, he was working cruiser shifts whenever possible. Life was right on schedule. Unfortunately, the competitiveness was intense. In the criminal justice field, Robby learned that experience was valued much greater than academics. So, when the strange opportunity arose in the department of correction, he jumped on it. Robby Cabral swore an oath to maintain care and custody of the state's incarcerated felons. It was merely a "stepping stone." Little did he know that the step would become a platform from which there was no escape. Months after joining the ranks, or brotherhood of correction officers, town politics had severely burned his bridge to the police department. With the exception of his cynical partner, Mike Ferreira, everyone said he was lucky. There were thousands waiting for a shot at corrections. The money and benefits were fabulous. However, Robby never felt fortunate. Instead, he understood that he was locked behind bars for eight hours a day. At a very early age, Robby understood that freedom was priceless, even if only for eight hours a day.

Robby Cabral's career had started differently than most others. Obviously, choosing a job concealed behind tons of concrete, bricks and steel, his family and friends could never witness the hardships he would face. His attitude and personality would gradually change. It was inevitable and necessary for survival.

There were only two ways of getting into prison work, depending on what type of work one was looking for. One was to rob a bank or commit a different felony. The other was to fill out an application and take the civil service exam. Though it was somewhat more competitive due to the absurd lack of employment available within the community, Robby passed the written exam and got his interview right away. The interview involved a small panel of senior staff who asked ethical and moral questions. It was their method of getting a glimpse into each applicant's character.

Robby nervously sat before four rigid men and one pouting woman. They barked out questions at him while never patiently waiting for his response. A gray haired Captain asked, "If you were riding to work in a car pool with your partner, who is your best friend, and he started smoking a marijuana cigarette, how would you react? What would you do?" Robby could feel beads of sweat form on his brow. The question was difficult, but he knew that staff and inmate safety had to be considered first. With confidence, he replied, "I would do everything in my power to stop him from entering the institution. If all else failed, I would inform my immediate supervisor. The man would be a potential danger to himself and all others around him!" The older man shook his head, but said nothing. Robby was sure that he had given the answer they wanted. Re-thinking the question, he wasn't so sure how he really would react to that situation. He hoped that he never got the chance. With little time to think, he was bombarded with one hypothetical question after another. They were mostly focused on emergency and stressful situations an officer may encounter during a tour of duty. Each response given was weighed carefully.

In the meantime, there were assigned security staff who were conducting a thorough investigation into Robby's background. There were random interviews of character references and so on. Robby passed with ease and was placed on a list of names to be drafted. Every applicant was more or less drafted by the institution most impressed with him, or her. Some preferred employment at a specific institution, but Robby didn't care where he ended up. He figured that they all had to be the same inside. Besides, he just wanted to climb aboard as soon as possible.

Once the hiring board determined enough applicants had been accepted for employment, they were handed over to the department's training academy. Robby Cabral was at the top of that list.

The academy had realized that there was always a small percentage of trainees who completed the requirements of training and graduated, only to quit within the first few months of service. Due to this fact, the academy required tours of various institutions. Different security levels were viewed making it possible to observe actual prison life. In the past, the turnover rates were considered acceptable. The profession was not meant for everyone. However, the tours had cut those numbers down. Touring different prison settings allowed each recruit a close-up look at the harsh realities inside, while enabling them to refuse the job with dignity. This saved the department money used to train them. Those that chose not to accept the job were never condemned or ridiculed. The first time anyone entered a prison, it was usually a terrifying experience. Robby and 35 other recruits boarded the bus, destined for the ride of their lives. It was a lesson in fear.

Within two long days, they were exposed to various security levels and unique types of institutions. It was mandated for a better understanding of the correctional profession. Each prison visited was a new experience in horror. Like most others, with every stop, Robby's doubts grew immensely.

The very first stop was the high maximum security or supermax, which was a newly built physical plant designed and staffed to prevent escapes and the introduction of contraband. Single cell occupancy and physical barriers prevented physical contact between inmates, between inmates and visitors and to rigidly control physical interaction between inmates and staff. In that environment, inmates were only allowed out of their cells individually. They were moved from area-to-area in restraints. Supervision was constant, as any inmate mandated by the department to serve time at this security level had demonstrated the need for total external control. Such inmates either had prior escape attempts from secure settings or were found in possession of sophisticated escape paraphernalia. Also, any inmate who had demonstrated assaultive behavior in the past was considered to be a danger. They were not allowed to physically interact with staff or other inmates who were housed there.

Bottom line, they were the worst of the worst, the incorrigible. In that very isolated environment, any human contact was cherished by the residents. Privileges to include personal property were few, while phone calls and visits were earned through good behavior. Again, supervision was intense, as this was deemed the last stop or the end of the line. The human spirit was definitely challenged there.

The next level down was maximum security or the 'Hill,' having the same perimeter as high maximum. In that environment, inmate movement and interaction was controlled by physical barriers. Inmates there were subject to direct supervision by staff at all times and could only leave the perimeter in full restraints. They had also demonstrated a need for constant supervision based on assaultive behavior, including use and/or introduction of contraband. Escapes or attempted escapes from lower security were considered, as was the refusal or inability to abide by the rules and regulations at a lower security facility.

That institution, with its giant concrete walls and shadowing gun towers, was incredibly intimidating inside. The inmates were housed in blocks, with three tiers reaching the ceiling of each unit. The population included many of the state's cruelest and most feared criminals serving multiple life sentences. This facility had two segregation units for the noncompliant, where it was not uncommon for an officer to have urine or feces thrown at him. The history of the institution was also astounding. It included riots, hostage situations, murders, rapes and so on. Due to the type of prisoners housed there, that environment was considered the most tense in the state. Though some maximum security institutions contained a 'Death House,' or chamber which held their state's electric chair, the Death House at the Hill was sealed off by concrete, as the death penalty had been abolished.

Lowering to the next level, medium security consisted of six very different institutions. Medium security was intended for inmates who had displayed the ability to abide by rules and regulations, while successfully interacting with others. There was no need for physical barriers, with the exception of emergencies, as inmate movement and interaction was generally controlled by rules and regulations. Supervision by staff was intermittent. However, any inmate leaving the perimeter would do so in restraints. These facilities had a similar perimeter as the maximum level due to the need for control and segregation from the community.

Scattered throughout the state, these facilities were each unique in their physical appearances, inmate populations and standard operating procedures. From the newest medium facility in the department with all its modern security technology, to an antiquated structure built in the late 1800's, each possessed its own character. Within this group was the Initial Classification Center for male inmates which also specialized in a protective custody program. There was also a facility exclusively for female inmates. Although the smallest medium security institution, it was considered no easy task to work there. Officers experienced the same problems regarding fights, drugs, etc. Depending on the institution, internally, there were those that housed its inmates in blocks, with tiers of single cells.

Others resided in housing units that resembled cottages, with shared rooms within, while still many offered dormitory or barracks-style settings. In any case, they were all overcrowded and understaffed.

Going further down the security ladder there were minimum security, pre-release centers, half-way houses, contract facilities, detox. centers and so on. As there was a decrease in security, so had the supervision decreased. Many of those facilities could have been easily mistaken for college campuses or camp ground sites. At those levels, inmates were preparing to reintegrate into society or were already functioning back within the community. It was hoped that the programs and treatment had helped to rehabilitate the convicted felon, preventing him from becoming a recidivist (a person who returned to prison).

There were three other unequaled facilities which Robby vividly remembered visiting. Each served a very different purpose.

There was the state hospital, or the "Bug House," housing the criminally insane. A bizarre environment because of the irrational and unpredictable behavior of the patients (not considered inmates), secured within. Probably the most difficult of environments to have worked in, many of the patients were aggressively assaultive, though never held accountable for their actions. With hundreds of officers seriously injured each year, that facility was run more like a hospital than a prison. It was alarming enough to visit for one hour, let alone forty per week. Some patients were locked behind plexi-glass walls, while others pranced about. Anything and everything was possible there. It was a world filled with heavily medicated manic-depressants, psychopaths and sociopaths. There were suicidal and violent patients who were capable of making an officer laugh uncontrollably, yet equally capable of putting him into retirement within the blink of an eye.

Then, there was the famed Treatment Center, built strictly to house the sexually dangerous. Within those walls were hundreds of men who had been deemed "not fit for society." A fairly quiet institution in comparison to others, their problems included homosexual rapes, sexual assaults and the like. Not so long ago, a practiced treatment for those sexual deviants included consensual homosexual relations while incarcerated. Intended to alleviate sexual frustrations, fortunately, this treatment had since been abandoned. That modern facility housed some of the sickest men alive who had been convicted of absolutely heinous crimes. Yet, those inmates went about their daily routines, as though they had never victimized children or the elderly, human lives they had ruined as a result.

The last stop on the tour bus was the department's pride and joy, the boot camp. It was an environment similar to that of the U.S. Army's basic training camps. The officers were trained and worked in the capacity of drill instructors, introducing non-violent, first-time offenders to discipline, self-esteem and a positive attitude. Though the program was still fairly new to the department, it was believed to have had made the difference in the lives of the inmates who had graduated from it. It was a different twist in the business of corrections. Unlike any other institution, the inmates there called each officer "Sir," while shining their own boots and completing assigned work duties around the camp. A rigid, but positive environment which was actually correcting the lives of those who were not yet beyond help.

As the bus sat idle in the parking lots of those facilities, it became easy to see how each was unique in its outside appearance. From the state hospital, for the criminally insane to the huge, intimidating walls of the maximum security prison, one look at those buildings made many recruits feel apprehensive, while others seriously started to have second thoughts.

The first time Robby had ever entered one of the facilities, he found it to be a disturbing and time-consuming project in itself. Each person entering was positively identified, then signed themselves in. At that point, a steel door automatically slid open, slamming shut behind the last person in. Every recruit was then located inside a trap or 'sally-port,' with steel doors to the front and rear. Nobody went anywhere without the officer's approval, located inside the outer control center. This officer was protected by bullet proof glass. It was that person who controlled movement in and out of the prison, by opening or closing the sally port doors. Inside the trap, the search for staff was conducted. Some recruits being searched had to empty the contents of their pockets. Others either walked through a metal detector or actually submitted to being pat searched by the trap officer. Robby had been one of the few who experienced the pat search. The search was uncomfortable for him, even humiliating for others, but done for good reason. It was to insure no contraband such as weapons, drugs, handcuff keys, etc., entered the institution, a safety precaution for every person inside that prison. Once the officer inside the trap was satisfied that all people entering were "clean," he signaled to the control center officer to open the second steel door leading straight into the court yard of the prison. Hearing that second door slam shut triggered certain normal emotions within everyone. Robby felt an incredible feeling of anxiousness while a knot seemed to form in the pit of his stomach. He realized for the first time, he was locked inside of a prison with hundreds of criminals, doing time for everything from killing cops to passing bad checks. The only way out was the same way he just entered, controlled by someone other than himself. What was felt was fear, a fear of the unknown. An emotion both understandable and expected, though it had to be masked from the inmates. He looked at the others and from their faces, he knew he was not alone. Though, he also knew it was acting time. It was time to put on the game face.

As the tour progressed, many of the inmates put on a show like no other. There were cat-calls, obscenities and frequent threats screamed directly at the new recruits. Those threats included anything that might induce fear or panic. This was an acceptable practice as seen by the other staff because it was like a test, or the start of a variety of tests. On two occasions, the yelling inmates had succeeded, as two recruits quit on the spot. They wanted out. Robby felt bad for them, but it was better to weed those people out early for their own sake, as well as the sake of the other staff.

Those initial tours were important in deciding whether or not a person felt cut out for the job. The recruits had to trust their instincts, as the information known about working in a prison was limited. Some would see past the fear, which would of course, be felt more than once if a career in corrections was chosen. In fact, Robby had sensed the adventure, the challenge of working in an environment where just about anything could happen at any time and without notice. No doubt, he was still young and impressionable.

Without question, no one could blame anyone for not wanting to work in a prison. After each recruit surveyed the daily operation of the prison, the living and working conditions, and most importantly, the diversified clientele inside, it was decision time. Most had decided to stay to be physically and academically challenged by the department's training academy. However, the last steps before beginning seven intense weeks of training were that an oath had to be taken and several related documents signed. It was then that Robby and the others had officially become employees of the department of correction. However, they could not hold the title of correction officer until they passed all of the mandatory training. Of course, there were always those who would never graduate.

The training began:

Corrections, being sort of a para-military organization with its ranking system, uniforms, etc., ran its training academy the same as most military basic training, or boot camps. The biggest difference was that correctional training was toned down a bit, as there was limited time to accomplish all training objectives.

Arriving in the parking lot earlier than necessary, Trainee Cabral read his instructions to report to some unknown area with several specific items in hand. These items included a gray sweat suit, gym bag, one note book and two pens (black ink). Nervously hurrying to the designated area, all of the fresh trainees attempted to line themselves up in some orderly fashion, with hopes of making the first day easier on themselves. Each had come to the academy carrying horror stories which had been passed on by previous graduates. Robby, who had prior military training in the Army's Military Police Corps., had abandoned his college career to gain experience within the department. He was determined to make the difficult decision worthwhile. Though, he was not looking forward to the head games that the drill instructors were sure to play in the weeks ahead. Also, being slightly overweight, he was reluctant to start exercising prior to attending the academy in order to shed those excess pounds. He was regretting his procrastination. Robby had been through this bullshit before, but it was not something anyone could get used to, nor would want to for that matter.

Expecting to start the morning at the time indicated on the schedule, the trainees were anxious. There was no training Cadre or staff there to meet the group, designated Class #141. As a matter of fact, it was now fifteen minutes past the hour the training was to begin. The trainees were beginning to mull about, talking quietly and introducing themselves to each other, curious about who would be working at which prison. Robby soon found that he would be training with four men and one woman who had been hired by his institution. He considered this a good start. There was trainee Donovan, the strong, silent type who also had prior military experience as an M.P. There was Olivier, just out of high school and relatively naive. Then there was Letendre, with a suspicious look about him and the distinctive accent of an inner-city kid. Trainees Johnson and Holt, both big guys, stood together just listening to the rest of the group, as did the female, Souza, who appeared small, but determined. As the group talked in whispers, one guy, standing in another huddle, lit a cigarette. This made him either extremely brave or really stupid. It seemed just at that moment when the nervous anticipation was becoming a little more comfortable, the air exploded with ear-piercing screams from drill instructors who were closing in on all sides. It was instantly clear that they had been closely watching the group. The trainees who had lined themselves up just minutes earlier were now standing in one mass glob, talking, laughing and even smoking. All hell broke loose.

At first, it seemed as if there were at least 10 of them, all sharply dressed in their starched uniforms, spit-shined boots and topped with those dreaded 'Smokey' hats. As time elapsed, Robby counted only four. He thought, "Damn, can they make some noise!" The screaming lasted better than an hour, but sure felt like longer. Each D.I. came nose-to-nose with every single trainee, spitting insults, while commenting and laughing at everyone's sloppy physical appearance. They were really pushing some buttons, trying to anger any trainee enough to solicit a response, which would display a lack of discipline in the trainee. The trainee would then be instantly removed from the program. Everyone kept their cool, some a little frightened from this type of rash, confronting harassment. Most had never encountered such radical instructions before and were visibly shaken at the start. There were only three females in a class of almost forty, however they received no slack whatsoever.

The big guy with the cigarette, Trainee Kirby, turned out to be just as Robby had expected, more stupid than brave. He was allowed to finish smoking the butt, while the remainder of the class was ordered into the front leaning rest position, or push-up position, without moving. The bastard seemed to be enjoying every drag, as he took his own sweet time. The drill instructors enjoyed this too because once the idiot had finished, all trainees were called to attention, only to stand and watch each D.I. go up one side of Kirby, then down the other, reaching decibels not known possible. At one point, the big baby, used as a guinea pig or training tool, looked as if he were ready for tears. Robby had to hold back a chuckle. It was obvious that Class #141 had just learned its first lesson.

The senior drill instructor, a black lieutenant who was tall, lean and apparently in very good physical condition, began to speak to the group in a monotoned, but authoritative voice. He introduced himself as Lt. Miles and stated that he did not care to know the identity of any of the trainees, as they were not worth his time at that point. He then ordered each trainee to double-time it (run hard) to the building located right in front of him. The games had just begun. There were three buildings located in front of him. Which did he mean? Did it matter? It was all a part of the head games. Of course, when he yelled to double-time it, there was mass confusion, with trainees ending up inside of all three buildings. In no time, each trainee was verbally flushed from the buildings and the screaming and push-ups started again. "Failure to follow directions will always cost you, both here and at your respective institutions," Lieutenant Miles would yell, although he knew his directions were so vague that nobody ever knew exactly what he meant, nor did they dare ask.

This type of fun lasted for the first week while the drill instructors laughed amongst themselves when they were sure nobody was looking. The job they needed to do was performed professionally and with great zeal. It was apparent that every word said, every action taken was for good reason and served some higher purpose. Within the first four days, the intimidation and intentional harassment had caused another two recruits to quit. This was probably in the best interests of everyone concerned, as both "flunkies" had demonstrated negative attitudes and may have not been there when another officer truly needed help. It was good-bye and good riddance.

That first week, the training seemed to concentrate on uniform inspections which were held every morning. Just as Robby expected, nobody ever passed. Physical training started slowly, with brief runs, some push-ups and sit-ups, but the momentum was building. On Friday, the last day of the training week, Lieutenant Miles entered one of the classrooms in the afternoon and all trainees sprang to attention. He took off his hat, placed it on the lectern, then ordered everybody to relax. Robby thought, "Now, that's definitely a different order." No question, it was time for a pep talk in order to boost the morale of the tired trainees. Lieutenant Miles, show-ing off his human side for the first time, began to explain the reasons for his rigidness, the absolute necessity of it all, to benefit the people that hadn't figured it out yet. He said, "If a trainee cannot handle my D.I.'s, or my screaming in his face, then how could he cope with a screaming inmate who might turn assaultive at any minute? There is the need to maintain composure under difficult situations, allowing yourself time to think or react properly." He continued to explain that his job was to instill disci-pline, to motivate, to train and teach, but more importantly, to prepare Class #141 for the demanding task of working in the most erratic environ-ment known to society today, prison. He then stood erect, placed his Smokey back onto his shaven head, called Class #141 to attention and smiled. He concluded, "Now that I've seen you people can be motivated, next week I expect teamwork! You are now released!" The class, resem-bling yelling school children, ran to their vehicles, more motivated than ever. Lieutenant Miles was a good instructor and he knew how to get the important messages across.

Robby started his brand new Dodge Dakota pickup truck, recently pur-chased from a nearby dealer. It was possibly a premature purchase, as he had not graduated from the academy yet, insuring his position in the de-partment. Robby, being only optimistic, had confidence in his abilities to complete the program, so he was extremely happy on this Friday after-noon. The first week had gone well. Trainee Kirby, the class "fuck-up," was assigned to a different prison half-way across the state and Robby dis-covered there were also two other trainees assigned to his institution. He thought, "The more, the merrier." Trainee Matos, older than most of the class, was a man in his early thirties. Having a unique sense of humor, he had joined the department because life was "boring him." O'Connor, the last of the trainees, had been a U.S. Marine. O'Connor showed every aggressive mannerism of his past training.

Returning on Monday, week #2, Robby's spirits were extremely high. It had been a relaxing weekend, the hardest week of training was behind him and for the first time, he was finally convinced that he was going to like the crazy occupation of a correction officer.

Just as expected, the majority of the bullshit given by the Training Cadre had subsided. The people of Class #141 were working hard toward becoming correction officers. Training staff were forever reminding the trainees that certain theories had been proven more than once. "Officers will revert back to their training during times of crises, as though it were instinct." There was also, "Something learned today may very well save your life or the life of a brother officer tomorrow, so pay attention!" and so on. The morning runs were getting longer, with Class #141's green and gold flag leading the pack. With each trainee loudly echoing Lieutenant Miles' cadence, motivation was high and morale could not get much better.

The academics were picking up as well. The topics, unexpectedly interesting, were taught mostly by guest lecturers. There were sergeants and lieutenants, formidable experts on the subjects they taught, who came from various prisons throughout the state. Following each class, there would be an allotted time period for questions. Then, the speakers would usually share what was known as "war stories." Those stories were actual incidents which had occurred inside different prisons. These people were not attempting to boast, but only pass on realistic advice and offer warnings about a dangerous job for which they knew well. Sometimes there would be more learned through the prison stories, than the entire formal lecture. Each would finish with roughly the same advice, "Above all else, be sure to cover your ass and take care of yourself and your brother officers." Words of wisdom spoken from the mouths of men and women who had seen it all.

A plastic card was then issued to each trainee. This card listed the radio codes used universally within the department. It was imperative that these codes be memorized and embedded into the minds of each aspiring officer, as each would use them for daily communication. More crucially, they would be used for the purpose of calling for emergency assistance, or responding to another officer in need. From 10-32, a radio check, to 10-2 "I read you loud and clear." Of course, there was the famous 10-4 meaning, "I understand," and the list went on.

More important were the vital codes covering emergency situations. The 10-70 meant a fire emergency and the 10-98, an escape. A code 99 indicated a medical emergency. However, the most broadly used code was the 10-33, emergency. This code was used when an officer needed assistance to break up a fight or because he, himself, was being assaulted. When those four emergency codes were called via radio, an automatic heart pounding reaction was triggered within every staff person in the facility. Officers, designated as responders, went from a stand-still to an all-out sprint in responding to the unknown situation. The normal operation of the institution would be halted until the incident had been determined under control. Those codes, especially the emergency codes, would eventually become second nature, as they were used more frequently than any of the trainees could have ever dreamed.

For the next several weeks, besides the usual uniform inspections and daily physical training, the remaining long hours were spent in the classrooms. The studies basically started with the goals and philosophies of the department. In essence, an officer's duties and responsibilities included the care and custody of the inmates in their institution. Supervision objectives consisted of keeping a controlled, orderly environment and also the safe-keeping of all staff and inmates. Priority one was to keep all inmates secured behind the wall. Priority two was removal or prevention of the introduction of weapons into the inmate population. Priority three was drug detection, prevention and intervention. The list went on. There were classes focusing on "How to deal with inmates." The class taught everything from reprimanding to supervising, from giving orders to handling requests. The stressed means of dealing with inmates was that an officer should be consistently firm, but fair. Corrections was one of the few organizations where the lowest ranking member was a manager. With hundreds of inmates in an officer's custody, the responsibilities were immense.

Training then turned to legal issues regarding Constitutional laws, prisoner's rights and lastly, the rights retained by the officers. Again, "Cover your ass." C.O.R.I., which stands for Criminal Offenders Records Information designed to protect the privacy of an inmate's identity, criminal history, etc., was also covered extensively. From there, it was on to classification issues which included explaining how an inmate serves his time at differing security levels, and an officer's involvement in that process.

The academy presented the job options within the correctional profession. The "Bluebook," or officer's code of conduct, Public Relations, Sexual Harassment and working with the disabled were all topics that were discussed at length. A class was given on interpersonal communication skills, which was actually just hours of instruction on active listening.

During these days of intensive study, quizzes and exams were given every other day, creating fierce, but friendly competition for class standings. If one trainee beat out another academically, though they shared the same starting date, the trainee with the better grade would gain seniority over the other. This mattered tremendously when it came time to bid for a shift, days off, vacations and so on. Trainee Robby Cabral, facing stiff competition from eight co-workers, studied hard each night.

In addition to the classroom instruction, three institutions, which had been previously toured, one maximum security, the other two medium security facilities, had requested the assistance of the training class in conducting major shakedowns. For the first time, every trainee, with the exception of the females, had to strip search several inmates. Robby found that this routine process, quite necessary in the search for contraband such as drugs, weapons and other illicit items, was both awkward and unpleasant. The inmate stripped naked. Robby then conducted a thorough visual check of the entire body. From the mouth to the anal cavity, nothing was left unobserved. Upon completion, the inmates clothes were searched and he was ordered to leave the unit so that his living quarters could be searched as well. Though it was well-known that trainees conducted the most meticulous searches due to the novelty of the experience, Robby found nothing. However, during one of the major shakedowns, one of his classmates made a significant find. It was tattoo related paraphernalia. The trainee discovered ink, stencils and some bleach (used for sterilization) under a sink in what was referred to as a common area. The area was accessible to all inmates, therefore no disciplinary action could be taken against any of them. Nobody got "pinched" with the goods. The tattoo gun was not found that day, but would probably turn up. Staff were now on the look-out. In the meantime, Class #141 had put a tattoo artist out of business, even if only temporarily.

The classes seemed to get even more interesting and more in depth. There was report writing, which literally took better than one day of composing incident and disciplinary reports. The following day, there was a class on communicable diseases, leaving each trainee completely terrified of hepatitis, T.B. and the H.I.V. virus which were being spread at an alarming rate inside of the closed-in prison environments. Teachings on transportation, along with outside hospital and court details finished off the week.

Special lectures on crisis situations, which explained the use of K-9 units were given. Riot and weapons squads, and the circumstances under which they were used, were discussed. The instructor spoke of hostage situations and informed the trainees that if ever taken hostage, "The administration will do everything in its power to negotiate for the officer's freedom. However, the ultimate demand of an inmate's freedom will never be granted, so you must prepare yourself for this reality!" Robby looked around the room to find that same blank stare on everybody's face. The thought of such a scenario was horribly shocking.

Other excellent classes were offered on gangs in prison, a rapidly growing problem, which were multiplying faster than the department heads realized. Also, Preservation of a Crime Scene instructed each person that, "Upon response, you must secure the scene, protect the evidence and leave the scene undisturbed until Institutional Investigators arrive." Several classes on contraband were taught, including identifying weapons, drugs, escape paraphernalia, etc., and the ways in which they entered the facilities. The means in which they entered could be through visits, mail, "dirty staff," any way imaginable.

Toward the fourth week, more practical, hands-on training was given. Searches to include body, cell and vehicle were shown, along with arrest procedures which focused on visitors "lugging in" or smuggling drugs and weapons into the facility. Then, it was into the Use of Force segment where the use of chemical agents was demonstrated. Fortunately for the trainees, during a rigorous obstacle course, everybody had the opportunity to experience for themselves the lasting impression of tear gas which caused temporary blindness, while the sinuses were literally emptied. From there, the class moved to the application of restraints, from an ordinary pair of handcuffs to waist-chains and leg irons. One instructor explained how there had been inmates who were powerful enough to snap handcuffs, while others were physically too large to fit in a pair. Yet, this did not even compare to the double-jointed men who could easily slide out of restraints to become just as much of a potential attacker. Next on the agenda was the unarmed self-defense class, where easy-to-learn martial art techniques were taught which could prove helpful in the future. There was baton training, where the famous "Lamb" method was taught. This was a method in which the enemy or opponent was rendered immobile without serious or permanent injury being caused to that person. In closing this block of instruction, Extraction Team or "Move Team" training was provided for very practical, important reasons.

If an inmate was "ripping out" or "tearing out" his cell, or was just adamantly refusing to move, he would be ordered to comply with instructions several times by the area supervisor, a lieutenant. After the orders were given, if the inmate continued to be non-compliant, chemical agents would be administered per order of the shift commander, a captain. If the inmate still refused to be handcuffed and removed, then the Extraction Team would enter the room and remove the inmate by force.

During this training, video footage of actual extractions was viewed in order to observe the proper removal of both assaultive and passive inmates. These graphic films showed violent inmates burning out and flooding out their cells. In one of the films, a fairly muscular, completely irrational inmate, who was stripped naked, had greased himself up with his own feces in order to make himself slippery. He flooded the floor with water, then disassembled part of his steel bed for the purpose of fabricating a weapon. Within minutes, he appeared ready to do battle with the five man move team. The team, suited up in protective padded jumpsuits and shielded helmets, awaited further instructions from the team leader. They were waiting for the green light to enter the cell. The largest of the group was to enter first and "bundle" the inmate with a concave, plexi-glass shield. There would be officers to his right and left to assist, with the restraint man in the rear waiting to apply handcuffs and leg irons. As the entire incident transpired, it was videotaped for the safety of all involved. The team, all psyched up, received the go-ahead to enter the cell. The inmate let out one loud scream and lunged for the shield, but was knocked to the back wall where he collapsed to the floor. With no fight left in him, he was restrained with ease and carried from the destroyed cell. After all the hype, the inmate had "laid down" and played possum. The show had been put on for the other inmates residing on the same tier, so he "went out like a hero." He knew otherwise, as did the members of the move team.

As required training, these extractions had been practiced. Luckily, Trainee Kirby was voted to be the inmate, while five others suited up into those bulky, uncomfortable jumpsuits. Robby, chosen as the right restraint man, was assigned to assist his burly friend, Trainee Donovan, who was the shield man. Upon receiving the cue from the instructor, the team charged into the room with a vengeance. Kirby never had a shot in hell. Before he could move, Donovan hit him square in the chest making a distinct popping noise. Immediately knocked on his ass and with the wind taken out of him, he just laid still. It didn't matter, the team sprang on top of him like a pack of wild dogs, enjoying every second while relieving weeks of frustration. Kirby was in full restraints in two minutes flat. Again, he looked ready for tears. This time, Robby couldn't hold back the laughter.

It was good to become proficient at those moves, as they were used somewhat frequently inside the prison. It was always better to make the mistakes in training. The inmates in the videos either "laid down," thinking smartly, while others had fought like animals. The team struggled in their heavy suits, sometimes wrestling with each other in the confusion. At the completion of the films, the instructor explained, "There are those that will always fight. They will never win because all of the resources lie in the hands, or if needed, the armory of the officers."

After completing the physical extraction training, another week was spent inside the classroom learning Fire Safety, First Aid and C.P.R.. Also taught was the Anatomy of a Set-Up. This fascinating class covered inmates "conning" officers into committing illicit acts such as sex or drug smuggling, anything imaginable.

Moving toward the end of the training, a whole week was spent down the firing range. Trainees were qualified with handguns, shotguns and rifles. Throughout any of the training involving the possible use of force, the fact that no excessive force was ever needed, nor would ever be tolerated, was strongly stressed. Only reasonable force, or the minimal amount of force needed to subdue, restrain or take control of an inmate would be used.

Week seven, the trainees progressed to the Physical Training Test. Although Class #141 was now running five miles, one shot, the test only required two miles to be run in a specified time. For Robby and the boys, it was no sweat. A certain amount of push-ups and sit-ups was easy enough. Then there was the final written exam which was a compilation of seven weeks of study. Robby thought that the test proved simple enough. It should have. He had studied hard.

On the last day at the academy, Robby arrived earlier than necessary, as he had that first day of training, weeks before. Sitting in his truck, he could not help but to reflect on the weeks spent training and studying. He thought of the new friends he had made in the meantime. When thinking about Class #141, Robby would always remember it with pride. Though, he would also recall it as a mixed crowd. Indeed, they had come in all shapes and sizes, races and genders, but this did not seem to matter at all. What did matter was character. It had become evident in the past seven weeks that the department's recruiting process was less than perfect. Of the original forty, most were the clean-cut, all-American types who possessed integrity, the right ideals and intentions going into this law enforcement field. On the other hand, there were those few who were probably criminals already, or at least displayed the potential to become criminals themselves. Whether they had just accepted employment in the department to supplement their drug business, or intended on faking an injury and retiring early, they would not be around for long. Trainee Robby Cabral, wondering why he was dwelling on such bad thoughts on this festive day, cleared his head and joined the happy group.

After weeks, seven to be exact, of hard work and determination, it was graduation day and a euphoric feeling was felt by all. During the ceremonies, the flag of Class #141 was presented to a female officer, who had demonstrated incredible heart throughout the training. Though it had not been easy for her, she persevered and now deserved the recognition. Trainee Cabral, no, Officer Cabral finished second academically in his class. He also finished first in the group he would be working with. Those long hours would forever pay dividends, as Robby had seniority over eight other officers. It was another good start. Those officers, destined to partake in many of the identical prison experiences together, would either create close friendships or strong dislikes for each other in the years to come. Officers Letendre, Olivier, Matos, Donovan, Cabral, Holt, Johnson, O'Connor and Souza stood at attention in their normal formation for the last time. Not one with a similar appearance or personality type, standing side by side. After graduation, Lieutenant Miles gave a brief speech which turned sentimental. He congratulated each new officer on a job well-done, then cautioned them all to take care of each other. He stated, "The working environments you are about to enter will change you, it is inevitable. I challenge you to keep as much of yourself as you can. Remain the same person that you are today. Negativity is meant for the inmates. They are the people being punished, but you must stay positive for yourselves!" His voice, once harsh, now sounded more like a concerned father than a senior drill instructor. Anyway, it was finally over and time to celebrate their recent achievement.

The class ended up at the local pub where most got drunk and spoke fondly about the tough seven weeks they had endured together. Robby, sitting with the eight officers he would be working with, had truly made some good friends in the brief time spent training. That night had been a glorious one. They toasted to each other's success and to the undeniable challenges that lied ahead. Little did they know that their lives were about to drastically change. Depending on their outlook, this change could be self-satisfying or terrible, with little room for middle ground. First off, this would be the last weekend any of them would see in years and most would end up on second shift or the graveyard shift. From here on, holidays would be spent in a prison. With only good intentions, each left that pub as an idealist, hoping to make a difference, maybe even help correct somebody's life. Officer Robby Cabral could have never realized that innocence should be enjoyed...no cherished for as long as possible because reality sets in quick.

❸

The last free weekend had flown by and it was now early Monday morning. That same nervous anticipation of starting something new was slowly slipping away, as Robby pulled into the crowded parking lot. It was time to go to work. Robby, along with his eight training comrades, had reported for their first tour of duty at 6:50 a.m.. It was a momentous day in each of their lives. It was the beginning. Only time would tell which officers would lead successful careers and which officers would not last long, or drift through the years like deadwood.

These officers, for better or worst, were assigned to the oldest penitentiary in the system. It was an antiquated facility which housed a population of hundreds of convicted felons, from the ruthless murderers to the despised child molesters. However, this prison was unique in two other ways. It included an Addiction Center for detoxing patients who were court committed to the program for a period of thirty days. There was also a Minimum Security unit attached to the large facility, housing close to two hundred inmates. It was a fantastically diverse institution providing an unequaled opportunity to learn the different aspects of the correctional profession. This would be the day the real training, or learning would begin. As each institution had its own reputation within the department, this prison was considered by both officers and inmates alike to be the "shit hole of the system." It had become a wasteland for many protective custody inmates, while also housing inmates with mental disorders or "bugs."

Therefore, it was considered an annex to the state hospital as well. Though many had called it the "Island of Misfits," with better than twelve hundred inmates residing in general population, the ancient prison also housed its fair share of arsonists, rapists and thieves.

Upon entering the pedestrian trap that morning, Robby noticed the shakedown of the day consisted of every sixth officer emptying the contents of all pockets. A random search which caught Officers Letendre and Donovan. Passing the search, the two officers punched their time cards and stood in the narrow trap to await entrance. While waiting, an older officer, choking on a potent smelling cigar, commented, "Just remember guys, once that last door closes, you're all considered expendable." With that said, a few officers chuckled at the old-timer's attempt to scare the new officers. It wasn't so funny, but the "rookies" had been expecting some taunting from the experienced staff. The last sally-port door closed behind Officers Letendre and Donovan, leaving the two men standing under the armed vehicle tower. They undoubtedly experienced that eerie feeling which was capable of upsetting the stomach. It was not so much fear, but the keen awareness of the potentials that awaited inside. This feeling would take some time getting used to. Perhaps it never disappeared, but remained as a reminder to keep the edge and stay alert.

All nine rookies, who were also called "boots," reported directly to the roll call room where there appeared to be at least sixty officers sitting or standing around in small groups, shooting the bull. The headquarters lieutenant, a short man wearing thick glasses, arrived and called out for silence. This took some time. The lieutenant then informed his shift that they had just received nine new graduates who would help in the lack of sufficient staffing problem. All officers were expected to answer any of the recruits' questions, while assisting them in the orientation of the facility. In other words, these day shift officers were tasked with "breaking in" the rookies. There was no clapping or booing, certainly no great welcome. These people could have cared less, or at least that was the impression given. The lieutenant then spoke about two fights, both isolated incidents, which had occurred the evening prior. Another notice was read about an increase in health insurance, then the roll call began.

The lieutenant started calling off names from the master roster in front of him. One officer after the other would respond, "present." The lieutenant would then inform them of their assigned post for the day. As each exited the crowded room, they reported to the inner control center, to draw portable radios and the proper set of keys for their assigned post. During roll call, Robby, wiser than his nineteen years, scanned the room. He observed the appearances and behaviors of the older officers. The most obvious behavior that morning was that the majority of the "Boys in Blue" were gawking at Souza, the newest piece of meat. Others sat unaware of the female officer's presence, still half asleep, coffees in hand. Most were dressed appropriately, with pressed uniforms and brush-shined boots, but there were those few who looked as if they had slept in their uniforms for weeks, displaying their obvious lack of personal pride. Being the day shift, these officers had the most seniority in the prison. Therefore, they were for the most part, older than the officers assigned to the second and third shifts. Showing their ages through paunchy physical appearances and faces that revealed some hard years of living, their sizes varied tremendously. The older were giants amongst men, proving that the department had once hired monsters years ago. The remainder were average size or smaller. It was apparent that the importance of size had diminished. Quite an assorted group, but each man had to have something special to survive years within the prison environment.

As roll call came to a close, each rookie was teamed up with a veteran officer, who was supposed to "show them the ropes of the business." Some were not too thrilled with the duty due to the questionable trustworthiness of the new staff. Others were happy to oblige, granting the nine rookies the benefit of the doubt.

The administration's plan was to have the new officers work the day shift for a period of one month in order to receive "on the job training." The intent was to expose the officers to the daily routines, different post assignments and the physical layout of the prison. At the end of that month, each rookie had to bid for an alternate shift, second or third. They would also bid for days off. Class #141 was about to be split up like a litter of puppies, just as soon as they finished nursing off their mother.

Robby found right away that seniority was definitely a big priority. Walking to his first assigned post, Robby heard an officer snicker, "Hey rookie, get some time in." Robby knew he was at the bottom of the seniority barrel. He optimistically replied, "When you're at the bottom, there's only one place to go." The heckler laughed at Robby's innocent response. He knew that within a few weeks behind the wall, Robby's reply was sure to be different.

The "on the job training" began. This training involved each new officer rotating through various posts each day, enabling them to learn more, all the while observing the different styles of the seasoned officers they worked with.

Robby had been initially teamed up with a sergeant of fifteen years, who remained quiet for the better part of the day. The post assignment was located in the sections, or housing area, where inmates resided in single cells, eighteen per tier, several hundred in all. Unlike modern, automated prisons, each cell here was locked and unlocked manually with a large skeleton key. The first duty was to get a proper head count of each inmate, insuring each was alive. Once done, an unlock was conducted. Robby felt anxious, as he stood alone watching the inmates leave their tiny cells and report to the I.D.R., or inmate dining room, for breakfast. Many refused, lazily staying under their covers for more sleep. With little direction, Robby had to more or less follow the lead of the other officers working within the area. It was sink or swim time, but Robby had decided to complete the required duties, with or without the help of the sergeant. Throughout the day, there were head counts, locks, and unlocks, as the inmates proceeded and returned from chow, work or school. There was also the hourly movement which allowed each inmate ten minutes every hour to move from one area of the prison to another. If an inmate needed to report anywhere outside of this allotted movement period, a written pass had to be issued by a staff member.

Three random room searches were required of each officer everyday. Robby conducted the searches. During this process, he took into account the property permitted to furnish the cramped quarters. There was a bed, night stand, metal chair and a plastic pak-a-potti (toilet). Oddly enough, there was no sink or running water. The inmates were issued plastic jugs to fill with water and given a chance to receive crushed ice two times a day. Personal property included a television, radio, clothing, magazines, cosmetics, letters, and so on.

Each cell's walls were covered with pornographic photos, calling Robby's attention for some time. Though the pictures were eye-catching, the cells also had a distinct smell of a foul septic tank, therefore his searches were thorough, but conducted as rapidly as possible.

After finishing the three room searches, Robby had discovered no contraband, but was fortunate enough to come into contact with an army of cockroaches. When he opened a foot locker, the little critters scattered everywhere, making him squirm. After only the first day, it had become real evident that hygiene was not a top priority of many of these inmates, so cockroaches, rats and other vermin were commonplace. He had expected uncomfortable working conditions, but was not really prepared for the deplorable surroundings he had chosen to spend forty hours per week in. Robby kept busy for the remainder of the day by "flagging inmates," by pat searching them and asking for their I.D. cards, so that he could start to learn them by name.

At the end of the day, Robby's sponsor, the older sergeant, complimented him on his efforts. "You did real good for your first day," he said, then started with some small talk. Robby reluctantly accepted the compliment. However, he could not help but to think that while he busted his ass all day, the sergeant only sat on his. Robby rudely excused himself thinking, "No thanks to you asshole!" The sergeant had gotten the message, but smiled, knowing this rookie would be good. He wasn't lazy and he had spite, two qualities needed to be a good officer.

Robby realized within the first day, that besides the fact that the physical layout was extremely confusing, there were also two transparent, unwritten rules which existed. Rule #1 was that each trained officer was issued a uniform, badge and hat. The hat was never worn inside and thrown into a closet somewhere. This was almost symbolic of other things expected to be thrown away and forgotten. Robby considered it to be an unwise philosophy. Rule #2, and even more undeniable, was that an officer, any officer, was not accepted by the others until that officer proved he, or she was solid. Solid referring to how an officer would back up another, or react to emergencies and stressful situations. It was basically whether the person could be depended upon. In this environment, trust was not easily given, making respect even harder to earn.

Robby learned later that Officer Matos, the lucky son- of-a-bitch, got teamed up with the smallest officer in the prison. This man, however, was not to be underestimated, as he possessed a commanding voice and the balls of a fiery bull, meaning that he took shit from no one. He was a perfect example of the old proverb, "The Lord never put the heart of a lion into an elephant." Both officers reported to their post, a dormitory, housing one hundred and twenty inmates. The first walk through was shocking for Matos, as he realized it was only him and the little guy for the day. The head count was completed and the inmates began to stir around, waking from the short nights sleep.

With eight separate dormitories inside this particular prison, the officer-to-inmate ratio was horrendous. But, with the system being phenomenally overcrowded, bed space was the name of the game. Some of the dorms weren't too bad, but others to include the Orientation Unit, was a dangerous stop to work in. Filled with new, unknown inmates, anything and everything happened there.

Matos, spending the day primarily inside the look- alike Army barracks, found that he was answering inmates' questions and filling their requests when necessary. They all wanted something. Matos told Robby that the first time he denied a smiling inmate's request, the inmate, without notice, turned angry and insolent, almost hostile. It was easy to see that the inmates were cooperative when everything went their way, but as soon as they were told "no," their attitudes toward the officer changed quickly. The word "no" was probably the hardest for some officers to say. They believed that granting an inmate's every wish was the easiest way to deal with them because they felt it would avoid a confrontation. However, the opposite was true. If an inmate felt that an officer would not grant their every request, they would literally leave that officer alone to find other means of getting what they wanted.

Officer Matos finished the shift with his partner for-the-day, who left the rookie with words to live by, "Above all else, be consistent. These inmates live very structured lives. They are institutionalized and do not adjust well to sudden change. If you choose the style of a prick, be a prick all of the time, so they'll always know where you're coming from." The short officer laughed, adding, "Just remember, being a prick takes a lot of wasted energy, it's better to stay firm, but fair, like the academy just taught you." Officer Matos felt he had been fortunate, learning several valuable lessons that first day.

Officer Donovan, the biggest of the crew, ended up getting bounced around like an orphan that first day. In the morning, he was assigned to assist the mail officer in the opening of incoming mail in order to check for contraband. The correspondence was forbidden by law to be read by the officers, but occasionally the photos sent were something to look at. From there, it was off to the Property Room for Donovan.

The Property Room resembled Grand Central Station. It was a bustling area of the prison. There, state clothing for the prisoners was issued. Inmates' personal property was received and sent out. Contraband items were destroyed. The searches for these items were necessary and constant.

Donovan felt as though he was getting in the way, but was soon saved by the bell. The female sergeant in charge hung up the telephone and yelled, "Donovan, report to the inmate canteen per order of Lt. Cook." "Where in the hell is that?" he asked in dismay. She pointed to a young black inmate, telling Donovan, "Follow him, he'll take you there."

She wasn't joking, before he knew it, he was standing in the canteen. The canteen was actually the inmate's supermarket where each inmate was allowed to spend fifty dollars per week on groceries which they could cook in their electric hot pots. From valuable cigarettes to snack cakes, cans of soda, spaghetti and cans of tuna fish, the shop was well-stocked. Orders would be placed one week in advance. The money would then be removed from the inmate's personal account, allowing him to pick up his groceries for the week. At the threshold of the canteen, Donovan's responsibilities were to allow only so many inmates in the area at a time and to prevent 'strong-arming,' which was when an inmate was forced by threats or physical assault to forfeit his food items.

Officer Donovan later told Robby that as he stood on the steps, he had two thoughts. His first being, "These assholes are really doing hard time, worrying about whether their cupcakes are going to get crushed at the bottom of the bag." His second thought was morbid, "There are two large cement yards to walk through, filled with hundreds of inmates awaiting the weaker prey...good luck boys!" One day behind the walls and he was already becoming cynical.

Officer Souza, the new female, had been assigned to the Inner Control Center in the morning. That area was actually the nucleus or main brain center of the prison. It was where all radio communication was controlled for the hourly ten minute movement, emergencies, etc. Her duties included collecting the entire count of the institution, dispensing keys, radios, emergency and other security equipment. Everything that transpired went through the Control Center, therefore, the basis for its title. Souza then spent the afternoon in the Outer Control Center which was responsible for every person, vehicle, or object entering or exiting the institution. It was another incredibly busy area of the prison. Visitors were processed and searched there prior to entrance. Being on the outside of the perimeter of the institution, the Outer Control Center was located near the armory where all weapons, ammunition, chemical agents, additional restraints, equipment and such were stored. It also consisted of a vehicle tower which allowed vehicles to ingress and egress the institution after being thoroughly searched. Officer Souza felt she had not learned very much that first day, as the areas were so intensely active, there was no officer available to instruct her on the routine duties.

Robby sensed that Officer Johnson had been an unfortunate recruit because he was stuck with a fairly young officer who possessed a piss-poor attitude. He was full of complaints and harsh criticisms for every staff member in the "joint." Their assignment was a recreation room referred to as the Shanty. Although the pool tables had recently been removed, a television set was available, as well as a small weight room located off to one side. The room was filled with inmates producing more noise than imaginable. A hang-out for thugs and groups of all races, the place really packed'em in. The Shanty's walls were lined with gym-style lockers and a large shower room, capable of holding maybe 30 inmates. The dreaded shower room where men engaged in homosexual acts, with or without consent, was located directly in front of the officer's station, a single desk. There was also a small, plexi glassed-in room containing sinks, three washing machines, three dryers and a barber's chair where the inmates received the latest hairstyles.

Officer Johnson listened to the poor advice of that bitter man for the entire day. "Treat'em all like shit, they're all no good," and "Forget what you learned in the academy, it's all bullshit," grumbled the malcontent. Johnson, smart enough to stop listening to the disgruntled employee hours earlier, sat in awe most of the afternoon just watching the behavior of every type of inmate. From the muscle-bound gang bangers grouped together, to the Biker's covered with tattoos and smelling ripe, the place was like a human menagerie. Then, there were the Bugs, who either sat alone or talked to themselves a mile a minute while pacing back and forth like expectant fathers. The place was a three-ring circus. Its history spoke for itself. Many of the major fights, or other disturbances occurred there. Directly above this recreation room was the Upper Rec., a room identical in physical appearance. Supposedly the more aggressive, problem-laden inmates hung around in the Upper Rec. and that area's reputation was even "badder" than the Shanty's.

Officer O'Connor, destined for a busy day, was assigned to the cement yards as a roving foot patrol. With a small guard shack and a steel door located between, and separating the two, he found the morning quiet. O'-Connor walked alone. Monitoring the inmates' movements and conducting some pat searches, he would occasionally check the rooms located in a building running along the right side of the front cement yard. Located in this building were the Catholic and Protestant Chapels, as well as the Muslim area designated for worship. All were quiet. Also, O'Connor conducted a security round of the school building, from the G.E.D classroom, to the college classrooms, filled with computers. Again, each was quiet. The library, containing shelves upon shelves of law books, was also located inside this building, but was being covered by another officer. Officer Donovan had the Inmate Canteen covered which was located at the very end of that same long building.

At one point, O'Connor stood, watching the games being played on the handball and the basketball courts. He was amazed at the differences in the inmate population. The sun was shining, the air brisk and O'Connor was getting the hang of the patrol business. Suddenly, before he could turn around, he heard it on his radio, "10-33 emergency, two inmates fighting, no weapons involved in the rear cement yard." At that time, O'Connor responded to what was actually his area of responsibility and within seconds, he was upon the scene.

There were two white inmates rolling around on the ground, one bleeding from his mouth. Attempting to separate the combatants were Officers Donovan and Stanley, who had called it in. Without thinking, O'Connor jumped in the middle, yelling for both inmates to stop. Pinning the more aggressive inmate and restraining him was the key, because the inmate who was losing couldn't take any more. In what seemed like a minute, a large crowd of inmates had gathered around and circled the scene. Immediately, a wave of blue appeared out of nowhere. The responding officers had arrived, ordering the congregating inmates to disperse, or they too, would be locked up. Handcuffs were then applied to the subdued combatants, as other officers escorted them away to the Health Service Unit (prison hospital unit), then off to segregation. As quickly as it had started, it was finished and everybody seemed to go about their business as if nothing significant had just occurred. A normal daily event was all it was.

Officers O'Connor and Donovan smiled at each other. Both knew what the other was thinking. It was only the first day and they had already "gotten into the shit." They shook hands, but Stanley couldn't understand their good spirits, as he walked away bitching. Officer Stanley was going to have to write two "tickets" or disciplinary reports on the fighting inmates. Stanley, like most officers, did not enjoy writing reports in the least.

As O'Connor walked away from the scene, his mind raced with the details of the situation that had just transpired. He then noticed his hands were trembling. The adrenaline was still pumping hard through his veins. It had been a rush. The "fight or flight" response from which some got addicted. O'Connor thought of how he had reacted without any hesitation. He conducted himself professionally. He was happy with his quick responsive actions, but now he started to think of what might have happened. Looking down at the blood covered sleeve of his shirt, he thought about the H.I.V. virus. His thoughts then flashed to the group of inmates which had surrounded him, as he knelt over the scene and a pang of fear entered his body. He later confided in Robby, "It was strange how the fear had never entered my body until the situation was over. Thank God, as it could have definitely interfered otherwise." It had been known that some officers became paralyzed by the fear, causing them to be unable to react. In those cases, a different occupation had to be sought out.

O'Connor then recalled the wave of blue which made him smile from ear-to-ear. The area lieutenant standing behind O'Connor startled him, as he asked, "What are you smiling about rookie?" O'Connor continued to smile which contagiously rubbed off on the older man. The lieutenant walked away saying, "Good job, but keep moving out here, you're supposed to cover both cement yards." He was right, the basketball game had been a distraction. His point was taken.

Officer Letendre, posted at the Health Service Unit, was paired up with a middle-aged, black officer who liked to talk, or at least liked listening to himself talk. Letendre's duties included taking head counts of the sick, lame and lazy during the designated medication lines. Each inmate, after placing one or more pills into his mouth, drank water, then showed Letendre that they had swallowed the medicine by widely opening their mouths for a quick inspection. This was needed to insure none of them were 'palming' their meds to stockpile, or sell them. It also insured that they weren't being strong-armed into giving them up. Psychotropic meds or sedatives were always in demand, so the dispensing of those narcotics had to be monitored closely.

There were two medication lines, then peace and quiet for awhile, if Letendre's partner, C.O. Smith would allow it...no such luck. "Smitty" continued to talk, but did offer one good piece of advice, "Play the cons straight, if you jack one up (set him up), they'll all know it and your credibility won't be worth shit, even amongst the other staff."

In the late morning, an older inmate entered the unit complaining of chest pains. An E.K.G. was conducted and a complete medical evaluation given, resulting in negative diagnosis of a physical problem. The old man was then issued a pass to speak with the mental health unit. He probably suffered from severe anxiety, possibly a panic attack. He would be back for the next med line to receive his prescribed sedatives.

In the afternoon, immediately following the fight in the cement yard, both inmates were escorted in separately to be evaluated. The bigger inmate appeared unscathed, while the other sustained two lacerations on the inside of his lips which required butterfly stitches. Both inmates were sent to the segregation, or the Hole to await their disciplinary hearings.

Officer Letendre, according to his post orders, was also required to cover the breakfast and lunch meals in the I.D.R. Upon arrival he met up with Officer Souza, also preparing for the new duty. After a brief hello, the chow hall sergeant told Souza, "You are designated to the outgoing silverware bin, where you will insure each inmate places his knife or fork in the proper bucket. We don't want the potential weapons to leave the area." Turning toward Letendre, he said, "You're assigned to pat search inmates leaving the dining room. Every fifth one will do fine." With that in mind, Letendre stood by the door awaiting for the meal to begin. Unthinkingly, he buried his hands into his pockets. The sergeant hurried over and told the young recruit, "It's not smart to leave your hands in your pockets, you may need them to defend yourself. If somebody attacks you, your first instinct is to make a fist, so you'll be unable to remove them, won't you?" Letendre smirked, thinking, "More good advice, everybody seems to be full of it. Anyhow, the man is right. It will be remembered."

Logistically the I.D.R. was amazing, as hundreds of inmates were fed within a fairly short period of time. Potentially, the place was a stick of dynamite. With hundreds of steel knives, the state figured long ago that plastic utensils were too expensive to hand out every day. As a result, any confrontation started had to be stopped instantly. Any inmate out of line was removed and isolated from the others. Too many bad ordeals had taken place there in the past. It was simply a case of money versus officer safety and the all-mighty dollar had prevailed.

Just outside of the I.D.R., 'Happy Hour' was conducted. There was a line of managers, from the Superintendent to the unit managers, standing in a row. They were approached by any inmate with a grievance, complaint, request, concern, etc. In essence, it was strictly a bitch session where inmates were afforded the fairest of opportunities to speak their mind. Officer Letendre was amazed at the long lines of inmates.

Officer Olivier, the high-spirited adolescent, was sent to work one of the institution's three segregation units, for the day. This particular unit was known as 'The Fort.' Teamed up with two of the youngest officers on the shift, Olivier fit right in. Within segregation, all inmates were continually locked up. They had to be fed three square meals which were brought to their cells. They were allowed telephone calls, showers and an occasional visit from disciplinary sergeants, case workers, etc. Each time they were removed from their cells, restraints were applied.

Segregation was where the non-compliant, disruptive inmates who had gotten into fights resided, along with others who had requested protective custody. The days were usually crazy there, with food or feces covering the floors and walls while some inmates attempted to assault staff. Some inmates would try to kick their doors down and it was all in a day's work to try to burn or flood out, causing extractions to take place. Officer Olivier's first experience in the unit was quiet however, as the coffee perked in the office and the radio played softly. The three officers seemed to cover every topic of conversation with the exception of corrections. That first day was definitely not what Olivier expected, but he felt fortunate for the easy duty.

Officer Holt, the last of the nine, was literally stationed out in left field. Assigned to the ballfield and main gym, he had a pretty cushy post for the first day. Robby thought him also unfortunate because he never got to meet the different characters who were also wearing the same uniform, only visibly more faded from wear. Alone for the day to observe sporting events, he knew there would be tomorrow and who knows where he would end up. It was like playing the lottery those first few weeks, with good and bad posts, competent or apathetic staff to learn from.

Finally, those first eight hours, uneventful for some, challenging for others, had come to an end. Robby and his new friends stood in the parking lot, exchanging the day's stories, following a full shift of prison work. There was one thing which was crystal clear to them. Upon entering the prison, most officers, depending on their own past experiences, were not prepared to deal with the type of people who were spending twenty four hours, seven days a week secured behind those concrete walled barriers. It would only be with time, the assistance and support of senior staff and most noteworthy, the drive of each individual officer, that would enable him to adapt and effectively function within this negatively, abnormal environment called prison. It seemed that the officers who were raised in an urban environment, possessed the street- smart instincts of the inmates and would adapt as though they were bred for the job. The other officers, like Robby, who had experienced a more sheltered childhood, would have a daily learning process to contend with. The schooling provided by the streets would definitely pay off in this profession. For Robby Cabral and a hand-full of others, it would be a constant struggle.

The following day, the fresh nine returned to do it all over again. Different posts, assignments, security staff to watch and learn from. This continued for weeks, four to be exact, of observing the routines, attitudes and interaction of the inmates. Strangely, the occupation of a correction officer was basically to care for and maintain custody of the inmates in the institution. During those first few weeks, although the recruits were well-aware of the inmates presence, the focus seemed to be on the other staff. Those men and women, slightly weathered from their time in, were extraordinary people once the rookies got to know them. Some were Vietnam Veterans and others also had prior military service. Many were well-educated people with educations ranging from high school diplomas right up to master degrees in sociology or criminal justice. Some had prior experience in various law enforcement fields. Most maintained fairly good attitudes, while possessing integrity and the right intentions. Almost everyone had a family which he, or she cared for, while working in a prison in order to provide for that family. Unlike the movies, starring those mythical large goons who carried big sticks used to beat inmates senseless, these people performed difficult jobs with the limited resources they had available to them.

Of course, like any other occupation, Robby found that corrections possessed its share of shit bums, its 'luggage,' which was carried by the other staff. The apathetic types who forced others to bear the work load. It became immediately clear to Robby that corrections was a self-motivated profession. To exceed was a personal choice. It was much easier to sit idle, doing as little as possible, collecting that same pay check.

After obtaining a good grasp of the physical layout, Robby and the others had gained confidence and experience with each passing day, but continued to learn about the complex system in which they were employed. Without being lost or walking into walls, other areas of the prison were visited or worked. Robby was escorted to the visiting room, where outsiders came in to visit with the inmates. It was a place of "sex, drugs and rock and roll." A hot spot to work, because much of the contraband entered the institution through that area.

Then, there were the areas in which the inmates worked. Besides cleaning the housing units, yards, recreation rooms and working the I.D.R., there was the laundry, the maintenance department and paint shop. Other shops employing inmate labor were the carpentry, plumbing, electrical and masonry trades. Vocational-type training jobs were available as well. Those included the silk screen and sign shops where all of the state's road signs were made. Besides the bindery shop, there was also teachings in welding, auto mechanics and construction engineering.

Most of the prisons produced items, used strictly by the state. For instance, mattresses, cleaning supplies and of course, license plates. Those industries departments would not compete with private business, therefore had never sold their goods to the public.

In completing the layout, there was also the Addiction Center filled with those 'thirty day wonders' detoxing from every narcotic available on the street. Those inmates resided in all dormitory settings with other addicts of unpredictable, and often aggressive, violent behavior. It was a site of communicable diseases, hallucinations, and projectile vomiting. It was also a place where illicit narcotics were desired more than anything else in the world.

The last stop for Robby in the institution was the Minimum Security Unit, with its own visiting room. It was a totally different world in itself. The adjustment was often difficult for officers, as the atmosphere, interaction with inmates, and the milder, lenient rules concerning inmate behavior were very contrasting to medium security. Although minimum security had no less problems on a whole, the visiting room, with one officer in charge, could have been mistaken for a state facility which allowed conjugal visits (permitting consensual sex).

After the month of day shift training had been completed, Robby and the other eight, whether they were aware of it or not, had just poured a solid foundation for their careers. Officer's Cabral, Letendre, and Donovan were assigned to the eleven-to-seven or grave yard shift. O'Connor, Olivier, Holt, and Johnson had been placed on the three-to-eleven or second shift. Unfortunately, Officer Souza had resigned before her nine month probationary period had expired. She accepted employment as a court officer, a job she had waited years for. She was congratulated and bid farewell, as her brother officers wished her the best of luck in her new career. This would, without question, be the department's loss because that small-framed lady had the makings of a good solid officer. She would be sorely missed.

The remaining eight officers left the day shift. They would meet new challenges, form strong friendships and become proficient at their occupations. On that last day, a gray-haired officer, preparing for his own retirement and known to be a wealth of knowledge in the correctional field, met with the group in the parking lot. He advised the men, "In reality, it's us against them. Even if you hate another officer, still consider him your brother and do whatever is necessary to keep him safe!" It was advice that would not be forgotten and actually the last real piece of formal advice these men were to receive, for the rest would be learned through their own trials and tribulations. Robby knew that from then on, there would be no experienced partners to depend on. He, like the others, were on their own. Robby desperately hoped that the training and brief prison experiences would be enough.

❹

J ust as each institution was unique, so was it true of the overall character of each shift. Robby, assigned to the third shift, decided it was adjustment time all over again.

He quickly understood that the day shift was the "laid back" shift. Not a whole lot of problems occurred because the inmates were constantly busy during the day. A busy inmate was a quiet inmate. Whether in school, at work, participating in treatment programs or perhaps at church services, the inmates were out of the yards and recreation rooms where there was usually nothing to do but hang around and get into trouble. The number of staff was greater during the day, from custodial to classification personnel. The inmates were often in the custody of the recreation officers, or the coaches, the drug counselors, teachers, mental health counselors, correctional case workers, clergy or their respective employers in the shops. The housing units, sections and dormitories were left somewhat abandoned, with the exceptions of specified count times, medication lines and such. However, with a full compliment of administrators, unit managers and other "brass" on site, the inmates found it wiser to remain in a calm state during the day.

There were always those inmates who refused to do anything but hang out '24/7.' Twenty four hours, seven days a week, they did nothing. However, it seemed they too stood relatively quiet. However, there was another reason for the general tranquillity. It was related to the burn-out factor of the more tired senior staff assisting to keep the day shift uneventful. There was no question that most of these older officers would not divert from their daily routines to search for trouble within the inmate population. These people had had their fair share of conflict and preferred the more dormant state of the environment they worked in. Peace and quiet was good, but nobody was fooled, for the Giant (collectively) was only resting.

At exactly 2:50 p.m., a magic time, the second shift, or "working shift," arrived full of vigor for their tour of duty. At that time the "climate" or atmosphere of the inmate population drastically changed. Non-custodial staff left for their homes. Inmates finished their work, school, etc., and it was time to play, and play hard. The behavioral changes were incredible to observe if an officer were to overlap his hours worked. The inmate who was quietly assisting the electrician all morning was now converting his trade into narcotic sales. The inmate who was taking a college course in accounting to better himself had quickly become the enforcer in a strong-arming, or extortion ring. The janitor of the Catholic Chapel and assistant to the priest, suddenly resented all authority figures, while playing the act of a maggot. The examples were endless, but the games had begun. The yards and recreation rooms were filled beyond capacity and the key was to realize that this game, often dangerous and always challenging, included each officer as a player. Like it or not, if you were in the arena, you were playing. Most of the crimes, con artist games and illicit acts transpired on the second shift, but fortunately the younger men and women who worked these off hours were up for the daily challenges. Granted, they were less experienced, so around every corner there was a hard lesson to be learned. Occasionally, the inmate would "get over on the officer," or win, but this business was designed around time. There would always be other chances to even the score. With every waking minute spent behind bars, the inmates were afforded more than enough time to devise devious plans or schemes of getting what they desired. In many ways, it was their back yard, their advantage. However, the officers, in the long run, always seemed to end up on top.

Officers Matos, Olivier, Holt, Johnson, and O'Connor started the shift knowing it would be a more interesting stop than the day shift due to the characters that worked it. The attitudes were much more positive. It was hoped that it took many years before the wind was taken out of an officer's sails. Robby stayed in touch with his five friends. It was important to share their experiences, their thoughts and their feelings about everything. Since bonding in the academy, they had become a support group for one another. Most of the time, they would laugh about each other's stories, though many were anything but funny.

Reporting to roll call each afternoon, the camaraderie felt amongst these younger troops was obvious. Those officers, wearing their uniforms with pride, were tougher on each other than any other occupation known. Whether it was crude jokes told about each other's family members or vicious pranks played on each other, it was as though they were continually testing the other's limits.

In one prank, a sergeant with the energy of a child, silently removed a set of cell keys, skeleton-type, from Officer Holt's belt clip while some officers looked on. Almost five minutes had elapsed before Holt went to his belt with his hand to insure the keys were there. His face went white and without saying a word, he began to frantically search the area around him. The poor guy nearly suffered cardiac arrest before the other officers erupted into laughter and the playful sergeant returned the key set.

As every officer knew, a lost set of keys was a huge breach of security because they could end up in the wrong hands. Although the loss of keys was unintentional, the officer could have very easily been terminated for such an accident. It was a funny prank because most officers were constantly feeling for their keys. To realize they were no longer there... Holt's facial expressions had said it all. The humor, although dark and dirty, was usually hilarious. This trait was frequently needed and used to cope with pressures that the job carried.

Robby had always felt that some of the funniest people alive worked in corrections. True comedians, with an endless amount of material to work with. There was always plenty of horseplay that often turned into tag-team wrestling matches. Those men and women had to create their own fun, which helped in tolerating their working conditions.

The second shift also had its daily routines which included the supper meal, med lines and drug programs such as, A.A., N.A., and Alanon. There was even a movie featured each evening in a designated area. Popcorn was optional.

Again, the majority of these officers possessed real integrity and a true sense of duty for their profession. Of course, there would always be those few who should be wearing con numbers rather than badges. Those who were the most vocal, professing to be this or that, normally showed their true colors when the heat was on. Officer Olivier quickly found this to be fact.

An overweight sergeant, in charge of one of the recreation rooms, was well-known for getting tough with inmates when, and only when they were in restraints. This man, along with a few of his "cowboys," who were considered aggressive officers, were sitting in a break room eating their supper. The rookie, Officer Olivier, entered the room. Grabbing his bagged lunch from the dirty refrigerator, Olivier started to sit at the same table with the overweight sergeant. At that time, fat boy said, "Hey boot, you can't sit at this table, only officers are allowed to sit here!" Olivier, without giving the comment much thought, replied, "This might be the boot that turns a corner to save your fat ass." The room went silent for a second. Officer Olivier shuffled down the table to seat himself right on the side of the ignorant man. Once he was seated, the other officers began to laugh, but the sergeant sat red-faced without any comeback whatsoever. Officer Olivier had not wanted any trouble, especially during his nine month probationary period, but he was not about to be bullied by anyone, especially a known coward. Olivier had gained the respect of the other officers, but more importantly, retained his own. Officer Olivier was learning about this brutal business quickly. Perhaps he was not as naive as he appeared.

The hard lessons of working on the second shift began at once. Officer Holt, assigned to the upper recreation room, was approached by a white biker-type inmate, who requested to have the shower room water turned on. Holt informed the inmate that it was no problem and that he would get right on it. The inmate walked away and Holt, continuing with his conversation, did not give the inmate another thought. After about five minutes, the inmate returned, this time angrily asking that the water be turned on. Officer Holt again replied that he would do it, waving the inmate away, only to resume with the conversation. He was completely ignoring the man's request. Less than two minutes had transpired before the same inmate approached the new officer. However, this time he had come in an aggressive manner, positioning himself into a fighting stance. The biker began screaming that Holt was nothing but a piece of shit, attracting the attention of everybody in the area. The area sergeant, intervening, could not defuse the situation, so the hostile inmate ended up in handcuffs and was escorted to the Hole.

Returning to the recreation room, the sergeant was not at all happy with Officer Holt. He explained to the rookie, "Once an officer tells an inmate that he is going to do something, it better get done. To just brush off an inmate, as though he does not exist, is the epitome of disrespect. In this environment, very few inmates will stand for it. Besides, it is always better to keep your word, so that you do not gain the reputation as a liar." What could have turned into a physical incident was stopped by the quick-thinking sergeant, but not before Officer Holt had realized that he had screwed up pretty badly. Holt, not desiring to be labeled as a 'White Hat,' (a liberal officer who gives the House away) failed to understand one thing. If an inmate was allowed or permitted by institutional rules and regs. to anything, then there was no reason for an officer to deny it. Some officers never wanted to give the inmates the time of day. As far as lying, well, officers were expected to play by a different set of rules. The inmates lied constantly, but officers were always bound by their word, if only because they were playing on that different level.

Officer Johnson, working one of the many dormitories on the new shift, learned that the need to be flexible was critical in the business of corrections. In one night, Johnson had locked up two inmates, one for being insolent and disruptive, the other for protective custody reasons. Officer Johnson had also counseled a lost inmate on substance abuse programming, issued several warnings to some inmates who had been horse playing, then hired another inmate as the unit janitor. A busy evening, as Johnson found that a correction officer wore many different hats in the performance of his duties. From disciplinarian, to protector, to referee. Among other roles, he was also a father figure and an adviser.

The old-timer, Officer Matos, got assigned to sections where the brick floors were visibly worn from over a hundred years of inmate traffic and the cell locks read 1875. Before long, he was getting used to his new post. Three hours into the shift, a '10-70'(fire emergency) was called via radio for the I.D.R.. Matos, trying his best to remain calm, cool and collected, grabbed the nearest fire extinguisher and sprinted toward the scene of the blaze. While en-route, the Control Center announced that the '10-70' was a drill, and only a drill. Slowing down to a jog, Matos found himself filled with mixed emotions, as he gasped for a full breath. He felt anger because there was already enough stress to deal with when real emergencies kicked off. He later learned that an officer had twisted and sprained his ankle responding to the false emergency, pissing everybody off. On the other hand, Matos thought to himself, those weekly drills, which were always timed, were conducted to insure that the staff were prepared for anything, at a moment's notice. There was also training experience gained in the meantime. Regardless, most officers had always felt resentment toward those shift commander's tests. Matos decided that he shared their attitude.

Officer O'Connor, destined to attract trouble no matter where he went, was assigned to the Central Prison Gate one evening. The huge steel gate controlled inmate movement from one side of the prison to the other. Without hesitation, O'Connor denied an inmate entrance because he did not have his I.D. card on him. Instantly, the inmate turned into a belligerent asshole. Surrounded by other inmates, the asshole began challenging O'Connor, claiming that he would kick his ass if it wasn't for the badge, adding that he would take care of him on the streets. O'Connor, smartly calling for back-up, attempted to isolate the inmate from the group, but could not. Within seconds, responding officers swooped down on the insolent man, restrained him, then dragged him away. O'Connor calmed himself down, realizing that not even his Marine Corps. training had prepared him for such confrontation. Later that evening, the area lieutenant informed O'Connor that the loud-mouthed inmate had apparently put on a big show and confessed that he owed several Hispanic inmates debts, for which he could not pay. The asshole had 'checked in' on a glorified protective custody move.

Being a fairly large shift, officers became tightly bonded with other officers who shared similar interests. Sometimes they hung around with their assigned partners, but there were definitely defined cliques. It was not as if the entire shift hung around in one big group. Within those cliques or 'inner circles,' close friendships grew. Outside of them, there was sometimes dislike, even hatred felt toward one another. Regardless of the feelings on the line, those officers functioned as a well-oiled machine, backing each other's play no matter the circumstances. In many aspects, all that these people could ever depend on within this uncertain environment was each other. No one could afford to lose that.

The five newly-appointed officers to the shift had bounced from post to post until the shift commander decided they were ready for a permanent post. Assigned as a 'floater,' or working different posts allowed opportunities to learn the different procedures of the numerous posts. Being assigned a permanent post allowed an officer the chance to get to know the inmates in his area, to gain a better understanding of the whole picture. The advantage of a permanent post was that the officer was more involved in the inmates' lives and daily routines, where he might deter some illicit activity. The drawback to the permanent post was the burn-out factor caused by being faced with the same problems day-in and day-out. Either way, both had their advantages and disadvantages.

After working their full eight hour shift, the rookies soon found that they were likely to be forced to work another eight hour shift if needed. As seniority prevailed, when officers 'banged in,' or called in sick, the institution would run at a minimal force. However, some posts had to be filled, no matter who was assigned. For example, if left unsupervised, a dormitory housing a hundred inmates or better, would be a tough area to clean up afterward. Anyhow, officers with less seniority were forced to perform another full tour of duty. It was just another fringe benefit of correctional work.

For Officers Cabral, Donovan and Letendre, there was the third shift, or graveyard shift. Basically a quiet environment, with the potential of being the most dangerous of all. The officers assigned to this shift were always kidded about their lack of inmate contact and their need for protective custody. However, those supposed 'Lames' worked on a skeleton crew that housed hundreds of its inmates in dormitory settings. Officer-to-inmate ratio was even worst during the dark hours. It was always hoped that it would be a quiet night, which Robby and his two friends learned was not always the case.

Officer Donovan was immediately chosen for the Orientation Dorm called the Bakery unit, because it was converted from such. Being a big kid with prior military experience, the shift commander had hoped he would do well.

Entering the dormitory on the first night, the count was fifty inmates, lying in bunk beds and playing cards. Some watched television. Donovan, though new to the business, kind of got the idea that somebody was giving him the business. He was alone and the area lieutenant had given him his instructions, "Insure a good head count every hour. Overhead lights go out at exactly 11:30 p.m., and the side mounted night lights get turned on. The television goes out at 12:00 a.m. when every inmate is to be lying in their own bed. Only quiet will be tolerated. Any talking, start writing disciplinary reports." It sounded easy enough, but somehow this country boy knew those fifty men would make it as difficult as they could. Donovan had no idea just how difficult.

The first count went well, with fifty, living, breathing bodies secured inside of a room that was getting hotter by the minute. Exactly at 11:30 p.m., the overhead lights were turned off, the dim night lights turned on. With the exception of a few obscene comments yelled out from the noisy crowd, the first half-hour went great. Unfortunately, the second half-hour was arriving fast. At 11:55 p.m., Officer Donovan turned the television off which caused the first problem. Like spoiled children, five or six inmates rudely complained that they were entitled to the remaining five minutes. The rookie ignored this and started to conduct the second count. The beds were lined along the walls in the shape of a horseshoe. There were also ten to twelve bunk beds located in the middle of the floor, causing a blind spot in the rear of the dorm. Up toward the front was the television set, with several park benches facing it. Then there was the officer's station, consisting of a desk and chair placed behind a steel cage. The cage was there for good reason.

As Donovan began the count, he noticed that the floor was extremely slippery. He discovered that someone had smeared Vaseline on it. Also, walking down the aisle, he came across overturned foot lockers and trash cans blocking the passageway. Some smartass had actually set up an obstacle course, hoping the young officer would slip and fall. The place went quiet, with each inmate tuned in to Donovan's every step. The count was successfully completed and Officer Donovan, returning to his desk, heard an incredibly loud amount of booing from the disappointed group. The officer had made it uninjured and the inmates had not liked it at all.

Before long, Donovan had to order each inmate into his own bed. Most bitched that they were grown men, but reluctantly complied with the order. One punk located in the rear yelled out, "Fuck you, Marine." Donovan, walking toward the area replied, "What's that?" and the stupid asshole repeated it, identifying himself. Officer Donovan got on the phone and within two minutes, three officers arrived to cart the heckler off to the Hole.

This left the dorm in an uproar, with inmates yelling and flicking disposable lighters. Then it happened, the last straw. Making the third count of the night, forty nine in their own beds, Donovan started back for the officer's station. In an instant, he heard something go whistling just past his ear. It smashed into the cage, causing the inmates to become hysterical. With his flashlight, he immediately spotted it rolling on the floor toward him. It was a battery. A D-cell battery which had just missed the back of his head. Enough was enough. More angry than frightened, Donovan considered this first night not a test, but a bad dream. Back on the telephone for some direction, a lieutenant arrived and sat for better than an hour until the dorm remained silent. Without so much as a word, he left. What a night it had been. Officer Donovan couldn't wait for the next.

Dreading the permanent assignment, Donovan returned to the Bakery unit where the battles continued. It took close to a month before he could truly admit that he had control. Within that long month, he was called every name in the book. More batteries and bars of soap were thrown at him, luckily never finding their target. Though, some had been close calls. Officer Donovan knew that the unit was no less than complete chaos.

Given the option to leave the toughest post on the shift, he declined, deciding that the old dorm would either make him or break him. In the meantime, twenty or more inmates were removed from the unit, with disciplinary reports to follow. At one point, Officer Donovan was approached by a sarcastic inmate who challenged him by demanding, "I've got at least thirty inmates that say the T.V. stays on an hour later tonight." Waiting for a reply, the inmate watched as Donovan unplugged the set, removing it from its cabinet. On the radio, he requested assistance, then using reasonable force, applied handcuffs to the confident spokesman, who could not believe he was getting lugged to the Fort, the worst of the segregation units.

Night after night, Donovan would escort inmates just outside of the unit to speak to them individually, man to man. It was always the same response, "It's not me man, I don't like it either, I haven't gotten any sleep." Fed up, Officer Donovan began throwing the bars of soap back into the crowd while leaving the overhead lights on for hours, until finally making a general announcement, "Do not hide in the crowd like cowards, let's deal with this problem like men!" Never was there a response.

Those were risky and unconventional actions taken on behalf of Donovan, but being at his wit's end, it was how he finally began to gain respect. It had taken a good month before Officer Donovan's reputation was solid enough. He would no longer have to endure the nightly attacks. It had been the hardest, most trying month of his life, but it had paid off. New inmates admitted to the unit were warned by the others, "Don't Fuck with the young guy, he's got no problem locking you up!"

The next five months of this six month post would be smooth sailing. Then some poor slob would take over the post, relieving Donovan and there would be talk on the shift, "The Bakery's going off again tonight." Donovan, hearing the comments, would feel sincere sympathy for the lone officer who was probably dodging the missiles, while trying to stay on his feet during the count. Donovan smirked, thinking, "And they say there is no inmate contact on the late night shift!"

In retrospect, as those officers, those enforcers of the laws of the prison dealt with inmates, they were being closely watched. Every word, every move was calculated and judged which would mold the officer's reputation. There would be tests, such as blatant challenges and heated confrontations. How these situations were handled would send the "Word" throughout the inmate population. After only six months of working with inmates, a new officer was no longer considered a rookie and within that short amount of time, that same officer would make the transformation from an idealist to a realist. It would not take long.

It was true that many had bid for the graveyard shift to relax, hoping they were not assigned a dormitory. Then, there were officers who held additional jobs during the day, some as construction workers or landscapers. Others even served as reserve police officers, picking up the day details. Each had there own reasons for working the crazy hours, but those people were far from lames.

Officer Cabral was assigned to the Penthouse. The Penthouse consisted of two-men rooms. While conducting his hourly count and security round, he observed the strangest act that he had ever seen in his life. As he pointed his flashlight into the observation window of each room, the entire room would become illuminated, allowing him to count living, breathing flesh. Arriving at the fourth room and looking into the small window, Robby had to do a double-take. He could not believe his own eyes. Robby found himself looking at an inmate, partially naked, with his double-jointed body bent completely in half at the waist. The man was performing oral sex on himself. Although the flashlight shined directly on him, he had never missed a beat. With no shame, the apparent contortionist did not have to depend on anybody else for sex. To see inmates masturbating was very common, especially during those late hours. However, that one would be tough to explain, though Robby had no problem telling his friends. As always, they laughed, but each one knew it was no less than sick.

Robby found that stress was just as much a factor on the late shift because many of the escape and suicide attempts were made during those hours. Besides the emotional wear and tear of the occasional and unexpected emergencies such as fights, fires, and so on, there was also the physical strains of fighting off sleep when the body naturally wanted to shut down. At 4:30 a.m., most officers tried everything from walking around to drinking cup after cup of coffee. There were those officers that would fall asleep. At those times, they had taken their lives into their own hands. They were also cheating their brother officers out of efficiently and effectively reacting to emergencies, possibly when help was needed most.

The graveyard shift had its own routine which consisted of making sure all inmates were accounted for, at least every hour. There were officers called "trippers" who conducted security rounds of the entire institution. Those officers insured there were no fires and that the facility was locked up tight. Officer Letendre had that nice assignment one evening, but soon decided it wasn't so great.

Trippers had to cover every inch of the prison. There were cat-walks located in the rear of one of the interior buildings. The area was very dimly lit and the narrow passageways were the home of bats, rats and other creepy crawlers. As legend had it, over five decades ago in that very vicinity, two officers had been decapitated by crazed inmates and their heads were rolled down the corridor, as though they were bowling balls. Officer Letendre, checking every door, couldn't help but to keep looking behind him. The secluded area had that haunting effect. On the late shift, quiet was good. It was normal. On any other shift, that type of quiet would be a serious indicator of a possible problem or future disturbance.

Robby and his friends realized that for each day that was worked in prison, there was something to be learned, considering any interest in the job remained. The shifts differed greatly in their routines and procedures, as did the styles and characteristics of the officers who filled the rosters.

It was easy to see that officers could be categorized as the good, the bad and the indifferent. More specifically, Robby took into account the various styles and characteristics which could be found in the officers of any correctional facility. There were those with big time in and were considered toast. "Put a fork in him, he's done," was a favorite saying describing these old-timers. There were those who performed at their best. Competent officers, who were real professionals. There were the hard-asses who gave inmates nothing but hard times. There were the aggressive, the assertive officers, those who took no shit. Some considered themselves part of the inmate's punishment. They were cynical and sadistic officers. On the other end were the white hats, the ultra-liberal who catered to the clientele. There were others who were timid, avoiding confrontation, always standing in the shadows. They never got involved in anything. There were the apathetic, or the public's perception of a state employee. Those who took up space to collect a weekly paycheck. Some suffered from identity crises', believing they were inmates and behaving in that manner. And then there were those who were most despised by their brother officers. The dirty men and women who wore the uniform, but smuggled in drugs or performed sexual acts with the convicted felons they were responsible for. Fortunately, most officers fell in between those styles, with the majority of officers on the better end of the spectrum.

To Robby's surprise, there were no nightsticks, no firearms or any weapons carried inside of the prison. In reality, there was always that chance that an inmate could disarm the officer and use the weapon himself. Officers carried a set of keys, a pair of handcuffs and a portable radio in order to communicate with each other. Unlike Hollywood's version of prison life where large, muscular men strutted around using brute force at will to maintain law and order behind the wall, times had changed.

Robby learned early that an officer was proven more effective if he possessed common sense and a quick wit in handling most situations. Of course, force was still used, but normally as a last option. When a bad situation escalated to the point where it may be deemed a major disturbance, those officers forever awaiting to do battle were called upon. There were spontaneous uses of force when an inmate went off and the situation could not be de-escalated. There were extraction teams and if needed, there were greater resources available for the use of force, with each officer having the option to join and become trained in.

First being the Tactical Response Team (T.R.T) which was normally a platoon size element. There were sixty members, who were highly trained in the art of riot or crowd control. Armed with batons, the Lamb method was preferred, as these troops could be activated at a moments notice to respond to their own institution, or to the mutual aid of others. This particular T.R.T. had been utilized in assisting house of correction personnel in the quelling of several riots. Upon regaining control, the institution was locked down and the team was withdrawn. Suited up in protective equipment similar to that of the extraction team, the T.R.T. competed each year against teams of other institutions. Proudly, the TRT of this institution had been victorious several times.

There were also the K-9 units. Those units utilized the breeds of the agile German Shepherd to the huge, intimidating Rhotweiler. Months of intensive training was required before an officer was appointed this position. The officer and his K-9 had to be ready in tracking escaped felons, sniffing out drugs and skilled in the techniques of crowd control. K-9 units found themselves continually assisting local police departments to render mutual aid. They too competed every year, skill against skill. Normally the dogs patrolled the exterior of the grounds. Occasionally, the dogs were brought inside the institution to help detect drugs, scaring the shit out of the inmates in the meantime. Many inmates had made it clear that they would prefer fighting a mob of officers before having to deal with a merciless K-9.

Lastly, there was the S.R.T. or Special Reaction Team. Similar to a police department's S.W.A.T. unit, those officers were trained experts in the use of firearms and chemical agents. From the handgun to the sniper rifle, they were expertly trained in the strategic takeover of hostage situations and storming buildings. At times, they were needed in riot situations. This team competed each year and was considered one of the best in the state.

As Robby became more educated about the profession, he discovered what job options were available to him within the institution. He could decide to hold a position as a line officer, considered the backbone of the prison. They were the men and women who worked the housing units, yards, rec. rooms, I.D.R., H.S.U. and so on. There were also specialized positions. Fire safety officers fell within this category. They were responsible for all fire safety equipment and the accountability of toxic, caustic chemicals. Then there were mail room officers, property officers and so on.

There were also superintendent pick positions which were criticized by many. Though often considered the best jobs in the prison, apathetic and negative staff complained that those were for the ass-kissers of the chosen friends. Robby believed it was probably the opinion of the envious. Superintendent positions included the I.D. officer, who fingerprinted and photographed the newly admitted inmates. The armorer, and assistant, who were responsible for all weapons, restraints and the accountability of all keys. There was the tool control officer insuring that all tools were accounted for. This was necessary so that hacksaw blades were not assisting in any escape attempts and to insure that screwdrivers were not found sticking out of anyone's head. Next position was the assignment officer, who was in charge of housing moves and inmate employment. The grievance officer handled all inmate complaints and allegations, a busy position.

Another interesting superintendent position was referred to as 'In-Service Training.' It was a challenging position as it entailed the training of every officer for forty hours per year. It was both demanding and challenging because those officers had to be innovative while providing the same old training every year. Inmate canteen staff and medical personnel had been recently privatized for fiscal reasons and as a result, they were no longer available as an option. Those jobs were strongly criticized due to the lack of inmate contact. Many officers felt that if an officer was not in the 'trenches' everyday with the cons, then he wasn't really a correction officer.

In concluding the superintendent pick positions there was the I.P.S. unit (Inner Perimeter Security). This team consisted of several security personnel who, essentially, were internal investigators. Initially designed as a unit which was used strictly for shakedowns, they were later referred to as a 'Goon Squad.' The nickname was derived because of their physical sizes and involvement in forced moves. Eventually the team's concept evolved. Because each line officer had numerous duties to accomplish each day, they did not normally have the time to look into illicit acts committed by the inmates. Essentially, the very need for these investigators.

Responsibilities of the I.P.S. unit included identifying breaches of security within the institution, to investigating criminal acts or infractions of the prison's established code of conduct for inmates. This unit specialized in various areas. There was the monitoring of gang members, escape potentials and climate of the general population. There was evidence preservation, urinalysis drug testing and sharp counts of H.S.U.(needles and syringes). There were the formal investigations conducted which included interviews and interrogations. These investigations sometimes called for the use of inmate informants, as well as the information provided by staff. Every incident, from fights to racial confrontations, work stoppages and boycotts, would eventually involve these officers. They would ask questions and get answers. To many, the job was considered the best in the house, equivalent to the detective squad of a police department. However, it could be a controversial position. Just as officer morale within a prison depends largely on administration style, the same was true concerning the reputation of its I.P.S. unit.

In addition to investigating inmate wrongdoings, these officers also investigated inmate allegations. Inevitably, this meant investigating other security staff, their fellow officers. If the integrity of the team was intact, investigations into excessive force, drug smuggling and illicit sex between officers and inmates were acceptable. There was a need for the check and balance system in order to keep all officers honest and professional. If an officer was on the straight and narrow, then he didn't need to be concerned. It was the questionable officers who hated the concept. Yet, even some honest officers would feel animosity toward the team. Those feelings were understandable, as no officer appreciated being questioned based on an inmate's word.

Most I.P.S. units focused on inmates, but there had been institutions in which the administration would use the team to 'head hunt' for security staff. Security tests were conducted to measure a shift's proficiency. For instance, an inmate was covertly removed from his cell to see how long it took the staff to detect the inmate's absence. Designed to keep all personnel on their toes, those tests were not appreciated by the already overburdened staff. However, the need for I.P.S. units had been proven in the past. Those units had busted 'dirty staff' while maintaining a solid overall understanding of the daily inmate activity. Sometimes called 'Rats,' those officers were the eyes and ears of the administration, keeping everybody abreast of the behavior of the inmate population. From covert operations and drug surveillances to room raids, confidentiality was of the utmost importance. Wearing an even darker shade of blue, those officers walked the prison with the respect of the inmates. They had the authority to lock any of them up, at their own discretion. Their goal was to work alongside the line officers to help maintain a calm prison, making it the most active job in the house. From the rooftops into the bowels of the institution, the team was always on a search-and-destroy mission regarding inmate's illicit activity, while maintaining damage control of acts that had already transpired.

Paralleled in some ways with I.P.S. was the superintendent's private investigator whose primary mission was to investigate staff. Those investigations sometimes led outside of the prison. Whether it was checking into fraudulent Industrial Accident claims or assisting the I.P.S. team in working with outside police agencies on drug cases, this position was an active one as well.

An officer could also transfer to other positions within the department, from correction officer/cooks to recreation officers. There were farm officers, grounds keepers and the list went on. Other personnel found within the prison were support staff. The clerical, fiscal and records staff who were often referred to as "non-essential" personnel, a completely unfair and ignorant assessment.

Some options available outside of the institution were specialized and frequently desired. There were transportation officers whose duties included transporting inmates from institution-to-institution, along with court and hospital trips. Stationed at satellite sites, this was a risky job at best. Located at central office were the internal affairs division. Those officers were investigators into the departments' major crimes and staff improprieties. The fugitive apprehension team hunted down escaped felons, while also assisting in the rendition (transportation from state-to-state) of inmates. Then, there was always the option of transferring to a different facility, such as the boot camp.

Robby also learned that it was imperative to understand the chain of command. The institution was composed of a two part system, the security branch and the classification branch. The correction officer was the lowly soldier, with his counterpart being the correctional counselor. Next up the ladder was the sergeant, considered the hardest position in the house. The sergeant acted as a buffer, or mediator between C.O.'s, the inmates and the upper echelon. Next step was the lieutenant, the area supervisor. This rank was trimmed in silver and considered one of the best positions in the house. Up to captain, who was trimmed in gold. The captain was either a shift commander or a unit manager. At that position, the officer was now considered an administrator and no longer allowed to be a union member. The chain then forked at the top with the security end including the director of security, the deputy superintendent of operations and finally the superintendent, once known as the warden.

The classification end included the unit managers, the director of treatment, the deputy superintendent of classification and of course, the superintendent. Good classification equaled good security. However, as overcrowding was an enormous factor, bed space often dictated the inmate's security level. It was a juggling act, for sure.

For career oriented personnel desiring upward mobility including promotions, it was no easy climb with numerous sacrifices to be paid along the way. Many believed that although a promotional test was taken, the administration would take care of who they wanted, promoting the well-liked. Promotions were difficult to accept because unlike other occupations, once promoted, that person started at the bottom all over again, with less seniority than any other person at that rank. This meant back to poor working hours, poor days off, holidays were worked, etc.. Each promotion was always a kick backward regarding an officer's personal life, but some had made the sacrifices while others displayed different priorities. Some officers had said that there were several ladders to success in corrections. Some would climb on their hard work and merit while others would ascend the ladder because of their friendly connections at the top. There were always those who would use people as the rungs of their ladder. For every person stepped on, another rung was climbed. Those were the henchmen, the department's head-hunters, and they did exist.

It had taken one full year of working behind the walls before Robby felt that he had a good grasp of his profession. He, Donovan and Letendre had taken their bumps and bruises on the late-night shift, while their five training comrades learned the hard lessons of second shift. Then, like so many officers who had passed before them, Robby watched his seven friends just sort of fade into that massive sea of blue.

For the next three or four years, they would each practice every aspect of their trade until finally finding their own style of getting the job done. Eventually, Letendre transferred to the boot camp, where he found his niche as a relentless D.I., while Holt switched to state transportation. Officer Matos was promoted to the rank of sergeant. Johnson retired early due to injuries sustained during a fight. O'Connor continued to find trouble wherever he was assigned and Olivier towed the line as one of the best officers in the House. Officers Robert Cabral and John Donovan, however, were promoted to prison investigators. They had been considered the most fortunate. It would be in that capacity where both men would learn everything they ever needed to know about prison life. In many respects, for the years ahead, their experiences would make them anything but fortunate.

The very day they accepted their promotions, Robby and John knew that corrections was considered to have the worst working conditions of any occupational group. It was thankless, frustrating and dangerous work. It was a public service which had to be remembered. Officers spoke about, "doing time," but it was their choice to remain inside. They had the option to leave at anytime. Senior officers claimed that after five years, a correction officer was locked into the job because their salary and benefits had been "maxed out." There was no turning back, or was there? In a normal twenty year career, an officer spent approximately six years in prison. Being stuck inside for years was true of many occupations, from the factory worker to the store clerk, however, it was undeniable that the conditions and circumstances were clearly different. There was no doubt that correction officers had their share of dilemmas, but for Robby and John, these dilemmas would be magnified. As investigators, they needed to take a closer look at the other side. In attempting to understand the criminals, the crimes that convicted them to prison and the daily lives which they led inside, it would become easier to understand the prison's underworld. From deceptive games to breathtaking violence, comprising every illicit activity imaginable...the fun never ended.

❺

They could have never guessed, but the morning that Robby and John reported to the I.P.S. office, would inevitably become the most important day in their careers. They were each issued a darker blue uniform. The uniform which carried more respect, but also more responsibility within the prison. The two young men knew they were up for the challenge.

John Donovan began to chuckle because his new uniform fit him like a wet suit. He was a broad-chested guy, with a serious look about him. He resembled Robby somewhat, with blond hair and blue eyes, but he lacked his friend's childish smile. As they got dressed, their new partner, Officer Keith Petrie, introduced himself. While getting acquainted, Sgt. Frank Gagne, Commander of the I.P.S. Bravo Team, entered the room.

Frank Gagne was no more than thirty years old, but had almost ten years experience in corrections. With salt-and-pepper hair, his tanned face revealed the lines of a worrisome soul. He extended his bony hand and with a genuine smile, he welcomed Robby and John to the team. Without delay, he explained, "The I.P.S. unit is divided into two teams, Alpha and Bravo. Lieutenant Redman has assigned you two, along with Keith, to my team. For the time being, it'll be the four of us working as one. I'll take Robby and Keith will break-in John." Robby and John exchanged a smile, never realizing that "For the time being," would gradually turn into three years. Sergeant Gagne continued, "I know that you guys have been around inmates for a few years, but now you need to change your way of thinking.

It's essential to get to know who they really are. Knowledge is everything! If you know who they are and what they're about, then you can start to think like they do. That's the key to this job!" The boys knew that Frank was right. They started their research right away.

It was already understood that corrections was a three part system consisting of probations, prisons and parole. The probations department, an alternative to prison, was handled right inside of court. The department of correction, or prison system included the parole department. The parole department was the committee responsible for determining which inmates were suitable and, or eligible for early release from incarceration. In many respects, the parole system had more power over the convicted felon's life than the court which initially sentenced the criminal to prison. Frank claimed that good connections with parole officers had always been an effective tool. No doubt, the inmates feared I.P.S. because of those connections.

It was also important to understand the steps of the road leading to a person's incarceration within the state's prison system. Essentially, the person committed a crime, a felony, and got caught. Once arrested, that person was arraigned where he would plead to criminal charges, guilty or not guilty. Without plea bargaining out, the person then had the Constitutional right to be tried by a judge. This consisted of a bench trial or a trial by a jury of his peers. Both sides would be heard. At the conclusion of the trial, if the person was found guilty, or convicted of the criminal charges against him, the presiding judge was responsible for sentencing that guilty person. More often than not and for different reasons, such as already overcrowded prisons, an alternative to prison would be imposed. There was probation, or suspended sentences, community service, house arrest, fines and retribution to be paid, as well as various other alternatives. Sometimes the convicted felons would be sentenced to jail, or the house of correction, which was designed for the incarceration of short term sentences for less serious offenders.

If sentenced to state prison, that person had just entered the 'big leagues' where inmates were incarcerated for much longer periods of time and for more serious crimes. A court order, or mittimus, was then issued to the department of correction charging that department with the custody of the convicted felon until the complete term was served or 'wrapped up,' or the inmate was paroled earlier. In essence, unless a blatantly heinous crime was committed, it was no easy task to enter the state system which was already bulging at the seams. It often took numerous felony convictions before the criminal was actually admitted into the state system. However, it seemed once they were admitted, this would become the chosen lifestyle of many. There were thousands who apparently enjoyed the living conditions, returning again and again. Frank quipped that those repeat offenders were, "Doing life on the installment plan."

Convicted felons were either sentenced to maximum security custody or the medium security classification center for men. Of course, females were directly transported to their exclusive medium security institution. Some convicted felons would be sentenced to the State Hospital for the purpose of evaluations, but end up staying for years. Others, who were deemed sexually dangerous by a state psychiatrist, would be mandated to the Treatment Center from which it was difficult to be cleared from.

There were two types of sentences. The first was a Concord bid. This bid consisted of a singular number, for instance ten years. Of those ten years, only one year would be served and the inmate would be paroled with the remaining nine years to hang over his head. A twenty Concord was only two years to serve with eighteen on parole. A Walpole bid was a split sentence, for example ten to fifteen years. This inmate would serve only one-third of the lesser (ten) for crimes against property, two-thirds of the lesser for crimes against persons. The state was attempting to stiffen those sentences, proposing that on a ten Concord, the inmate actually serve the entire ten years and not just one. That legislation was not yet passed, though Robby felt it only made sense.

The court system had once allowed statutory good time in which inmates were allotted generous amounts of time taken off of their sentences for no reason. The good time system still remained intact, although those generous gifts had recently been stricken from the lawbooks. An inmate had to earn this time subtracted from his sentence by working, attending classes, substance abuse programs, etc.. There was a cap of seven and a half days which could be removed from the inmate's bid each month.

Upon being admitted to their sentencing institution, the inmate's criminal history and prior prison history were reviewed. Interviews and counseling sessions were conducted before the inmate was classified to maximum custody or lower security.

Once classified and admitted into a particular institution, the inmate was issued several outfits of state clothing, a bed to sleep in, usually located in a dorm (single cell would come later), medical treatment, to include any medications that were needed and three hot meals per day. Robby thought, "Our nation's homeless should be so lucky." During the mandatory Orientation Program, the inmate was informed of the classification process and what was expected in order to reintegrate, as quickly as possible, back into society. The inmate was also introduced to treatment programs available to him. Those included education, vocational training, psychological counseling, substance abuse programs, religious services and so on. This was the fork in the road where each inmate would choose to either rehabilitate himself or continue on the path to nowhere. Though many opportunities were offered, the rehabilitation process could not be forced. It had to be voluntary and the changes desired by the inmate intensely.

Most inmates were well-aware of the rules and regulations that governed the behavior of the inmate population known as the disciplinary procedure. A code of disciplinary offenses were listed, from lying or being insolent toward staff to fighting, extortion, even self-mutilation and killing. This internal judicial system was designed to prevent intolerable inmate behavior while punishing the inmates in violation. If an inmate was found violating any of the institutional rules or regulations, an officer would write, or issue a 'ticket.' This was a disciplinary report, charging the inmate with the appropriate offenses. The inmate was often secured in a segregation unit to await his disciplinary hearing. This hearing, held by an impartial, objective board would hear both arguments of the alleged infractions, then make a judgment of guilty or not guilty. If found guilty, the inmate would receive a sanction, which could include loss of privileges, isolation time in a segregation unit, loss of good time and possibly a transfer to higher custody. The inmate had the right to appeal, as the accumulation of tickets could affect future classification moves or even his parole consideration. This system's intention was to maintain law and order while keeping a calm environment within the prison. Realistically, those rules and regulations for which all inmates were required to comply was not always a deterrent. Robby had already witnessed that the same individuals, who chose not to comply with society's rules or laws, were even less likely to conform while incarcerated.

After concluding the orientation program, an inmate would begin his own structured routine. Instantly, they became a member of, or an associate of a group for the purpose of protection. Most would say, "I came in alone, I'll do my time alone and I'll leave alone." Robby laughed. It was a crock of shit, as it was very seldom that a loner would be found amongst the hundreds. It was usually only an inmate who was criminally insane, who could survive alone. They would avoid being constantly victimized due to their instability.

Most inmates had been through the system numerous times. For Robby, it was amazing to watch a newly admitted inmate enter a unit and be greeted by ten or more friends which had all done time together at various detention facilities. For some, it was like coming home, as they played their card games, sports, watched television and laid around all day. They didn't have a responsibility or worry in the world. Many became involved in illicit activities. However, there were a small percentage of others who attempted to better themselves, hoping to rush their stay through the system. They would gain employment, with the average salary being one or two dollars per day. Some had half of these earnings transferred into their personal account. They would use this money to purchase canteen items. The other half of their salaries were deposited into their savings account, so they would have some money to start their lives over upon leaving the system. Those savings accounts could not be withdrawn. The exceptions would be the inmates serving the 'book,' or life, or when special permission was granted. Frank advised Robby that close monitoring of those accounts was important. Inmates had tried to launder dirty money right through inmate accounts. Receiving large amounts of money only to send it back out weeks later, while an outsider was cashing state checks. It had been tried.

Education, vocational training and substance abuse programs were also attended, keeping the inmates busy and productive, while earning good time. Robby had always heard that an inmate entered prison as an angry, non-productive citizen and left even meaner and more likely to victimize another human being. However, he knew this may have been true in many cases, but again it was the inmate's sole choice to either make a positive change to better his life or slide deeper into the life of darkness.

In their new, dark blue uniforms, Robby and John's closer observations of the inmate population hanging around in the vast cement yards, were intriguing to say the least. With their assigned partners, for the first few weeks, they patrolled through the yards which always contained several hundred inmates. Immediately, Robby noticed the unsubtle diversity of the racial groupings or cliques. It was phenomenal. Leaning against one of the interior walls or huddling in large groups, there were the black inmates. Some were Jamaicans, others allegedly radical Muslims with the majority being Afro-Americans. Large numbers of inner-city 'gang bangers,' talking over one another loudly. Their street rap of communication was difficult to interpret. They seemed to be forever attempting to display unity by 'sporting,' or wearing the same haircuts or footwear styles. They would do anything that would tell other inmates that they possessed strength in numbers. This behavior was forbidden, keeping I.P.S. busy trying to stay on top of it all.

In a completely different area of the yard were the white groupings, consisting of Outlaw Bikers, covered in tattoos, wearing long, greasy hair and beards growing wild. Included in this group were Aryan brothers or white supremists, a dangerous sort. Fortunately, they did not possess the numbers to cause any major disturbances. Much like the black inmates, the whites congregated with their 'homeboys,' or friends from a particular city or geographical location. The Irish with the Irish from Southie, the Italians with the Italians from the North end, each clinging to the safety their numbers provided.

Then there were the Hispanic inmates, originating from various countries and sharing many similar cultural traits. The most obvious would be their native tongue of Spanish. Those inmates were normally found in very large groups and were known to be tightly knit, allowing very few outsiders in.

In concluding the racial breakdown, there were the Orientals, also originating from different countries. Those inmates were a smaller group with the difficulties of a language barrier. Normally they were quiet inmates, whose main concern was deportation after serving their sentences. Many of them would face an automatic death penalty upon being sent back to their native countries. There were still countries that refused to tolerate the criminal behavior those men had displayed. Many had dishonored their Motherland and would pay the ultimate price upon being returned.

Within these various ethnic groups, those men had brought elements of their own cultures, which consisted of prejudices, biases, religious and political beliefs, as well as varying opinions on most everything. Lacking a reputation for possessing high ethical or moral standards, each brought his anger and aggressiveness to the group. Together, they created an altogether different sub-culture inside the walls. On the majority, each would offer negativity and their own criminal skills in creating the unbelievable sub-culture. There was some interaction between the groups. Sometimes, it was passive and friendly, but frequently to gain illicit goals. Far too often, it was violent, as the strongest or most dominant group at the time would attempt to victimize and control the others. Each group had its own leader, or leaders who possessed the 'juice.' They had the power to influence, persuade, even control the other members. Frank informed Robby that those were the inmates to speak to when racial unrest between the groups existed. Quite often, they could easily bring about peace by their own word. Again, as strength was found in numbers, many of those inmates were singularly weak, but collectively, they could survive without a problem. However, there were the predators, the strong, unfearing and vicious hunters who would victimize any inmate who walked within. Robby observed that those men did not discriminate. Everybody was open game.

Before long, Frank casually pointed out the less predominant groups which were also found in the populated yards. Groups who could survive in small numbers for various reasons. Within those groups, were the Old-Timers, many being lifers or doing 'smoker bids'(lengthy sentences). They were real con-men who knew exactly how to manipulate the other inmates and staff. After being locked behind bars for years, they had become hardened men who wore a smile on their faces, but had cold blood running through their veins. Those old-timers were still living by the old 'code' for convicts which had become quite weakened and confused. They were not real happy with the younger inmates. Up front, they were compliant with institutional rules, but often they became the real player's controlling a good percentage of the prison's illegal underworld. Robby had once over-heard some of those older cons complaining about how times had changed. They said that the younger inmates spoke to officers. Informants were abundant and allowed to live. They felt respect and honor had been lost. Some of the younger, candy-ass inmates did not even contemplate escape. Times had certainly changed. Frank strongly advised his young friend, "These are the men who have been involved in, or witnessed the riots, hostage takings and numerous murders of the early 1970's. Though time has taken its toll, don't be fooled. They will still fight at the drop of a hat, never allowing another man to strip them of their honor, pride and respect within the population."

Walking through the yard with his new boss, Robby listened atten-tively, as Frank described one of the characters associated with the old-timers group. "He was an Italian man called Dom, serving big numbers for mayhem and manslaughter. It was said he had no choice, but to take the fall for another man while being heavily connected with organized crime. An old leg-breaker for the mob, he would deny his crime, but laugh about crimes he had gotten away with. Dom was a dangerously, frigid man with the capability of taking more lives and sleeping like a baby for it. Living in a preferred housing unit, 'the Penthouse,' the inmate lived as comfortable as it got inside, with money dropped off into his account every week. Young ladies visited him routinely. It was clear that somebody with money was taking good care of him."

Frank chuckled, saying, "Dom was in his cozy room one Sunday after-noon, along with three or four of his trusted friends. He had just finished cooking a large spaghetti meal. His friends, sitting around an improvised table, were just preparing to dig in when I opened the door. I took a head count, then turned to leave. To my surprise, old Dom asked me to sit and join him in the Sunday feast. Of course, I politely declined, adding that I didn't think it was appropriate. My host, visibly insulted, asked, 'If I come to your house and you invite me to eat dinner with you and I refuse, would that not insult you ?' I responded, 'I guess it would.' The old man, smiling, replied, 'Well, this is my house, so sit down, eat and don't insult me again.' I felt confused and afraid, so I sat down to a small plate of what turned out to be a delicious meal. More importantly, I learned that the old-timer had controlled the situation, displaying his cunningness for friends to observe and enjoy." Frank shook his head, laughing, "Like I said, watch out for the old guys, they'll try to beat you every time!"

Robby shared Frank's laughter, as they continued patrolling the crowded cement yards. He noticed that another group left untouched were the homosexuals and transvestites who were plentiful within the prison. Protected by their stronger lovers or pimps, those men survived better than expected in general population. Regarding transvestites, most were admitted with female breasts and no testicles. They did have a penis, therefore had to serve their time within a male prison. Serving time for prostitution to drug dealing, some had been saving money for sex change operations. However, they had not finished the complete transformation. Referred to as she or her, most were actually treated like ladies and acted as though they were on cloud nine. One particular inmate, called Josephine, who was always shaking her ass across the court yard, had the tight body, permed hair and distinct mannerisms of a seductive woman. If Robby didn't know her, there would have been no second glance, but a wide-eyed stare. This inmate conducted herself as a highly paid call girl. Once a close-up look was possible, it was easily noticed that Josephine had the face of a homely man.

As they walked, she passed Robby and Frank. She winked at Frank, to which he jokingly responded, "Well, good morning sweetheart." Robby laughed, knowing it was a good example of what was considered normal behind the wall, but obscene in outside society.

They watched, as Josephine met up with two other 'Shims' called Margaret and Shelley. Margaret had the calf muscles of a middle line backer. She would cut and sew state jeans into mini-skirts and fabricate halter tops. She would create her own make-up by mixing dry Kool-Aid powder with Vaseline. With ruby red lips and lavender eye shadow, she always looked ready for a hot night out on the town.

Her friend, Shelley, was probably the strangest of inmates known to have resided within the system. She was a large, muscular, black inmate convicted of a double murder. While serving her sentence at maximum security, this vicious killer took another inmate's life. She also put countless officers into early retirement. A violent freak, lacking any conscience, she eventually went insane for unknown reasons. This murderer started to believe that she was a woman by the name of Shelly. If an inmate or officer referred to her as anything but Shelly, there would be, without question, at least a brutal assault. Wearing homemade skirts and a turban shredded from a bed sheet, this fruitcake began carrying a mustard-style squeeze bottle wherever she went. During a breakfast feeding, Shelly was seen squeezing a white liquid on her toast, spreading it out, eating it and giggling the whole time. It was later discovered that Shelly had passed the bottle around, so that other inmates could masturbate and ejaculate their sperm into it. Shelly, still feared by many, was using the sperm as a condiment for her food. Needless to say, it was a struggle to remove that nasty squeeze bottle from Shelly, who probably still feels lost without it.

There were also many homosexuals who were very open about their sexual preference. Occasionally, they got 'pinched,' or caught having intercourse with each other. Those inmates received disciplinary reports because sex was not authorized in prison. However, the reports had not been a real deterrent for those men. Some inmates claimed to be married with others and were constantly quarreling with each other. One inmate, a young blond slut, enjoyed performing fellatio on his friends. He was always getting into trouble for his kindness. This inmate could not understand why there had to be a problem. He was not charging fees or being forced to perform his services which were provided to many inmates who claimed to be heterosexual. There was a famous saying that, "It doesn't count in prison," due to lack of female contact. It was an accepted practice by many, especially the inmates serving big time. A bizarre environment to find love, but with a late night stroll through a dimly lit yard, the moon shining off of the razor wire, anything was possible. One inmate admitted to Robby that he could not sleep without at least a good night kiss.

The last group to really stick out of the crowd was actually just a collection of individuals doing their own thing in their own world. Those were the criminally insane, known as 'bugs.' They were able to function within the general population without the threat of sane inmates bothering them. On occasion, when they acted up and got out of hand, those inmates were sent to the State Hospital for 'tune ups.' Many had problems with medication, or displayed assaultive or self-mutilating behavior. Sometimes, it was just the need for more intense observation. They were normally gone for a month or two, returning heavily sedated and fattened up. In this group of individuals, there were some real characters.

Robby had already met quite a few of the bugs. Their bizarre behavior never ceased to amaze him. One inmate, a completely bald man, continually filed grievances, as he truly believed that he had won millions of dollars through a famous mail-in Sweepstakes. He had received the large envelope in the mail indicating that he was one of several lucky millionaires, so he was convinced that the state was stealing the fortune from him.

Another bug, not overly concerned with bathing, would pace the shanty floor for hours in search of 'snipes,' or poked out cigarette butts. He would either relight the cigarette and smoke the remainder, or empty whatever tobacco was left, then roll his own. Greasing his hair back, he would do a hilarious, but realistic impression of Jack Nicholson. "Wait 'til you get a load of me," he would repeat over and over. Once, he was locked inside of a segregation room on mental health watch where he was checked every fifteen minutes. He had filled his pak-a-potti, then began defecating in the drawer of his night stand. The awful aroma had made Robby gag.

Others included an old deviant delinquent, incarcerated since adolescence. He knew no other life. Released from prison, the lost soul stole a bicycle and rode it off of state property. Almost one year later, he returned on some bogus charges. He was home at last, for the real world had been too much to handle. This pain in the ass, a small man, but well-endowed, enjoyed exposing himself while boasting that he had serviced some nurses in the old days, "They loved me," he would reminisce, as he fondled his genitals.

A different character, finally classified to minimum security after years of wall time, got a job working in the cowbarn as a cleaner. One winter morning, he was caught by a farm officer attempting to sodomize a calf. He was immediately returned behind the wall. Officers would "moo" each time he walked past, pissing him off to no end. He would respond with a middle finger salute and a loud "Fuck You!"

Yet, the one that Robby found most disturbed was a unique individual who was extremely intelligent in his own right. He would talk for hours about Roman history on one day, Greek mythology the next. Before long, officers would say, "Kenny's lost it again." Then, Robby would be see him walking through the yard with dried feces smeared across his face, forming a perfect mustache and beard. This unusual inmate, diagnosed as a manic-depressant, was convicted of butchering his sleeping wife to death with a hatchet. Crazy Kenny, forever showing remorse for the gruesome crime, claimed that it had occurred because his psychotropic medication had not been regulated properly at the time.

The examples were endless. The crimes which had convicted those inmates were just as strangely horrifying. Yet, those inmates were not considered troubled enough to be admitted to the State Hospital full-time. With a range of mental disorders from severe chemical imbalances, to the abuse of L.S.D., and P.C.P. these men, if in sight, had to be watched closely. Very few were harmless, however, the peculiar behavior displayed by some was sadly entertaining. Robby remembered always laughing, as one inmate would cover himself in moistened bread crumbs, then laugh out loud, as a flock of pigeons would feed right off of his body. This became a daily morning ritual until he was transferred. Curiously enough, Robby seemed to miss the eccentric "Pigeon Man."

As Robby became more familiar with the inmates he was dealing with on a daily basis, he started to hear about some of the crimes that had imprisoned those men, from Frank and Keith. Many of the stories seemed far-fetched with Keith saying, "Don't talk to that one, he's a sick son-of-a-bitch." With his curiosity peeked, Robby started to research the inmate's records for the official police version of the crimes in every heart-wrenching detail. Many of the inmates appeared normal, behaving as ordinary, decent people. Robby soon found the opposite was true and that Keith was not exaggerating. It was simple enough to find out any inmate's criminal history. Though it was a good idea for Robby to know the crimes for which the inmates were convicted, it was usually better not to know the details. It was not his job to judge or punish the inmates in any way, that had been the court's responsibility. Yet, after discovering the gory description of a brutal killing, the sick and demented acts of a child molester and the heartlessness of a punk who violently assaulted an elderly person for pocket change, it was difficult to remain objective and not think or act differently toward those same men. It was natural for Robby to picture his family as the victims of those heinous crimes. To help remove the hatred which he started to feel toward those inmates, it was essential to deal with them as they behaved in prison, regardless of the inhumane acts which had sentenced them.

The majority of inmates lied about their crimes and many spoke freely, boasting about their offenses. The lies were intended to cover up sex related offenses because the truth could cause them enemy situations, or other problems down the road. For every crime there was a victim, and quite often, those victims were related to other inmates residing in the same prison system. From all walks of life and completely different backgrounds, there was no way to generalize race, color, age, social status or education level when it came to criminals. It was not worth trying to figure out why a particular person committed a certain offense, there was usually no rhyme or reason for any of it. There had been inmates who had adamantly denied their crimes, claiming that they were unjustly convicted. On the other hand, those same men admitted that if they were caught and convicted for the crimes they had committed, chances were they would be serving longer sentences.

Besides the dominant racial groupings, the old-timers, homosexuals and bugs, the prison hierarchy, or pecking order was still in existence. However, unlike years ago, the 'solid cons' were perishing while the sex offenders and gang members, who were just beyond adolescence, were flourishing in large numbers. Robby had known the order well, but with Frank's assistance, he started to meet many of the criminals who filled its ranks. Frank had been right, it was time to get inside their heads. It was time to understand them completely, though it would never be easy, or pleasant, for that matter.

At the height of the pecking order were the cop killers. They usually entered prison blocks receiving standing ovations from the other cons. There were also serial killers, mass murderers and a cannibal or two which would always be housed at maximum security, or in federal institutions. As the media focused on certain criminals who had committed outrageous crimes, they were brought into the limelight and the public became absolutely horrified that such animals existed in society. However, there were other men who were not as publicized, perhaps because of more pressing social issues at the moment. Yet, these men had committed equally inhumane acts. They had the capabilities of committing worst deeds, only they were limited to destruction within the confines of a prison. Robby knew these men, though they were the men who the public were fortunate enough not to know. He considered it a blessing, as those men could easily be the root of terrible nightmares which could quickly become reality. Unfortunately, society had become numb as more atrocious crimes were a frequent occurrence. Fear was an emotion that could save lives, to become numb was dangerous within itself. Years earlier, Robby Cabral had been introduced to that fear, but he had always masked it well.

Some of these unknown animals maintained a low profile for years. They were serving life sentences with the chance for parole after twenty five years. Others serving natural life, multiple life sentences or life and a day, would fortunately never interact with society again, condemned to die inside of prison walls from natural causes, suicide or at the hands of another animal. The controversial death penalty was not in existence. Again, Robby felt it was a blessing, though a very expensive one, that those inmates never saw the light of the real world again.

Murderers, seated at the top of the order, mainly resided at maximum security. Others would reach medium or even minimum statuses. A great number of those killers entered prison, boiling in their own rage, with the attitude that from here on, they had nothing to lose because everything worth living for had already been taken away. It was a destructive outlook on life. They possessed blank stares that could penetrate straight through steel. Their blood was as cold as ice water. Some had not finished terminating human lives and would kill while serving the 'book,' or their life sentence. Those murderers would spend years in isolation. They were just unable to interact with other people.

Robby had met other inmates who entered the system, convicted of similar crimes, such as murder and manslaughter, who would display a different attitude. After the initial adjustment and depressing realization that incarceration was their lives and their futures, many decided they would make the most of it. For better or worst, they were compliant with institutional guidelines and considered some of the best, most cooperative and quiet inmates serving time. One convicted murderer doing life for stabbing his unfaithful girlfriend to death had told Robby, "I had a problem, I fixed the problem. I no longer have any problems." That was one way of looking at things, however, that inmate had no problems while serving his sentence. Though compliant, those lifers would fight tooth and nail with litigation, often using aggressive means, if the administration removed privileges and the like. It was those men who the changes affected most, and for the rest of their lives.

During some intense research in the records room, Robby learned several of the inhumane crimes committed by a few lifers. Obviously, they were just a small portion of the offenses known of in the prison's population. One inmate, who was a passenger in his girlfriend's car, kept telling her to pull over so that he could drive. She firmly refused because he was blown out on drugs. Becoming enraged, he unbuckled the girl's infant from the child safety seat and threw the baby out of the window, as the car was moving at better than fifty miles per hour. The infant died on impact. The inmate claimed that he could not recall the terrible incident because he was so high. He told Robby that he felt that he did not deserve the long sentence the judge had imposed. He would try to justify the crime by calling it an accident, but no excuse could bring that baby back to life, or other lives for that matter.

There had been endless others, murders by stabbings, mob-style slayings and forced hangings. Other victims of these men fell prey to electrocutions, forced drownings and one inmate had even set a man ablaze, who must have suffered an incredibly agonizing death. Most premeditated, many were committed during the commission of another felony such as robbery or rape. Because of this fact alone, the prison hierarchy had become somewhat confused with kidnappers, thieves and rapists who professed to being cold-blooded killers. Due to the nature of their hideous crimes, Robby considered that some of the murderers should have been found at the very bottom of the pecking order.

One old timer, called Woody, was taken into the home of a kind priest at a very early age. The priest had vowed to take care of the homeless boy. After several years of pious upbringing, the priest left his home for a short time, leaving the young man to care for the house and himself. During the first week of the priest's absence, the seventeen year old man abducted a young woman and tied her up, so that she could not flee. For three straight days, this deranged individual raped and tortured the woman until he completely cut off both of her breasts. Leaving the corpse to rot inside the house, Woody tied both breasts to his belt and was using them as ashtrays, until finally being apprehended by the authorities. Woody was tried, convicted and sentenced to death, by means of the electric chair. Sitting on death row, two weeks before he was to be seated in that notorious chair, the governor of the time commuted, or reduced the young man's sentence from death to a life sentence which had to always be served behind a walled facility. For over fifty years, Woody served time with the majority spent at maximum security. Once he had reached this old, run down medium security prison, he appeared to be the age of ninety or better. A broken man, he wore a baseball helmet while regularly drooling and urinating all over himself. Obviously, he was not well-liked by the other inmates. They had not killed him, but some valid attempts had been made.

More than once, Woody had been thrown off of three story tiers. The falls had turned his head into what could have been mistaken as a deformed squash. The old man, like a doll with a pull string located in its back, had only three or four sayings that he would repeat when spoken to. One was, "Not gonna send me back to the Hill, it's a whorehouse up there," recalling with fear the countless times he was raped. This man had served hard time because the other inmates had punished him dearly for his gruesome crime. After serving fifty consecutive years behind the wall, a state record, Woody received a cake, as though it was his birthday. It was a strange ceremony indeed. He died shortly thereafter in his sleep. Looking back, it was questionable whether that governor had done Woody any favors. He was sometimes told to enjoy his days on earth because only God knew what punishment he faced once he reached the other side.

In a similar case, an inmate who resided in the Penthouse of the prison, had also kidnapped a young woman. He had tied her to a chair and tortured her for days with lit cigarettes and cutlery found in the house. Eventually, bored of his own twisted games, he hung the woman by her neck, putting her out of her misery. This man, serving life, lived a comfortable life by prison standards. Times certainly had changed. Woody apparently committed his atrocity during the wrong era, or more likely, the other sick bastard had never gotten his just desserts.

Robby knew of several cases where inmates were convicted of breaking into houses, restraining the man of the house and forcing him to watch his wife and children get repeatedly raped and violently beaten, often to death. One related case involved two youths entering a secluded, wooded area. They had found a pair of young lovers having intercourse in the back seat of an automobile. Without much planning, they removed the naked lovers from the car and beat the male senseless before throwing him through the windshield where he was left to die. The girl was then gang raped for hours, but lived to suffer mentally and emotionally for the rest of her life. These co-defendants bragged about being cold-blooded killers, but were only vicious sex offenders who got carried away. Robby, overhearing their boasting, privately reminded them that they were cowards and skinners in disguise. The pep talk had shut those boys up for some time. Robby had reminded them that some people did know the truth.

Other inmates, serving life for murder, were actually real human beings who were positively guilty of not using good judgment resulting in the death of another human being. For instance, the driver who, under the influence of alcohol, struck two pedestrians, killing one. Returning from work, he had consumed three beers. That was all it took to end an innocent person's life. Another inmate was serving thirty years for engaging in a fist fight outside of a convenience store. His opponent, knocked to the ground during the struggle, struck his head on a curb stone and died instantly. They had each committed acts no different than that of thousands of other people. However, the outcome had made the real difference.

Then, Frank explained the case of inmate Dale, leaving Robby dumbfounded. "He was an ordinary man who had just started dating a divorced woman. The woman's extremely jealous ex-husband repeatedly threatened to kill Dale if he continued to socialize with his newly divorced wife. Dale ignored the threats and stubbornly continued, but found himself running for his own life one day, while the ex-husband, wielding a baseball bat, chased him for blocks. After two weeks of peace and quiet, Dale was sitting at a red light in his pickup truck. He looked to his right to find the obsessed ex-husband pointing a handgun directly at him. Immediately picking up his twelve gauge shot gun located under the seat of the truck, Dale fired once at the armed man, blowing his head clean off his shoulders. Arrested and tried for murder, Dale discovered that the ex-husband had only been pointing a starter pistol and not an actual handgun at him. How was he to know? The prosecution, basing their case on the shot-gun being placed in the truck for the purpose of killing the ex-husband, had Dale convicted of second degree murder. He received a life sentence." While absorbing the unique story, Robby figured it was probable that Dale was more guilty of hiring a poor defense attorney than anything else. In prison, inmate Dale's nickname was the "citizen." He acted nothing like an inmate and most people knew of his case. There weren't many, but this may have been one man who fell through the cracks of a less than perfect justice system.

There was a long list of inmates doing life for taking the lives of others and they all had to be considered dangerous. One murderer, convicted of three slayings, put it to Robby this way, "The first life is the hardest to take, the rest come easier." This same philosopher struck another inmate over the head with a pipe because the man abusively kicked one of the wild cats that roamed inside the prison. He was certainly a real animal lover, but a humanitarian, he was not. That same killer reminded Robby, "One thing which you always have to remember concerning us lifetime members...the prison is our house and if another inmate serves thirty years inside, he is only a visitor passing through our house."

Moving down the pecking order, there were the inmates incarcerated for Mayhem, or the maiming and disfiguring of another. Serving a long sentence for such a crime, one inmate bitterly stated to Robby, "I cut up one of my enemies on the streets in a fair fight, scarring his face real bad!" Laughing at the thought, he added, "I should have finished the job because I would have gotten the same time for it." Robby shook his head in disgust. It was just another prime example of some ordinary prison logic.

There were also the violent, abusive men serving time for aggravated assaults with the use of dangerous weapons. Those assaults included breaking the knee caps of another, beating one's wife or children into a coma and one who even viciously assaulted a seventy year old man during an argument. Those types of inmates were also in abundance and for the most part, Robby considered them the hardest to deal with. Those inmates would generally have the behavioral traits of being loud-mouths, non-compliants who resented authority while either fighting, or aggressively verbalizing with other inmates and staff. One of these inmates, by the name of Pereira, was known as the toughest and craziest inmate in the house. Usually locked up in segregation, he was discovered one day holding a freshly killed pigeon and a cup of his own blood, while melting a string of rosary beads. Those were rites used in a grotesque ceremony of worshipping the devil. Both arms tattooed with devil heads, this nut was always working out, increasing his strength each day. Eventually, even he would be released some day. This was a petrifying thought. Robby knew it would only be a matter of time before he permanently injured or killed his next victim.

The next step down were the inmates serving big time for kidnapping. Kidnapping was a risky crime, always searching for that easy money, the big ransom. Many kidnappers ended up with more trouble than they bargained for. Careful not to cross state lines which would turn the crime into a federal offense, one inmate, an enormous man of over seven feet, had been convicted of the crime when he was very young. Allegedly stoned on P.C.P., he and his partner panicked and threw their victim out of the speeding car which caused him to die days later. This inmate complacently served the remainder of his days in prison for murder. Other kidnappers, stuffing their victims into car trunks, later found that they had suffocated to death. From kidnapping into a 'murder beef,' it was not so uncommon.

Below them were the burglars, the B. and E.(breaking and entering) artists and the thieves. Lazy men who had never held down any formal employment, they would steal for a living to support bad drug habits or even their families. Those were many of the inmates constantly in and out of the system. They never seemed to be sent up for many years at one time, nor did they ever seem to change their choice of trade. Until they were deemed a habitual criminal, whereas a judge could impose a life sentence, many of those men would do life on the 'installment plan.' Amongst this motley crew were the inmates serving 'smoker bids' for house invasions. This term was used when criminals, who normally worked in pairs or small groups, forcibly gained entrance into a home when the family members were awake. The family was then held at gunpoint while their house was robbed and vandalized. One inmate, after serving eight years for such a crime, confided in Robby, "It was the thrill of it all that got me hooked. Just watching the man of the house on his knees, crying, pleading for mercy and sometimes pissing himself from fear right in front of his family....it was a powerful feeling!" The inmate could hardly contain his excitement while Robby could barely contain his temper.

On the same level were the bank robbers and the armed robbers. They were criminals in masks carrying sawed-off shot guns who were always looking for the big heist. Many were serving mandatory sentences for firearms charges and had been shot during the commission of their crimes. Some had shot back and were also serving life for murder. Robby had asked a particular bank robber what he would do when he got out. The punk snickered, "Next time, I won't get caught." This was a dominant attitude shared by inmates of all convictions. Robby thought, "Now that's rehabilitation working its wonders." Serving alongside these men were the less dangerous criminals imprisoned for unarmed robbery, larceny and petty theft. Although, inside the wall, they could be just as dangerous as the rest.

Further down the ladder were the arsonists. Conceivably the most volatile inmates to be incarcerated, those men were capable of wreaking the worst destruction. They were feared by the other inmates because there had been a few incidents where cells were set on fire. One arsonist, named Keaton, was serving a multiple life sentence for setting a tenement house on fire which resulted in several cruel deaths. He was found by the police parked across the street in his car, masturbating, as he watched firefighters struggle to save lives. The building was turned into ashes. This had not been his first fire, but this was the first time the lunatic had gotten caught. As they walked past, the pyromaniac yelled to Frank and Robby, "Don't play with fire, you might get burned." Keaton was a real comedian, though the two investigators never laughed.

One step down were the drug dealers and the inmates who were busted for using and abusing illegal narcotics. Those men were not completely liked or respected by the other inmates. Many of those other inmates were fathers of children hooked on crack-cocaine or heroine, therefore, the reason for the animosity. Though most of those inmates were serving mandatory sentences, they also frequently returned into the revolving door of corrections, as they could not beat their addiction. They would steal or sell more drugs to feed their uncontrollable, engulfing habits. Some would say they felt best when in prison because they could stay clean, but those were the same inmates being 'pinched' for lugging in illicit narcotics. Many were caught with dirty urines. The numbers sent to state prison for these crimes were growing and the inmates sentenced were getting younger. As one nineteen year old cocaine dealer told Robby, "I can either work at a fast food joint for minimum wage, or drive a B.M.W. and always have at least two grand in my pocket. My options are limited." Another claimed that, "Crime does pay," bragging that although he would have to serve a five year mandatory sentence, he had stashed away money. Enough money to take care of him for the rest of his life. In essence, he had traded five years of freedom, so that he would not have to work again. Somehow, Robby knew that his greed would probably tell another story.

Within that group was an increasing number of H.I.V. virus carriers, who were mostly I.V. users. They were introducing the deadly disease into the prison population at an alarming rate. Those inmates, once found to be infected (since their medical records were confidential, even staff did not know who was infected with what), were feared most within the population. One fight could mean death. Drug convictions were often coupled with other felonies. This was a result of criminals who were 'under the influence' during the commission of a crime.

Also right around that area of the pecking order, Robby found the white collar criminals. They were also not truly respected by the solid cons. After a guilty conviction and upon entering the system, most were sentenced to federal facilities, with the exception being few and far between. Convicted of fraudulent crimes such as embezzlement, tax evasion and the like, those men normally came from affluent backgrounds and professional careers. Those who were admitted into the state system, normally brought with them a snobbish attitude. The majority emitted an aura of being better, or above the others. They felt as though they did not belong with lowly street scum. Eventually, they would adapt well and survive comfortably inside. Adapting quickest would be the smarter, more devious con-men, always looking for something for nothing, the ultimate deal.

Many were also known as great story tellers. One inmate, called Cody, regaled an audience when speaking about his scams. He once revealed to Robby that he would go into various banks and open up new checking accounts at each. With every new account, he would receive several blank checks to get started. He would deposit different amounts of money into two or three different accounts. The following day, he would withdraw money from these accounts before the checks would clear. This had gone on for some time until his own greed and a smart detective had caught up with him. There were other stories of Cody trying to beat credit card companies. In one scenario, he had ordered hundreds of dollars of mail order products. When the delivery service arrived at his house, he did not answer the door. In this case, they left the packages at the front door. When the service drove away, Cody picked up his goods. He was later billed for the items, but refused to pay, claiming he never received the items. With no signature from the delivery company, the mail-order company could not force restitution. The items could have been stolen for all anyone knew. Cody never paid a dime. He was always thinking.

Below the white collar criminals were inmates doing time for motor vehicle theft and involvement in 'chop shop' operations(the stripping of a stolen auto in order to sell separate parts). On the violent side of that coin were carjackers. This was one of the newest criminal crazes where drivers and passengers of vehicles were being forced out of their cars, usually at gunpoint.

Creeping down the order were men serving time for male prostitution. The majority were homosexuals and were most likely AIDS carriers. Their trade did not stop upon being sent to prison. One of these men had made Robby laugh. "Business is better than ever," he would brag. He wasn't kidding. In the business world of supply and demand, he was the supply and there was plenty of demand for his costly services.

Reaching the bottom of this dark list of criminals, the prison's hierarchy possessed the hated sex offenders. There were the rapists called 'skinners.' Below them, the lowest of them all, were deviants not to be considered human. They were the despised child molesters, the pedophiles called 'diddlers.' Many of those madmen were not even recognized as being in the prison's food chain. Those demented men had infested the system in the last decade or so, proving sexually related offenses had become the dominant, or popular crimes. Perhaps, a more accurate account would be that those twisted acts had only started to be reported recently, therefore the phenomenal increase in numbers. Even Robby once believed that if sentenced to prison for a sex crime, the inmate's life immediately turned into a living hell. Strangely, the truth was that this was not always the case. Many would ban together, creating some strength in large numbers. Others would dream up bold stories of fearless bank robberies and brutal assaults, masking their true identities.

Occasionally, inmates who were identified as sex offenders were unable to survive in population due to the cruelty of other inmates. Under those circumstances, the administration would make other living arrangements and place them into protective custody,(P.C.). Almost all P.C.'s were sex offenders. Along with police and correction officers sentenced to prison, P.C. units also housed the weakest and most timid. There were those who claimed fierce enemy situations mixed in, but nobody ever really bought their stories.

The sex offenders were making up a majority of the population in some institutions. The old pecking order had become unbalanced. Sharing many of the same characteristics, most sex offenders were meek and fearful of other men. In total compliance with institutional rules and regulations, they tended to cooperate and made up a big percentage of the informants within the population. It was in their best interest to maintain a safe and serene environment. Though believed otherwise, most were unable to be identified by just a look. Others could be spotted from a mile away. Those were the inmates who ended up in protective custody upon being admitted.

Wallowing at the bottom of the barrel, those sick men could only victimize each other. Most would deny their crime when confronted. Many claimed to be victims of an unjust judicial system, however their appalling records spoke for themselves.

Robby had researched several of their cases in order to cultivate new informants, but as he read one case after another, he decided that it would be best not to identify any of the sick freaks any further. He had read that one diddler, nicknamed the "dentist," had raped several children. He would pull their teeth out with pliers prior to forcing them to perform oral sex on him. Another sick bastard, called "Bozo," would dress as a clown, luring children into his van, where he would brutally sodomize them, physically damaging them for life. Another case involved an inmate who, on Thanksgiving, had tied up his own wife like a turkey. After sexually abusing her, the man forced their young son to perform oral sex on his own mother. Yet, another diddler had forced his way into a home where he removed an eight year old girl from her bed while her parents slept soundly in the very next room. Placing a sock in her mouth and a pillow case over her head, he carried her into the backyard where he raped and sodomized her for hours. Afraid for her parents' safety, she never screamed out. When the maniac finished, she crawled to her front door and rang the door bell. Her father opened the door to find his little girl naked, covered in mud and bleeding from her vagina and rectum. Rushed to a nearby hospital, several surgeries were required to mend the physical damage. This diddler later confessed he had mistaken the small child for his girlfriend who enjoyed rough sex. His best friend, a skinner of course, had raped a woman in an elevator, as her six year old son looked on in horror. It didn't take long before Robby wished he had never learned the details of their crimes.

There were, without exaggeration, hundreds of similar episodes of rape and sexual assault. Nothing, or no one, was sacred. The victims included newborn infants and toddlers. The mentally retarded, both young and old were victimized. There were also physically handicapped people, the elderly, and of course the dead, for the necrofeliacs. Those numerous victims were sodomized and forced to perform fellatio. They were tortured into performing unnatural acts, leaving them all physically and emotionally scarred for life. Others, perhaps the fortunate ones, had died.

Though unsuccessful, some sex offenders were incarcerated for attempting to rape their victims, but were still seated at the bottom with the rest. Inmate Farley was an avid sailor who had invited two young ladies onto his boat for a pleasure cruise. Once out into deep waters, the shit-bag threatened if both girls did not provide sex for him, they would have to find another ride back to land. The two refused and Farley threw them both overboard, after which he sailed away. Luckily, another vessel happened to pick the girls up, saving their lives, leaving Farley a long sentence which included attempted murder.

It was a fact that most victims of sex crimes personally knew or were related to their abusers. Fathers, uncles, brothers, even sons, had used various instruments or their own penises to rape and molest their supposed loved ones. Rape, a crime of controlling, or overpowering and humiliating the victim by sexual means were ingredients that made those men the most dangerous criminals alive. They had a sickness, a mental disorder with no known cure or rehabilitation proven, which could stop those traumatic crimes. The official versions of those offenses were enough to make Robby want to vomit. Yet, those were men who were not considered sexually dangerous, therefore it was not required that they reside at the Treatment Center. The criteria to being deemed sexually dangerous was unknown to Robby and other staff. Obviously, it took some doing to earn a ticket into that facility for deranged, sexual beasts.

Many sex offenders only received Concord sentences to serve. One or two years for aggravated rape, or rape of a retarded child under the age of seven. Other inmates complained that it would have been better had they, "skinned a kid, rather than robbed a gas station." They would have certainly served less time. Those demented creatures, once released from this warehouse of sex offenders, would return to the community. Robby warned his family and friends that there was no such thing as being overly-protective. They were out there in numbers.

Only once had Robby found a rare exception to the rule of sex offenders. He was a young inmate of eighteen, serving two or three years for statutory rape. His record indicated he had dated the same girl for four years. They were in love and planned on a future together. The girlfriend, who was only sixteen, was discovered by her strict parents having sexual intercourse with the young man. Becoming enraged, they pressed charges against him. The girl, herself, testified that not only had she consented, but often initiated the sex. No matter, the man was convicted of rape and sent to prison. Oddly enough, this young inmate ended up being the roommate of a rapist who had brutally assaulted several victims with instruments. He always sliced them up after the sexual abuse, but left them to live. Both inmates were stereotyped as skinners, the details of their crimes unimportant. There was no excuse for rape in the eyes of other cons. Two extremely different crimes and totally opposite criminals, yet they shared the same label and suffered the same abuse.

Amongst all of these colorful characters, Robby had discovered the thugs, the enforcers, the leaders and the followers, the predators and their prey, the con-men, the players and the informants who assisted I.P.S. in maintaining law and order within this pool of piranhas.

Those men, those inmates whose reasons for incarceration varied from murder to rape, would complain non-stop about their living conditions. Forever weeping about their loss of freedom. They complained about being removed from their families. They were forced into celibacy. They were also forced into associating with other criminals for prolonged periods of time. In essence, they were being deprived of the better elements of life. Many did not fully understand the concept.

It was difficult for Robby to feel or show any compassion for men who had terminated lives at will, or had ruined and traumatized the lives of their victims. They had proven total disregard for the laws of society. Those criminals were paying their debt to society in time taken from their normal lives, a form of compensation. Many of Robby's friends said this was not payment enough because it was not hard time. They felt it was considered enjoyable to some. "Isn't it evident through the huge return rates?" they would ask. Those same friends wondered why Robby and other officers did not allow inmates to kill or victimize each other as part of their punishment. Robby knew they could never see the whole picture. Again, Robby's job was not to judge. Though a difficult task, he had to remain unbiased while accomplishing his assigned duties. Those duties included protecting the public from criminals by keeping them behind bars, while maintaining order within the prison. If possible, he was to protect convicts from each other. The idea was to maintain a safe environment, obviously in the best interests of every person located behind that wall.

However, for reasons due to overcrowding, understaffing and the very nature of the criminals housed within, Robby would see the fights, the strong-arming or extortion, the con games and every illicit activity thinkable. For many inmates, being incarcerated only changed one thing: There was less ground to cover, but the victims were still walking about, so the crimes would continue. There was drugs, prostitution, gambling, loansharking and violent assaults including the use of a variety of weapons. The only way to observe the inmate's way of life was to get right in the thick of things, from the yards to the dorms. There was always something suspicious, always something illicit going on. That was the way of this world. Robby had to keep his eyes and ears open, because he could walk right into it at any time. However, with Frank by his side, and Keith and John only a call away, the Bravo Team would face it together.

6

After several weeks of concentrating on the prison's clientele, Frank decided that it was time to go to work. He told Robby and John, "The rest, you guys will have to learn from day-to-day," and so they did. For the next three years, the foursome became an intricate part of life inside the walls. Robby and John began to understand the inmates' strong desire for drugs and weapons. Between intercepting that contraband and shutting down every illicit business, from prostitution to extortion, they kept busy. Each would cultivate his own informants, who would even assist in detecting the continual con-artist games. The four men would become the closest of friends while breaking their backs to keep the prison safer. Somehow, the inmates would never appreciate their efforts.

Money, the root of all evil, dictated a person's social status from the wealthy to the poor. Money also determined how an inmate did his time in prison. The ultra-rich were a rarity in state prisons due to their vast resources in hiring the best of defense attorneys. However, there were those men entering the system who were financially comfortable, or had families willing and able to support them during their incarceration. Those inmates did easier time, as they were able to wear better clothing and eat better food. They had means to pay for protection, and if necessary, purchase any contraband item, or illegal service they desired from the other cons. Less fortunate inmates, who did not have substantial personal and savings accounts, depended on the state to clothe, feed and protect them. Those inmates were referred to as 'vikings.' They were the poor, and many would beg, borrow, steal or use any means necessary to improve their standard of living within the prison's social setting. Like any human being, priorities existed. If shelter, food and water were provided, personal safety came second. Once established, each inmate would focus toward living better, often at the expense of others.

The contraband and illegal services were sometimes paid for outside of the walls. A family member of one inmate deposited money into the account of another, or they would deliver the cash to that inmate's own family. Within the walls, the exchange rate consisted of cigarettes in place of currency. One pack, two packs or a crate (a carton) could buy anything on the inside market. Robby noticed that all inmates possessed cigarettes, whether they smoked or not.

The most forbidden items in prison were those which were most sought after. They were defined as contraband, which was anything not authorized for an inmate's retention. More specifically drugs, weapons, money, escape tools, tattoo guns and related paraphernalia. Sometimes even seemingly harmless items were forbidden, such as dental floss, which could cut through steel bars. Non-dairy creamer was also not allowed because it was highly flammable.

Although every reasonable precaution was taken to tighten security and prevent the introduction of this contraband, the inmates possessed a strong will and they were always finding ways to get them in.

Contraband items could be hidden anywhere. However, more often, they were hidden in common areas, or in the cell of a weaker inmate who had been forced to 'safehouse' the drugs or weapons. In those constant searches for anything that might interfere with the safety or orderly running of the institution, Robby discovered that contraband was normally found in the dirtiest, smelliest and nastiest areas conceivable. From the bottom of a filthy trash can to the inside of a full pak-a-potti, anywhere he would rather not place his hands, the jackpot was usually found. There had been hacksaw blades found in book bindings, heroine discovered in the false bottom of an ashtray, a fake dummy concealed within a mattress (escape tool) and a gun that had been smuggled inside the prison with five bullets located in a molded ceramic pot. That find was a true eye opener, proving that the possibilities of smuggling contraband were endless and the intent would probably have cost the lives of staff.

While searching, Robby tried to match his thoughts to the mind of an inmate, imagining the best places to conceal the illegal items. Some were found right under his nose and strangely, from shanks to paper money (needed for escape), many had been discovered on his gut feeling. Very often, the contraband was held right on the inmate, or inside the inmate himself. This caused the need for 'skin,' or strip searches.

In prison, the rectum was called the vault or the bank. That was where sets of works (needles), drug packages that were the size of oranges and even a Derringer-type pistol had been found. Having years of practice, they greased themselves with Vaseline. However, whether they were buttered or left dry, many inmates relied on 'tucking' their loot for safekeeping.

Illicit narcotics were drugs including heroine, marijuana, cocaine, acid and crystal meth. All pills, uppers and downers, you name it, also fell into that category. They were, by far, the contraband most coveted by the inmates. Not very different to the outside world, those junkies, addicts, users and abusers would go to any means to get their fix. Though entering the system through various ways, the drugs were normally 'lugged' in by visitors and introduced through the visiting room.

Officers assigned to the outer control made hundreds of arrests. The majority were drug related. Elderly mothers attempted to supply sons. Narcotics were concealed in wheelchairs and hidden in baby diapers, wooden legs (prosthetics), canes and under false dentures. This was to name a few of the attempts that had been made.

Frank and Robby had discovered an obese woman in her early fifties, concealing both heroine and cocaine taped under rolls of fat. Her only wish had been to take care of her poor son. The woman soon found herself in tears and in handcuffs. She should have known better, as all visitors had to pass a metal detector and a pat search. If a visitor was suspected of being in possession, an extraordinary search, or strip search would be ordered. If the search was refused, entrance was denied until further notice. Even the exchanging of sanitary napkins was proof that every effort was made to insure no contraband entered the system. Although such cautious procedures were taken, contraband still got inside. Only a fool would believe that there were no drugs within this population, however, the Bravo Team did everything in their power to keep this to a minimum. It was always better to intercept the package before it entered the facility. Once inside, the odds of making the bust became increasingly difficult.

It hadn't taken very much time, before Robby learned that nine out of ten times, drugs would normally enter the prison in the same manner. The visitor usually wrapped the narcotics in cellophane, or tied it inside of rubber balloons. The package was then tucked up into the vagina or rectum. Unfortunately, the outer control search was passed with ease. Upon entering the visiting room, some were visibly nervous. Others remained calm and cool due to their personal experience in these illicit matters. During the visit, the package was removed and the 'pass' was made via a kiss, or placed into a bag of popcorn. At which time, the inmate swallowed the bundle or tucked it himself. Upon completion of the visit, the inmate would remove the package from his ass. If swallowed, more than likely he would drink shampoo and hopefully vomit the drugs up. There was always a chance that the big score could not be puked up. If this should happen, he had to wait to shit it out, desperately hoping the wrapper did not break or dissolve, causing an overdose.

Once the drugs were in hand, they were dispersed throughout the prison in a flash. This was a big business. Normally, the product had already been purchased for ten to fifteen times its street value by customers who were impatiently awaiting their fix. Similar to street sales, there were differing levels of seniority within this drug business. There was the big man, the inmate whose money had purchased the drugs. It was usually his connections which got the drugs in from the street. Then there were the 'mules' who lugged the drugs in from the visiting room. They were entitled to a cut, as personal risks had been taken. Then, there were always some inmates, who were forced into performing this dirty and dangerous job, receiving no payment for their troubles.

Many of those passes had been intercepted by the Bravo Team. An inmate, who had been profiled for this type of dealing, was monitored closely using electronic surveillance. Frequently, informant information would also assist in the pinch, resulting in Frank and the boys storming into the visiting room. Some heavy wrestling matches had ensued during those incidents. In several cases, the inmates who were trying to swallow the drugs, were stopped as Keith and John grabbed their throats, forcing them to cough it up. That was an ideal situation. If swallowed, which had happened in several cases, the inmate would be placed in full restraints and secured in a segregation unit. He would be watched around the clock or until he defecated. One inmate, who under went this procedure requested a sedative. He then produced fifty Valiums within a few short hours. Robby, who was assigned to the eyeball watch, was fortunate enough to be the sucker who had to unwrap the pills. They had been inside of a greased-up plastic baggy.

During another case, Frank observed an inmate accepting a pass on camera. The man later confessed that he had swallowed a balloon of cocaine. This inmate took four days to defecate. He sat in full restraints the entire time. Frank and Robby, who were watching him, were on overtime. Filled with bran muffins, prune juice and a liquid sedative, the con finally shit so much that the bucket provided had overflowed. Frank, who had to cut through the watered-down feces, began to gag. As his eyes watered and his face turned pale, Robby looked on and laughed uncontrollably at his poor friend. The tool used to search through the excrement was a tongue depressor. It had been disgusting work, but Frank had been thorough and there was only one empty balloon found. The bundle had broken open, leaving the inmate high, but alive. He had been lucky because even the evidence, which would have been used against him, was gone. This had not been the most glorious day in Frank's career, but even he had to chuckle at the gross duty he had performed.

Not one month later, another similar situation occurred in the visiting room. Two females, who had entered the area, were watched closely by Keith and John because they had never been in to visit in the past. They were also under scrutiny because the inmates they wished to see were players, real drug addicts. One female paced nervously awaiting her visitor, while Keith picked her up on camera. It was impossible! This one was too easy to be real. The girl had a huge bulge protruding from one of her cheeks, apparently it was a package. As the area was rushed, the girl swallowed the ball of whatever had been in her mouth. A quick interview revealed that the girl was either extremely high on drugs herself, or men-tally handicapped. She immediately admitted that she had been coaxed into bringing in muscle relaxers for an inmate she did not even know. Keith then advised her to promptly report to the emergency room. It was later discovered that this 'special needs' person had been manipulated by two inmates. The other girl, who was one of the inmate's girlfriend, lugged in a large quantity of downers which would have killed her, had her stom-ach not been pumped. The inmates were transferred to higher security. Before leaving, they swore vengeance upon Keith and John, who had in-vestigated the incident. Wrapping up their bids only months later, the Im-migration and Naturalization Service deported them back to Africa. Keith had to laugh, saying, "So much for empty promises."

It seemed that for a time, the drug busts were non-stop. One inmate, admitted into the institution's detox program, suffered from a terrible limp. Keith, the street-smart investigator, picked it up. An initial interview, along with a strip search was conducted, but the vault looked clean. The inmate claimed that he had sustained serious hip and leg injuries, as a re-sult of an old motorcycle accident. Keith, acting on a hunch, began screaming at the con, telling him that staff had knowledge that he was at-tempting to introduce illicit narcotics into the drug program. Keith threat-ened that if the inmate did not remove the bundle from his ass, then he would, without hesitation. The inmate panicked, pulled three balloons of Xanax from his rectum, swearing all the while they had been intended for his own use. He was a heroine addict and needed them to survive. It had been a good bust on mere intuition.

Drugs had also entered the facility through the mail. Acid had been hidden behind stamps and marijuana had been found sealed inside of stuffed or padded envelopes. Cocaine had been sewn inside incoming per-sonal property. Needles with heroine had been located within the soles of brand new sneakers. Still, other means were through newly admitted in-mates, especially the thirty day wonders who had been through the detox. program more than once. Minimum unit inmates, with freedom of the grounds, were allowed to interact with medium inmates within the law library. Many deals had transpired there. Then, there were the inmates who were strong-armed for their psychotropic meds, often sedatives, which left them unbalanced. Unfortunately, there was also dirty staff who supplied inmates because they chose to supplement their income. Some staff allowed themselves to be blackmailed. In other cases, there were previous street connections.

Bizarre incidents had occurred where drugs were placed inside of softballs, or dead pigeons, and thrown over the wall. A true topper was when marijuana had been shot over the high wall inside of an arrow, proving the sources of transference could be the most unexpected. Whatever it took to get the product inside would be tried. The ways in which those drugs entered did not matter to those men who would break open a disposable pen and jam the jagged edge into their forearms. Then, they would use a sneaker pump to 'boot' the heroine into their thirsty veins.

Drugs in prison was an enormous problem because drugs often encouraged violence. The inmates who were caught and did not provide the already purchased pills to the user would always be known as having had 'a deal gone bad.' It became part of their reputation. Their customers were usually unforgiving. This turned the dealer into a protective custody issue for I.P.S.. One never knew how a person would react when high. This increased the danger level of working with those already unpredictable people.

There were the chances of overdose and death. There were also risks with those people of spreading AIDS and other blood diseases.

Like it or not, Robby's job was care along with custody, therefore it was frequently necessary to protect an inmate from himself and his self-destructive vices.

Incarceration for dealing drugs did not always put the dealer out of business. Some maintained their outside contacts and controlled things from behind the wall. In one extraordinary case, a sting operation was ordered by Lieutenant Redman to target a well-known drug dealer residing in the minimum unit. Frank and his Bravo Team went undercover and were placed in the visiting room. With the use of sophisticated surveillance equipment, the operation commenced. Receiving different male visitors each night, Robby found that the targeted inmate would only use the pay phone and talk for a brief period. Then, he would put the visitor on the phone who would finish the conversation. Some nights, five to ten of these calls were made.

This inmate, called Sly, also enjoyed fingering through hundreds of dollars which would be brought to him, but always returned after the visit was done. Apparently, he truly missed this part of the business, holding his own cash. An outside police agency took over the investigation, as it had become completely out of the team's jurisdiction. Before it was over, the inmate, who was smart enough not to peddle small drugs in prison, was locked up for being in possession of too much currency. It had been a petty reason, however, it had paid off. After being returned to higher custody, John Donovan had inventoried his personal property and confiscated a beeper watch, along with an address book including most of his drug connections. Inside, there were phone numbers of both dealers and customers. Sly was running his drug business, as though nothing in his life had changed. The police were doing everything in their power to shut him down.

The man was no slug. Within his property was also a photo album, picturing him on the hoods of very expensive cars. They were taken in European countries and showed professional rap singers shaking his hand. Before Sly was shipped out, he said, "Business is business, but I have to respect you guys for not setting me up. Don't worry, though, because you may have slowed me down, but only death will stop me! The money is just too good!" Robby jokingly advised the cunning convict, "If things don't work out for you in the drug trade, a career in corrections is always an option. The salaries have to be almost the same." They all laughed, though Sly the hardest.

Meanwhile, one of the bonuses added to the undercover operation was the fact that several inmates were also lugged back to medium security. The Bravo Team had observed them engaging in open and obscene sexual acts with their visitors. Many of these perverted acts were performed in the presence of other inmates' children. This caused hostile situations, as they were taken as a blatant showing of disrespect toward each man's family. According to most inmates, it was a valid reason to assault and beat down a fellow convict.

The strong desire for the use of drugs on behalf of the inmates caused the team to work that much harder. It was a game of 'hide and go seek.' Sometimes the game even turned to 'beat the clock.' With room raids being conducted in the middle of the night, some inmates were caught sleeping. Some literally and others figuratively. The drugs were always confiscated.

One afternoon, Keith had another one of his hunch's. He was sure that there had been a set of works circulating inside the prison. He was also convinced that it was being used to shoot a recent shipment of heroine. Keith Petrie began his own feverish quest. Not one week later, he came crashing through a drop ceiling. He almost snapped his neck, but he had found the set. He was finally satisfied with the positive results of an ex-hausting week. Robby, his partner for-the-day, began snooping around while he searched the ceiling. To his own amazement, Robby found a cache of pipes, broomsticks and one baseball bat concealed in an old wall. The weapons appeared to have been there for years. Apparently at one time, some inmates were planning for a big brawl. There had been two big finds in one day. When it rained it poured, even in prison. As in most of their searches, many contraband items were found by chance. It was the luck of the draw.

Inside the walls, another popular path out of reality was through 'home-brew,' or homemade alcohol. This booze was concocted from fruit and sugar stolen from the kitchen. Pieces of bread were also placed inside the large containers for its yeast. Left hidden for awhile, so that the beverage could ferment, some inmates had been known to make a good, potent batch of brew capable of knocking a large man on his ass. Those brewmasters got really busy around the holiday season. On one winter evening, Frank and Robby found a couple of those men shit-faced. They were just sitting in the cement yard, drinking out in the open, as though they were at a Christmas party. Both were locked up and one of them, the happy drunk, decided to quietly sleep it off. His partner, however, grew beerballs and wanted to fight with the entire I.P.S. team. The uncooperative lush was eventually held on the floor, as his clothes were cut off of him with scis-sors. Frank laughed uncontrollably, explaining to the drunkard, "We need to conduct a proper strip search, for your own safety, of course!"

The various methods of detecting the existence of drugs and alcohol within the population were based upon the most credible information there was, staff observations and discoveries. There was also electronic surveillance, shakedowns of cells, yards and common areas, along with pat and strip searches of inmates. There was the monitoring of inmate's criminal records, or 'profiles' and their financial accounts. Then, there was always the reality of busting visitors, or even staff, smuggling it in. Trained K-9 had been useful in detecting drugs, and when all else failed, the last line of detection was through both subjective and random urinalysis drug testing.

Robby, assigned as the team's urinalysis technician, thought it was a fantastic tool in measuring the amounts used inside. Sometimes it was even a deterrent. However, he knew it was like being a day late and a dollar short. A positive urine meant that drugs had made it in and that they had been enjoyed by the user. Nevertheless, it was valuable because the inmate paid for his misconduct by losing visiting privileges for a period of time. In the long run, classification moves and parole consideration could be hampered as well. While testing urine specimens, Robby found one that tested positive for cocaine, so decided to interview the provider. The inmate disclosed, "There's no money to be made in a poor camp loaded with rats, so I don't deal. I have it brought in for my own use." Robby laughed. How could he question a man who was only recently incarcerated for selling crack-cocaine to kids? How could he question a man who had just been caught using coke himself? The inmate had to be telling the truth! Robby locked him up.

Robby soon found that the drug testing system which was used, was often beaten by the junkies and addicts. Men who had been around the block a time or two. Inmates, whose bloodstreams were saturated with narcotics, would place dried bleach under their finger nails, or pour bleach on their fingertips, letting the fluid dry. While urinating into a specimen cup, they just made sure that the urine stream hit their fingertips which would instantly contaminate the sample. Others would flush their systems by consuming gallons of water, causing them to urinate over and over. This practice was slightly more risky, but it too had been known to work. Unfortunately, the testing system was not flawless and there had been a fair share of con-men who had 'gotten over' on the young investigator.

The second most dominant contraband item that the inmates attempted to possess was a weapon. In prison, a weapon could be anything which was intended to bring bodily harm to another. They were found around every corner, from a broomstick to broken glass removed from a window. Though those items were dangerous in their own right, and had caused some serious injuries, the weapons that the team was most concerned with, were the obvious ones. The weapons that were purposely fabricated and hidden for future use. The list of weapons would include homemade edge weapons or 'shanks,' pipe bombs, molitov cocktails, padlocks or cans placed inside of socks or pillow cases and even zip guns. Those zip guns, or improvised pistols, were normally fashioned out of wood with holes drilled out for the bullets. A nail, or some type of firing pin, was used to strike the primer. Known for being inaccurate, those firearms, though medieval in their design, had still taken human lives. They generally used small caliber bullets. When found, the institution usually had more problems than they ever realized.

Weapons, intentionally fabricated, were sometimes found in common areas, or carried on the inmate for self-protection. The weapon of choice was normally a shank. Shanks were historically carried by the weaker inmates for self-protection. A popular model was a toothbrush, which had been mcltcd down until gooey. Razor blades were then stuck in the end and the shank allowed to dry. Referred to as a 'skinner's shiv,' those small knives had sliced many inmates who had doubted their capabilities.

Weapons, for the most part, existed because of inmate- to-inmate assaults, or altercations. From icicles, which were perfect weapons because all evidence, including fingerprints, just melted away, to pots of scalding water. Fights that involved the use of any weapon would bring forth criminal charges. Though, through the ages, some officers had been cut up, most inmates knew that additional 'on and after' sentences were a direct result of such an attack. The inmates also knew they would find their time much harder to serve afterward. Searches for fabricated shanks smuggled out of Industries were common. Flammable liquids, such as lighter fluid and cleaning supplies, were monitored as well.

When weapons started popping up everywhere, a thorough assessment of the inmate climate was necessary. This was a strong indication of a possible gang fight or racial confrontation. Sensing some racial unrest, John soon discovered shanks which had been strategically stuck in the ground of the ballfield. The knives had been placed, blades down, so that they were readily available. However, John, conducting a broad sweep with a metal detector, forced the inmates back to the drawing board. It was a never-ending search-and-destroy-mission. One older inmate, finding out that John had located the stash, said, "Big deal, the inmates around here have finally wised up. There's no longer the need to risk being caught with a blade when it's just as easy to take a man's eye out or stick a dude with a pen or pencil!" He was right. Most inmates conveniently carried a writing instrument on them at all times.

Contraband items such as paper currency, along with other tools of escape, had been discovered just in the nick of time. During a random search, Robby stumbled upon a rope, a grappling hook and a life-like dummy. The inmate, who owned the valuable escape tools, had waited a day too long. He soon wished it had been just a shank that he was busted with. His punishment would have certainly been less severe.

The methods of detecting weapons, escape tools and other contraband items were identical to the constant search for drugs. However, as I.P.S., Robby and John quickly learned the tremendous value of informant information. In their constant fight against criminal activity behind the wall, those informants became the most effective weapon in the I.P.S. arsenal. Frank always said, "There are no secrets in the big house and the walls had eyes!" Though unrespected by the investigators they assisted, those 'rats,' or 'stool pigeons' were always lurking in the shadows, just waiting to report what they had seen or heard. They existed in large numbers, definitely more than Robby would have ever guessed. Each had his reasons for exerting the effort. There were the thrill seekers. Those inmates who killed the monotony of their days by watching other inmates squirm and run for cover. There were the self-righteous, possibly attempting to right some of their wrongs. Then, there were those who suffered from an identity crises. These inmates believed that they too wore badges. Some would say they had personal reasons. Their reasons varied from bigotry to enemy situations. Perhaps, some were merely removing their competition. Robby and John found that the inmates involved directly in the illegal activity would always become the best of informants. Who better to have on the inside? Either way, if cultivated correctly, those men would tell all. Each one of them wanted to talk, but needed to justify the dishonorable act to themselves. Some informants produced incredible results. They worked, as though they had been sent to the best of investigative schools. Robby sensed that some of them knew his job better than he did.

The rules of the institution dictated that no officer could give an inmate anything for their information. Reality was that a couple packs of cigarettes, or a housing move in trade for drug information, or valuable clues to a recent assault, was not considered so unethical by the Bravo Team. Those snitches kept the remainder of the population walking on egg shells. Inmates never knew who was solid or who was "working for the cops."

One inmate, pinched for strong-arming by Keith and John, had been betrayed. He had always considered the informant to be a trusted friend. After being busted, he informed John, "If there are three inmates who know a secret, in order for it to remain a secret, two must die." John ordered him to keep quiet, but knew he was probably right on the money.

Informants had to prove themselves reliable or their information held no credibility. Often the best information was received during termination interviews. This was when an inmate was leaving the institution and was questioned about the prison's underworld. Many would provide valuable information due to the elation of wrapping their sentence up. Frank loved to conduct those interviews and during one, some grinning inmate revealed, "There's some big contraband right inside the Catholic Chapel." Frank called the team together and a major shakedown was conducted. Sure enough, an old set of keys and a wig were found. The keys had been outdated. However, somebody had obviously had plans of leaving the prison a little prematurely. Exiting the sacred area of the altar, Robby asked, "Hey guys, can you imagine how difficult the job of the clergy is?" Each man guessed on how long the confessions took and laughed at the thought.

John's first informant was an inmate who was also a burglar by trade. He kept insisting that there were a lot of drugs within the population. Code-named Eagle Scout, he was sent out to prove his claims. In the meantime, he was followed by John and Keith. It was found that he was associating with the leader of a hispanic group, a strange connection. After two days, information was provided and a small marijuana bust was made. It had become quite clear to Keith that he was playing both sides of the fence. He was creating a diversion for his hispanic friend while wiping out the man's competition. Both inmates were transferred and John learned a hard lesson about informant information. Before the move, Eagle Scout, who was a real storyteller, explained his recent escape from a minimum security camp. "I was tired of the same old scenery, so I walked out the front door and climbed a tree in a nearby forest. Everybody, and his brother, was out looking for me. Nobody ever looked up. Even the dogs didn't have a clue. My biggest problem that night was that although I had taken enough cigarettes, I forgot a lighter or matches!" Laughing at the vivid memory, he added, "I was almost tempted to call down to the officers below to ask for a light!"

Robby's first experience with an informant was just as bad. The inmate was an Aryan brother who held a deep hatred for all minorities. He provided information about weapons. Looking into the older man's claims, Robby and Frank found two shanks lying on the beds of two black inmates. It became clear that this racist had planted the homemade knives. Alas, there were no fingerprints found on the weapons, so even he could not be punished. Left inside the same population, this inmate eventually became a protective custody issue, as his body was covered in Nazi tattoos which the black and hispanic inmates did not seem to appreciate.

Robby and John, embarrassed for believing the con-men, also learned that most informants provided good information. Many were quite useful in detecting illegal businesses, or services provided within the prison. Robby found that every man had to make a living, so some of those illicit businessmen were unbelievably resourceful and busy.

There were the tattoo artists, talented men who drew with brilliantly engineered tattoo guns, stencils, bleach for sterilization and ink. The ink was made from melted plastic, pen ink and anything else that would dry inside the skin. They catered mostly to the white biker-types who marked their bodies with satanic designs and other status symbols. Other inmates had themselves permanently marked, so that they could eventually leave with a souvenir, a conversation piece for boasting about their hard days spent in the "Big House." Many Hispanics and Orientals had gotten tattoos of significance, which were usually located on their hands. Sometimes consisting of only a series of dots, those markings identified previous crimes, or possibly their status in an established group. Frank swore that it was fantastic and handy intelligence information.

For several months, Lieutenant Redman ordered that the team concentrate their time on cleaning up the tattoo business. The boys went on a tear and in one week made a bust. The inmate, with only three days left before wrapping up his bid, was being tattooed in his cell by one of the camp's better artists. The peek man (an inmate lookout), who had his head up his ass, daydreaming, did not 6-5 his friends, thus allowing Frank and his restless crew to walk right in, confiscate the bootie and lock up everyone involved. The inmate, being tattooed, ended up leaving his second home, only to get shot weeks later in a drug deal gone sour. Hearing this, Robby thought, "For some, it really is safer behind the wall."

Immediately following that pinch, another one was made. The tattooist, a thriving businessman, had gotten careless one evening and kept one of his valuable guns inside of his own room. It was a stupid and costly mistake. Holding a morning appointment, he had not expected the early raid. John, confiscating the tattoo gun, had made this inmate his hobby. For some reason, he hated the inmate. The inmate was infuriated because his livelihood was being taken away right from under his nose. With fifty to a hundred dollars per tattoo being deposited into his wife's bank account, the distraught inmate complained, "I have no other source of income!" He had been shut down. The inmate expected sympathy. John nearly pissed himself laughing while he cuffed him up. Not four months later, that same tattooist had completed some sloppy work on an unsatisfied customer who 'dimed him out' (ratted on him). The money was too good to stay out of the trade for long. Though this art form was a permitted avocation in some prisons, the administration had forbidden the service, which also helped to spread the deadly H.I.V. virus.

Other inmates would clean rooms or fold and press laundry to make an extra pack of cigarettes here and there. The barbers, who were listed on the prison payroll, making it a legitimate job assignment, also received gratuities of a couple of packs for a job well done. Then, there were the artists, the men who drew greeting cards and sketched portraits for their living. Robby considered this a God-given talent wasted, but those men lived like kings inside. The artwork was allowed, but could not be sold, or so the story went.

One eccentric inmate, busy at work during the Christmas season, was pinched by Frank and Robby with eighty packs of cigarettes in his own foot locker. They had found the mother-lode. The Bravo Team held a long interview with this fellow, followed with questions of strong-arming and loansharking. They knew his greeting card business was responsible for his wealth, so their only intention was to inquire about the wrongdoings of other inmates who resided in his unit. The angry inmate bit the hook and began telling his interrogators, "You guys are wasting your time with my small business. Had you been on your jobs, you would have figured out that two inmates escaped one week ago!" The story, though initially entertaining, did not make sense. There had been no escapes. Robby persuaded him to give details. The man reluctantly revealed, "Two inmates (parole violators) were involved in a ninety day drug program, which was mandatory to regain parole. However, they didn't completed the program, or finish their court committed time. They forged paperwork indicating their completion of the three month, intensive program, provided it to the parole department and were released more than one month earlier than they were supposed to." In essence, a paper escape had transpired without any staff ever realizing it. Frank and Robby later verified, through the parole department, that those men had indeed beaten the system. With no personnel confirming the paperwork, they had written their own tickets out. Within that week's period of time, one of the escapees had committed two armed robberies and was already in custody. The other, on the run, would eventually be found and returned behind the wall. Needless to say, a more competent checks and balance system was set up, but not before several people had been embarrassed into explaining the ordeal to their superiors.

There was the prostitution trade, also one of the oldest in this business, which did quite well. Homosexual men selling any type of sexual favor imaginable for cigarettes, food and protection. The weaker prostitutes were controlled by pimps who reaped the benefits of the gay inmate's long hours of labor. Those situations were no different than the outside world excepting the gender always being male.

In a quite bizarre situation, Sherry, a large, black transvestite and hard working girl had fallen in love with her pimp. For the sum of two or three packs, with some "on the house," Sherry would perform oral sex on her customers. Living in a preferred housing unit, the business she received soon became overwhelming. She finally went to Lieutenant Redman for help. Sherry disclosed, "It's not that I mind, but it's become too much. This girl is tired...real tired!" Redman had her shipped out.

There were also the thieves who stole food and property. In turn, they sold their goods on the prison's black market. This business often led to violent endings, as even most inmates hated a thief, especially one who was trying to sell the man's own clothes back to him. After cleaning up the mess, Robby chuckled, saying to Frank, "At least they can never be accused of being intelligent." Frank replied, "Just remember buddy, every inmate is a two time loser. Once for committing the crime and secondly, for getting caught!"

Robby became most intrigued by the 'jailhouse lawyers,' who kept the boys constantly running around. Those were the inmates assigned to the law library to assist other inmates in their legal needs. A prison paid position, the smarter inmates received more than a dollar a day. Most made a killing from their clientele, another similarity of the outside world. As Frank put it, "There is power in knowledge." Every single convict was hoping to overturn his case on appeals. Each had a strong wish to receive a revise and revoke, the court's ticket to freedom. This was where the inmate walked right from the courthouse, every inmate's dream. Due to those strong hopes, those legal beagles had bigger caseloads than many legitimate attorneys.

Inmate Stanford, a para-legal, actually supported his family from inside the prison walls, while he was allegedly doing free legal research for a reputable law firm. Robby could never figure out why this legal whiz never overturned his own case, until his demanding wife started to visit regularly in her shiny, new Cadillac.

Frank discovered another inmate, who was not as wise, rendering legal services. He was easily caught taking pay-offs. Certified checks were being sent to the institution via mail to be deposited into his account. Terminated from his law clerk position, he started to live like a Viking and at one point, slapped a civil suit on Frank, who had fired him. It was probably best for everyone concerned that the man did not last long. He couldn't even win a suit brought against a Correction Officer, which was considered by many to be the easiest. Lord knows that thousands, maybe millions, had been won in court with the state providing the inmates with legal assistance. In turn, the state would normally fork over some small fortunes, helping to cut its own throat.

The Bravo Team also investigated a 'jailbird lawyer,' who ended up meeting a brutal fate. He was an intelligent character, who burdened himself with so much paperwork, that he started to produce shoddy work for all of his merciless clients. Returning from court, those men knew that they hadn't had a chance for freedom, with the obvious poor defense that had been provided them. Somehow, he continued to convince them that he was their only chance. It was really only meant to save his own neck, but like all good things that must come to an end, so did this inmate's profitable charade. Though continuing to accept outside money transfers for his legal services, he began stalling for time, putting the inmates off. One highly respected inmate had gone to this law clerk months earlier, but received no results. He was being transferred out of the institution and 'punked off'(disrespected) at the same time. All the other inmates knew this. So, while the jailhouse lawyer was sitting on the throne, trying to enjoy a quiet moment, he was approached by his very unhappy client. Witnessing inmates later said that he begged for mercy, as the reputable inmate brutally assaulted him, knocking him off the toilet and onto his knees. Everyone there had laughed at the chump. At the completion of the simple investigation, the ex-law clerk still showed signs of a beating, but he laughed it off like a little weasel. He told Frank, "At least I still have the tough guy's two hundred dollars."

From these illegitimate businesses to more illicit activities, other inmates found easier and more profitable ways of getting by. There were the loansharks, those inmates who loaned out food and cigarettes on an old two-for-one system. It was designed to double the loanshark's riches on a weekly basis, but realistically, the interest was compounded even higher, making it virtually impossible to pay the debts. The borrower found himself indebted to the shark. They had enforcers, paid hitmen, who were hired to collect and occasionally rough up a deadbeat. Those activities, more often than not, seemed to turn into enemy situations and in turn, become protective custody issues.

Even more fierce were the inmates who strong-armed, or extorted from others by brute force, or intimidation and threat of serious bodily injury. Those were the sharks who fed on the weaker guppies for canteen goodies, food, cigarettes, slave labor, and so on. Some victims were turned into the strong-armer's 'kid.' When that occurred, sexual favors were forced to be provided, sometimes to other inmates as well, depending on the generosity of the strong-armer. Some were coerced into lugging in drugs or having money deposited into the accounts of the men they so desperately feared. There had been instances where some inmates, who were labeled 'kids,' would confess to illicit acts they did not commit. However, this caused suspicion on behalf of the team, usually forcing the predator out of business for awhile.

For the Bravo Team, strong-arming was a constant problem to deal with. In one case, Frank set up surveillance of the cement yard, just outside of the canteen. It was amazing to count how many wolves were sitting and waiting for their little lamb to walk by. There were even arguments over which terrain was being covered by which group. Robby watched as two muscular, black inmates were approaching some feeble detoxing inmates and with just a look or a threatening word, food items were being stolen like they were taking candy from a baby. Upon further surveillance, the bigger babies were being left alone. The whole thing made Robby angry. Like most other officers, even in prison, he hated to see the stronger inmates always win. After some time, Frank, Robby and the rest of the team rushed the yard, ordering each inmate to grab the wall. They all complied, but one. He was the bigger of the two thieves and he wanted to go out like a hero. After a hands-on escort into another yard, isolating him from the remaining inmates, he decided again he would rather fight than give up the goods. A use of force was needed and of course, he lost the struggle. However, John's thumb had been broken during the incident. After it was over, Robby thought that the self-professed tough guy must have used a firearm on the streets because, like so many of the younger inmates entering the system, he was not good with his hands. Carted off to the Hole, all the stolen items were confiscated. Later, it was noticed that besides the broken thumb, a bag of barbecue chips was also crushed, as a result of the small tussle.

Weeks later, another strong-arming situation involved an inmate who was filling out canteen slips and forcing another inmate to purchase the food items. This had gone on for months, until finally the victim could not afford to support the bully any longer. A handwriting analysis was taken and comparisons were made, proving that the strong-armer had been a dependent of the smaller, weaker inmate for six months. He was locked up and while removing his handcuffs, Robby called him a coward. The asshole grinned, then snickered, "It'll only be a matter of time before I choose my next fish!"

There were inmates, who were literally walking victims, having bags of canteen taken from them weekly. They were forced to give up their radios and televisions because they lived in constant fear of everyone around them. Very often they were sex offenders which enabled some inmates to blackmail them by threatening to reveal their crimes. Robby thought this was a joke because those meek characters could be read like open books. He thought, "A man, afraid of his own shadow, is probably not doing time for assaults or robberies."

Keith picked up an extraordinary case, where an inmate, who had publicly won thousands of dollars in a personal injury law suit, watched it slip through his fingers. He walked around the prison in state clothes and was always bumming cigarettes from the sympathetic. He finally confessed to Keith, that for over two years, he was being strong-armed by two older, influential inmates. He revealed, "My mother has been writing their families monthly checks of one thousand dollars, or more. They told me it was protection money, in payment to prevent other inmates from stealing from me." This inmate, who was once worth a bundle, was now penniless. The sharks had found a lame duck and squeezed him for all he was worth. This sad story, seemingly unbelievable to Keith, was later confirmed with the inmate's elderly mother. She had figured something was wrong, but as long as her son was being taken care of, it was only money. Keith advised her, "Don't worry, he was being taken care of, and good!"

Strong-arming was a fact of life in prison. Though the team intervened when possible, by monitoring accounts, canteen activity and through informant information, it was an unavoidable game of the strong preying upon the weak, the foundation of this sub-society. It was almost like being picked-on in school, but magnified a million times.

When they weren't bogged down in strong-arming cases, the Bravo Team tried to stay on top of the gambling. Whether it was the numbers 'pool,' shooting craps with unauthorized dice, playing card games, or betting on sporting events, both professional and institutional, hundreds of inmates enjoyed participating in the illicit activity. There were the point spreads and there were the bookies who would take all bets, regardless of the odds. In front of staff, the inmates did pushups as payment. Behind the scenes, cigarettes were exchanged in the joint, money outside.

Keith and John tracked one book maker. He was a cunning con-man who eventually got caught with a betting slip written on a paper towel. It included the point spreads, coded initials of the players, the numbers of packs wagered and the teams picked. Taken out of his lucrative little business, the man was not happy. It was football season and he had been doing well. Once locked up, he pleaded with Keith, "When someone places a bet with me and loses, if they don't pay up, they don't play again. I don't deal in violence, it's too expensive." He was being truthful, but he was an exception to the rule. Most bookies were just like the bookies on the streets... the loser would pay, one way or another. In prison, collectors were paid generously, keeping all of the gamblers honest. A good percentage of assaults were a result of unpaid debts, causing the team even more work during the NFL season.

One inmate, an ignorant kid, had placed outrageous amounts of cigarettes on some real longshots. As expected, he had lost his shirt. Unable to pay the bookie, he had been threatened with a time limit. If this time limit was not met, he would be made an example of, for future deadbeats. Assigned as a canteen worker, he began stealing cigarettes and smuggling them out. It was not enough. Like every other con in the system, this bookie was tripling the interest and the threats were getting more detailed.

The stupid kid then started issuing fifty dollar canteens. When the canteen staff's attention was diverted, he would destroy the slips intended to be transported to inmate accounts, so that money could be withdrawn for the items purchased. What the inmate failed to remember was that a monthly inventory, which was due, showed a huge deficit. Frank fired all three canteen workers from one of the best jobs in the house. He initially believed it to be a conspiracy. The kid checked in, or P.C'd himself because his ex-co workers wanted him dead. The bookie wasn't at all happy either. Knowing he was in some hot water, the young inmate 'rolled over'(ratted) on the bookie. Robby found the man waiting at his own cell, property packed up, as he knew the kid would squeal. That bookie swore vengeance on his new enemy. Robby had no doubt that it was only a matter of time before revenge would be his. The old lifer had vast connections throughout the system, so sooner or later, the kid was all done.

Robby often marveled at the level of deceit within the prison's population. A good informant told him about another book maker, who was a quiet inmate, with a smile forever plastered on his face. He resided in the minimum unit and the informant claimed that he had stashed away thousands, as a result of taking bets. The man worked inside a greenhouse during the day and he loved to take care of the stray cats that lived in the area. A fellow inmate, placing a wager with this old bookie, was actually only trying to con-the-con. Evidently, it was not an easy task. He placed a five dollar bill on a basketball game, but had soaked the money in tuna fish juice, days beforehand. After the bill had dried and the bet was made, the scheming inmate followed the old man's cats around for days, hoping they would lead him to the big stash. It never happened. The stash was never found and the inmate had even lost his five dollar bet. The informant giggled, "So much for easy money, but it was a valid attempt!"

When considering all the illegal acts, Robby noted that the braver, more ingenious inmates, would involve themselves in bigger and better deals. Reaching way outside the walls, those con-men, or scam artists, fraudulently preyed on giant businesses, to include the U.S. government. With the payoffs a potential goldmine, the risks taken were much larger. Those risks could pay off well, but they also landed many of the con-men back in court to receive additional sentences. For the amount of time and effort needed to investigate the scams, the Bravo Team had to work together. Month after month, Frank, Keith, Robby and John had their hands full.

Inmate Bradley, for instance, was not satisfied with gaining money from only one source, but chose to fraudulently target private companies, along with the state and federal internal revenue services. An extensive investigation of both mail fraud and tax fraud were conducted simultaneously. Through an authorized mail cover of the suspected con-artist, astonishing information was gained. To begin with, Robby discovered that Bradley was in possession of 10 Consumer Reports magazine pages which contained a list of various defective, or dangerous products. These products had been recalled and completely taken off the market. Attached to these pages was a list of nine companies, or manufacturers and their addresses. Bradley had been writing each company, falsely claiming that he, or his beloved family, had sustained some serious injury, as a result of their poorly designed products. In each identical form letter sent to these manufacturers, inmate Bradley would request a refund, but never a product replacement. He then threatened that he would be forced to contact the U.S. Consumer Safety Commission if his needs were not met. Bradley's mail was monitored for a brief period and the correspondence sent and received were both entertaining and devious.

In one accident, as detailed by Bradley, the subject had informed a well-known company that his already-ill wife had suffered a terrible injury from a defective hair dryer which they had recently recalled. Writing both the manufacturer and distributor, covering all bases, the inmate received two totally different responses. One had replied with a half-hearted apology, coldly informing the dissatisfied customer that the product had been discontinued and that it was no longer for sale, or a danger to any person, period. The other quickly sent a check for twenty dollars. Apparently, this company was less willing to call the man's bluff and involve themselves in litigation.

Inmate Bradley wrote to at least three formidable toy companies which had all recalled a flammable canned spray string. The con-man informed these companies that while the candles were blown out during his son's birthday party, their product had ignited a paper table cloth, slightly burning his young child. Again, the request for a full refund, followed by threats of contacting the U.S. Consumer Safety Commission. One of the companies replied by asking the customer to contact them by telephone, so that they could clear up the unfortunate matter. Another company replied with a refund check of 10 dollars. The last sent a heart wrenching apology and enclosed a catalog, informing the poor man to choose any of their other toys, free of charge.

After monitoring this fraudulent activity, inmate Bradley was interviewed. This also proved to be entertaining. As Keith asked questions, Bradley calmly responded. He said, "In all sincerity, my only concern is the safety of the public consumers. I feel that I have been acting in the capacity of a scout for dangerous children's products. My only intent was to assist my good friend, Ms. Joyce Greene, who is a consumer advocate." At the completion of the investigation, Frank found that Ms. Greene had been the victim of inmate Bradley. She had been the victim of a sex offense, for which he was currently incarcerated. His idea of humor was not appreciated by any of the team members. Records indicated that he had been divorced from his wife for years. She resided out west and had never been injured in a hair dryer accident. Frank and the boys also found that inmate Bradley did not have any children on record. The companies which had been scammed by this convict were advised of the fraud. However, not one chose to pursue the issue any further. It was considered small potatoes to these corporate giants. At the completion of the investigation, Frank snapped, "That's exactly what Bradley had counted on." Bradley was disciplined internally, though there were much bigger problems in this thief's future. Problems which involved Uncle Sam, who the scam-artist would surely find less forgiving.

Inmate Bradley had masterminded a scheme while incarcerated within the prison walls. He and other inmates received a total of almost twenty two thousand dollars in fraudulent refunds after filing phony federal and state income tax forms. Recruiting several willing inmates, Bradley filed twenty false returns. Eleven of them were federal, the other nine, state. In every instance, the inmate receiving the refund had been incarcerated the prior year and could not have earned any taxable wages. Even the dollar or two per day, earned inside the wall, was non-taxable, another prison perk.

Bradley filed false W-2 forms in order to provide evidence of phony wages and withholdings. Though Bradley had never filed a claim for himself, each refund was for at least seven hundred dollars. All inmates agreed to provide Bradley with a generous portion of their refund, as payment for his services. Hoping the paper trail would not lead back to him, many of the tax refund checks were sent directly to the institution. This caused the Bravo Team just a tad bit of suspicion. The phony tax scheme was prosecuted and a plea bargain was met, whereas Bradley smartly agreed to serve two to three years in federal prison, after his state sentence was completed. He chose not to take the strong case to trial.

Accountant Bradley's clients were prosecuted as well. All were convicted without one single trial. This at least saved the federal government court costs. A con-artist to the end, Bradley had filed several civil law suits. He claimed that his rights had been violated. He also decided fifty thousand dollars would compensate for his mental anguish. Forced into the minor leagues, Bradley was attempting to draw blood from a stone. Eventually residing at maximum security, inmate Bradley's wheels, along with others like him, were still spinning out of control, searching for that easy ride. Inmate Bradley, a stubborn, but stupid man, filed more tax returns the following year and was caught again. Robby had no doubt that some federal judge would no longer find any humor in this inmate's games. The team laughed at his stupidity, as John commented, "Bradley will probably never get a chance to collect social security, so he had better get used to the food. I have a feeling that he'll 'be down' for a very, very long time!"

Almost one year later, another ingenious scam involved Ma Bell and every pay phone within the prison. On the word of a radical, thrill seeking, but reliable informant, Robby initially discovered the on-going telephone scam. It involved hundreds of inmates state-wide. The informant, who was nicknamed the Inspector, revealed that the money-making scam basically involved five major players which he identified from a photo array. For a couple of days, the telephones and players were monitored closely by the entire team. Nothing appeared too unusual. On the third day, the Inspector called the hot line. This was a direct phone number to the I.P.S. office. He excitedly informed Robby, "I'm standing in the Shanty and one of the players is in the next booth. I think he's busy with some customers right now!" Robby advised him to remain on the telephone and act, as though he was speaking with his mother. The remainder of the Bravo Team was dispatched to the area. Frank, Keith and John rushed the telephone booth and locked up the alleged player. The Inspector could hardly control himself, screaming in Robby's ear, "You guys got him! It was great!"

The con-man was escorted to the I.P.S. office where he underwent a strip search. Four pages of countless telephone numbers, both local and long distance, were found. Within the first few minutes of the interview, the inmate became increasingly afraid of losing his parole eligibility. Of course, Frank had to show him the error of his ways. He started singing like a hyperactive canary. Explaining the entire scam in detail, the inmate disclosed, "An inmate must make a collect call to an outside business, for example a large bank or corporation. The bigger, the better. The inmate will then tell the operator or recorder that he is calling collect from A.T.&T. or New England Telephone. The majority of the time, the business will accept the collect call. Upon accepting said call, a story is fabricated such as, 'Hi, I'm an employee (repairman) for A.T.&T. and I am presently working on your telephone lines. Can I please get an outside line, so that I can call my supervisor?' At this time, an outside line is usually granted, without questions and the inmate can call anywhere in the world for free, staying on the phone for as long as he desires. Various fabricated stories are used to gain access to outside lines for free. Most businesses are scouted out first to ensure that they will fall for this scam. Most are too busy to verify the inmates true identity. Of course, it would always be easier to open the line than investigate the true source of such a call. The average cost for one of these outside lines is two packs of cigarettes, which is charged to inmates unable to pull off the bullshit talk. The price is worth it for inmates who don't wish to burden their families with high phone bills. This way, they're able to talk for hours." Every well-spoken word had been the truth. The inmate hadn't dared to try bluffing the sneering I.P.S. unit.

Other inmates were also bagged in the scam and they received disciplinary reports as a result. The telephone companies were informed of the ongoing fraud. Their security people had continued the investigation on their end. The eventual goal was to devise a system of stopping this type of fraud, especially where the recorders were concerned. The confiscated telephone numbers were called and the businesses, or companies made aware of the scam, so that they could protect themselves from this costly illicit activity in the future. The smaller companies showed great appreciation. They could not figure out the incredible increases in their billing. The larger businesses displayed little concern, stating, "It's nothing more than a tax write-off." Robby knew that with such apathetic attitudes, the fraudulent activity would never cease.

The Inspector, after months of good investigative work, began to become a problem. It was as if he would create situations and set up other inmates. Apparently, it would break up the monotony of his long days. Providing some valuable information on drug deals, outside police agencies began using him. That was until he hired a thug to blow up his father-in-law's car. Charged in court for conspiracy, he was convicted of the crime and transferred to higher security. A final interview of the once credible spy was conducted by the team. The informant, hoping to awe the investigators, revealed, "I am the prodigy who created the entire telephone scam. I showed a few others how it worked and then sat back to enjoy the show." The foursome laughed at him. Robby then informed the young smartass, "We've been aware of that fact from the beginning, but you had become too good to take down. It didn't matter, we knew it would only be a matter of time before you hung yourself anyway. Of course, our theory proved true enough!" The Inspector smirked, adding, "Maybe you did know, but did you guys know that it's been raining in France for the past three days?" The nut had been calling Europe for the weather, just to kill time. More than anything, he enjoyed knowing he would get away with it. Robby laughed hysterically.

7

W hile the Bravo Team investigated the illicit businesses and con-games, Robby learned that violence was somehow woven into almost everything they did. It was considered part of corrections, but for I.P.S., it became a part of their daily routines. That very fact insured that the boys clung together on everything they did. Their dependence upon each other brought them closer than four men could ever get. Robby enjoyed that tight bond more than anything the job had to offer.

The illicit business of inmate-victimizing-inmate very often led to incredibly violent acts. Every man had a boiling point. Some needed to only get burned once to retaliate fiercely. Respect and a solid reputation was everything. It was essential to maintain one's own safety. To become the victim of another inmate in prison was normal, but to leave the act unanswered, or unavenged was like asking that all other inmates violate you. Those men, who were unwilling to stand up and fight, were open season for the band of hunters who prowled the concrete jungle everyday. Any weakness that could be exploited, would be. Property, self-esteem and even life could be taken away as a result. Therefore, there were brutal assaults and bloody fights. The use of weapons was commonplace and sometimes there were murders. For some, the only hope of surviving within this harsh environment was through the quick responses and constant intervention of the people the inmates hated most, Frank Gagne and his Bravo Team. Unlike other areas of society, those men literally fought for their lives and each situation differed. Physical size and fighting skills, or capabilities, would only go so far in a world full of weapons. In this world, the real strength was found in numbers. Whether it was one-on-one or ten-on-one, most fights occurred without warning. Robby observed, all too often, that very seldom was there any mercy shown.

Physical altercations in prison were as commonplace as rats in a landfill. There could not be one without the other. Besides the gambling debts, strong-arming and loansharking factors, there were a multitude of reasons for the unavoidable violence. There were basic personality conflicts which became even more magnified within the enclosed setting. Enemy situations were created everyday, another reality of life behind bars. Though these situations were monitored closely and administrators attempted to separate and protect all inmates, quite often the team was unaware of a problem until an assault or fight transpired. Then, there were retaliations and vendettas. Those occasionally occurred because of prior victimization and enemy situations which may have been carried over from another facility or the streets. The Bravo Team seemed to investigate at least two-to-three fights a day. Unlike other investigations, they simply reacted to these situations after everything was over.

There were men who retaliated against another because they had been backed into a corner and were forced to react. One inmate, who had been involved in an unreported fight at the house of correction while awaiting trial, was admitted into the institution. He soon found that his old friend, who had beaten him months earlier, resided in the same dormitory. Within the first day, the tougher inmate attempted to strong-arm cigarettes from the man. The weaker man refused to give up the smokes. Into the bathroom they went, only to return minutes later, the strong-armer victorious. That night both men went to bed. The weaker inmate had woken with two swollen eyes and a loss of self- respect. Embarrassed by his injuries, he decided to retaliate. He placed a can of soup into a tube sock with which he intended to open his enemy's skull.

Approaching the larger inmate, who was sitting on a bunk bed talking with a friend, the victimized man swung the weapon at his enemy. He clearly missed. The weapon had, however, struck the inmate's friend in the side of the head causing a wide-open laceration. This inmate, accidentally hit in the cross fire, commenced beating the hell out of the smaller man. In a desperate search for respect, that inmate only found himself another vicious beating. He just could not win. Laughed right out of the dorm, Frank and Robby escorted him to segregation. From the look on his face, even he knew that he would never be able to interact in general population again.

Another inmate was attacked from behind while sleeping in a dormitory. He was punched several times in the face. The pain had caused him to awaken dazed, confused and short three teeth. Apparently, the victim's bitter girlfriend had requested the 'hit.' She had asked another inmate, the assailant, to do her a favor for which he was happy to oblige. She and the assailant soon became engaged because of his cowardly assault on the unsuspecting man. Locking up the assailant, Robby couldn't help, but think, "There certainly are better ways to wake up."

Just hours later, another inmate, who had sworn to avenge the rape of his friend's daughter, made his move. In the middle of a crowded recreation room, this inmate approached a known sex offender and struck him several times in the head with a small lead pipe. The skinner fell to the floor in a puddle of his own blood while the room erupted into cheers. The attacker, satisfied with the damage he had done, dropped his weapon and waited to be taken away by I.P.S. During the escort to the hole, the assailant told Frank and Robby, "I've waited almost two years to get that skinner and now all I feel is relief. I never wanted to kill him, but just give the demented freak a taste of what he's sure to receive by my buddy when he gets out!"

Many assaults or fights were racially motivated. For reasons that reached beyond Robby's logic, each race found it necessary to beat the hell out of the other. Years of hatred and prejudice were passed on through generations. Amidst prison life and forced association with each other, problems arose almost daily between races. The administration and its staff attempted to maintain a racial balance throughout all areas of the prison because it was not so uncommon that a racial problem would turn into a race riot.

Robby and John, assigned to work late one night, happened to walk upon a nightmare in progress. There had been a basketball game involving eight black inmates and two white inmates. Evidently, it started to get rough. Pushes turned into punches. The whites, who were outnumbered, were easily beaten down. All staff were unaware, as the infuriated white inmates began recruiting for retaliation on the attack. Approximately forty inmates met inside of a cement yard, both sides somewhat evenly numbered. Only a few heated words were spoken before each inmate was exchanging blows with a counterpart. A somewhat spontaneous riot was taking place. Very little planning was done to create the dangerous situation.

The first officer to arrive on the scene was John Donovan. He called in the emergency via radio. Just seconds behind him, Robby witnessed as his brave friend began calling out each inmate by name, letting them know that they had been identified and would eventually pay dearly for their involvement. This act alone, though risky to John, helped to de-escalate the volatile situation. Some inmates stopped fighting when they heard their names called. Others continued to scrap and responding officers soon found themselves in the middle. Robby, John and other officers exchanged punches with some of the inmates who had lost control. Before the melee was taken under control, five officers were injured. The rest were left extremely stressed out. Hours later, John told Robby, "It's weird, but I didn't feel any fear during the incident. Now, looking back on the entire episode, I'm sure it's taken at least two years off of my life!" Unfortunately, the spontaneous confrontations had to be dealt with in this manner, force versus force.

On several occasions, the Bravo Team had discovered planned riots just prior to them taking place. Those were easily prevented by locking up the leaders and advising all inmates that staff had knowledge. Anyone choosing to become involved in a group dispute would be dealt with accordingly. This general warning would usually stop any major incidents. Frank informed Robby, "No matter how strongly an inmate feels about a situation, he will always look after himself first. Most only involve themselves with hopes of being unidentified."

One summer evening found a popular white inmate walking across the large cement yard, with his midnight snack in hand. A group of young black inmates standing on a wall had been harassing each passerby. For some reason, they chose to target this lone man by threatening him. Given the ultimatum of giving up the sandwich and milk, or eating concrete, the white inmate stopped in his tracks and gave the fairly large group an unusual reply. He challenged any of the black inmates to remove the snack from him. He then told them that they were all heartless. Within seconds, three or four of the black youths jumped the challenger, knocking him to the ground. They began kicking his face causing blood to fly everywhere. An emergency was called and when Robby and John arrived, the white inmate was on his feet. His face was badly beaten, but oddly he was speaking to the group in a calm voice. He reaffirmed, "You're all heartless punks, who find bravery hiding within a group, but you couldn't even take a little cheese sandwich away from me." He then explained to the group the reason he was enjoying a late-night snack. He informed them, "I'm in the latter stages of the AIDS disease. The sandwich is meant to keep my strength up. You boys better get yourselves some blood tests!" With that final warning, Robby handcuffed the white inmate. He cooperatively walked away with Robby and John, laughing at the ignorance of the punk-ass group. All of the black inmates were carted off as well. When Robby and John finally found time to get answers, one of the assailants wept, "We were only out 'wilding,' or having fun, but the fucking hero wouldn't give up his shit. Instead, he challenges us." John replied, "What did he have to lose? You're the one that needs to worry now. I hope it was worth it." The inmate's eyes swelled with tears. A night of 'wilding' may have condemned him and his homeboys to a terrible death. The partners removed their rubber gloves and went home.

The following morning, not twelve hours later, Robby and John reported to a fight in the Shanty. A white Irish punk had decided to take on several hispanic inmates and he was doing quite well for himself. Throwing everything he had, the two investigators finally had to concentrate on restraining him in order to break up the altercation. Once restrained by Robby and John, Keith handcuffed him. As the tough guy was being escorted out of the area, another hispanic inmate appeared out of nowhere and punched the Irish kid square in the face. The Shanty exploded into screams. The white inmates, so far uninvolved, circled a group of hispanics and got ready to do battle to avenge the attack on their friend. It had taken the smooth negotiating of the quick-thinking Keith Petrie to quell the disturbance. This could have easily turned into a bloody mess. Instead, a thick tension filled the air. It lingered for days. The officers assigned to the area felt the tension as well. One told Robby, "It seemed like for a good two weeks something big and bad was going to kick off." Fortunately, it never did.

Immediately following both altercations, Lieutenant Redman ordered the team to monitor the growing racial tension within the prison. He especially wanted the young gang bangers monitored. They were inner-city kids who entered the system with a total disrespect for authority. With many having already established enemy situations, most gang members would align in prison to control illicit activities. They also united for protective purposes. Some rival gangs would never unite and whatever transpired on the street would reflect the climate between the groups within the institution. If a drive-by shooting claimed the lives of certain gang members outside, quite often retaliation would also take place behind the wall. It was imperative that the I.P.S. unit stayed on top of gang activity on the streets. This created intelligence information inside. With no striped uniforms being worn inside, those bangers attempted by any means to identify their loyalties through clothing, footwear, haircuts, etc. For some, hatred ran deep because they had experienced great losses at the hands of other gangs. Vengeance was always a possibility. Occasionally, a hit called from the street would be carried out inside. Often, this involved the use of weapons. Any assault or altercation involving weapons were the worst, for obvious reasons, but the Bravo Team still needed to deal with those situations. Keith was assigned as the I.P.S. gang liaison, but as the numbers of extensive enemy cases increased, inmates were moved from institution-to- institution. It was no less than a dangerous chess game. However, the number of pieces continued to increase, while the size of the board remained the same.

The Bravo Team also monitored the outlaw bikers and Aryan brothers who had randomly attacked a minority with no motive other than sheer ignorance. To belong to the white supremist group, an inmate had to take the life of a minority. He would then display a tattoo of a teardrop directly under one eye. Some possessed more than one teardrop and needed to be watched closely. They were transferred from one prison to another, so that their connections could not become strong. Their recruiting was kept to a minimal. One Aryan brother, received from out of state, had entered prison at a young age and was gang-raped by a minority group. In retaliation, he burned one of the men to death in his cell. As part of the Aryan nation, he found protection, along with a life bid. His roommate, a white supremist, serving big numbers for manslaughter, became a fantastic informant for John, due to his hatred of other races. However, he was soon caught assaulting weaker black inmates. There was a constant power struggle, with racism playing a large part in the vicious assaults and frightening fights which occurred regularly.

Others had been the recipients of merciless beatings due to their own stupidity, or failure to own up to a dirty deed, for which another had taken the fall. One stupid inmate had gotten beaten because he had found two inmates fighting in a cell. The clown locked the cell door. When the Bravo Team discovered the two in the same room, both showing visible wounds, it had not been difficult to figure out that a fight had occurred. The clown should have minded his business. Because they could not flee after the fight, both combatants received disciplinary action. The inmate population was not impressed with his prank and just minutes later, Robby found himself responding to another fight in the main yard. The prankster had been brutally attacked by a group of angry gang members. He was placed into protective custody.

Another inmate, who neglected to rightfully save the hide of an innocent man, was beaten down with a broomstick while his legs were burned badly from a pot of boiling water. Frank searched for an inmate who had stolen a telephone from one of the counselors' offices. The suspect was attempting to conceal it until a working phone jack could be located. The item was found, but all evidence led to another criminal. Therefore, that inmate was locked up, pending investigation. The real thief, given the opportunity to come forward with the truth, did not, at which time several inmates took justice. He soon became the recipient of a brutal beating. Afterward, Frank had no problem finding the true thief.

Inmates exacting justice, an ironic part of the correctional picture. There had been inmates who had formed their own committees and decided to take justice into their own hands. They would positively identify sex offenders by watching which men attended a special program which was designed strictly for rapists and child molesters. These inmates would later hold 'Court Sessions' and punish the guilty, which of course, were all of them. The guilty would then be punished by receiving extraordinary beatings. Eventually, the team intervened and stopped the popular game.

In a similar case, inmates who wished to take care of their own problems within their house and not get caught, had discovered a dorm thief. That thief was a stupid man with a dismal future. A blanket party, military style, was held, whereas a blanket was draped over his entire body, including his face. Unable to identify his attackers, this man was severely beaten, as one inmate after another took a shot at striking the thief with any blunt, heavy object they could find. In the morning, the thief was covered in bruises from head to toe. Frank and Robby removed him from the unit and everybody involved in the attack lived happily ever after, or they were at least satisfied that they had gotten rid of the bum. Robby saw the irony in both cases because every inmate, from an arsonist to a child molester, had assisted in beating the sex offenders and the dorm thief, feeling they had exacted justice on men who had done wrong.

Sex offenders were constantly being attacked and assaulted. It was certainly one of the most common reasons for much of the violence within the prison. But again, those inmates could only victimize their own kind, so very often they would prey upon each other. In one very unusual case, an inmate, who was a medical doctor by profession, had been convicted of sexually abusing his elderly patients. Once incarcerated, he had taken on the guise of being homophobic. Arguing with a well-known homosexual in the library, the gay inmate pinched the good doctor on the ass. Fighting words were exchanged and the doctor, with the demented bedside manner, eventually received a terrible beating. The gay inmate, who loved to fight almost as much as performing oral sex, was far from being passive, as he smashed a wooden table over the doctor's head. He then used a leg from the table to beat the older man down.

Both inmates were locked up. Robby collected and inventoried their personal property. The doctor's property was found to contain several hundred color photographs. The majority being of young children. There were approximately twenty nude photos which appeared to be taken at different times and places. Several angles and poses of the young children were used in these photos and eight (xerox type) copies were also found in the subject's property. These had been photocopied from the twenty nude photos found. An investigation regarding child pornography was conducted by Robby and Frank, with both the U.S. Postal Service and the local Defense Attorney's office involved. Due to the fact that there had been no penetration within the pictures, criminal charges could not be filed. The inmate, who intended to distribute the photos to other pedophiles, was charged internally. At the conclusion of the investigation, the correctional legal department ordered that the photos be returned to the sick doctor, as they were his rightful property. Due to the department's fear of liability, Robby knew that justice had not been served. He also found it very difficult not to take the perverted man's actions personally. No doubt, the man continued fantasizing about the nude children and had probably made a few dollars on the side selling the valuable snapshots to other child molesters. Robby hated the fact that he couldn't do more.

Some inmates just snapped and would lash out without reason or warning, a benefit of working with the criminally insane. Frank and the boys never knew what a man was thinking. There was a neighborhood bug known to be harmless to staff, but merciless on himself. John, who was hanging around the Shanty one afternoon, was having fun by teasing the young kid. Suddenly, the bug snapped. Grabbing the nearest weapon he could find, a mop handle, the inmate swung the weapon at one of the biggest officers in the joint. He had made the wrong choice. John Donovan, a powerful man, disarmed the inmate with ease. He then informed him, "If it ever happens again, the stick will be rammed so far up your ass, you'll walk around this prison for days looking like a popsicle." The problematic inmate was escorted off to segregation. Not twenty minutes later, a code 99, medical emergency was called for that exact area. Upon arrival, John and rest of the team discovered both the floor and walls covered in blood. That same inmate had removed one of his false teeth and had begun to carve deep cuts into his forearm. He had been crying, sorry for his assault on Big John. He was now punishing himself through self-mutilation. Immediately sent to the Bug House for a tune up, this mentally-ill inmate would spend at least a month with other inmates who enjoyed pain. Men who would stick foreign objects inside their penises, burn themselves with lit cigarette butts and perform any other form of self-mutilation they could dream up in their nightmares.

Robby found that even the sane lost it at times. One inmate, informed of the death of a loved one, was harassed while he headed for his cell. That man, in a fit of rage, doled out one of the worst beatings in the history of the prison.

There were an infinite number of other reasons for the violence. From being under the influence to strong varying opinions, some seemed almost valid, yet never condoned. During Operation Desert Storm, an inmate of Arabian descent had made comments about the American troops getting killed in mass, as they deserved. That inmate was beaten senseless and left crying on the floor of a shower. Robby, hearing about the story, privately smiled, thinking, " National patriotism is alive and well, even inside prison."

There were basically two philosophies believed by correction officers when breaking up fights. First being, when observing a fight in progress, the officer called the emergency over the radio and waited until sufficient backup arrived before attempting to separate the combatants. This was the method taught and encouraged, mainly for officer safety. The idea was to let the cons fight it out and jump in, only when enough help arrived. The other theory was that when a fight broke out, the officer called it in. He then jumped right in the middle of the fight, doing all he could to stop the altercation while responding officers were still en-route. Those officers believed that any confrontation should be broken up as soon as possible because the chance of the situation escalating increased with each second. Onlooking inmates who chose one side or the other, could get involved, causing a more serious problem. This thought, along with the emotional factor which shot the adrenaline, made most officers jump right in without waiting. Common sense prevailed in all cases. If a weapon was involved, assistance would definitely be in the best interest of any officer. The number of inmates involved in the ruckus had to be taken into account and so on. For one reason or another, the men assigned to the Bravo Team always chose the second theory when breaking up fights.

Robby recalled one savage fight which had snapped off right in front of an officer. The officer called the emergency in and waited for help, without even ordering the combatants to cease. All of the inmates, who had witnessed this, had lost all respect for the officer because they too relied on this man's help for their own safety. It was the officer's discretion. It was considered a judgment call each time, but even if waiting for assistance was the chosen method, the officer should have controlled the scene. Within seconds, other inmates interfered by yelling and causing more confusion. The officer had let all hell break loose without even a word. Upon arrival, Robby and the others discovered a potential riot which could have been quelled long before. Both combatants were locked up, along with several other inmates who had become cheerleaders.

Those fights which occurred right in front of staff were usually the inmates who wanted the altercation to be broken up before either man got hurt. Possibly, they were forced for some reason into dukeing it out. For many, it was a last desperate cry for help. Those were glorified protective custody issues and it was referred to as 'going out like a hero.' Other means of achieving protective custody were also used. John had experienced an inmate going off on him for no apparent reason while Keith interviewed another who had self-inflicted wounds, while telling a tall-tale of an unidentified attacker. Those men, for one reason or another, could no longer hang in population. They wished to 'check in,' or P.C.. The real serious cases would find the need for transfer because those petrified inmates could no longer cope with the on-going violence. John often grumbled, "If only their victims had had the same luxury of being so strongly protected." Ultimately, P.C. didn't make a difference, because they could run, but there was nowhere to hide in the system. Inmates working inside of the property room kept other inmates informed of who got shipped where. By 'flying a kite,' or writing letters, inmates corresponded between prisons. If an inmate was wanted, he could be had, unless he was locked up in seg. for the sole purpose of protection.

The other inmates, who were serious about fighting, would find a secluded area to 'throw hands.' In those instances, either one or both of the combatants wished to cause the other serious injury and not get caught. When Robby or his partners happened upon those fights, they usually had a really tough time trying to break up the enemies. Those were the genuine beefs. In such cases, Frank stressed that it was better to play it safe by smartly waiting for backup. From the back stairways, to any nook or cranny that could be found, those inmates would fight while a peek man kept the watch. The injuries sustained normally left some scarred for life.

Concerning all fights, assaults or any type of physical altercation, the team's biggest concern or more specifically, fear, was the chance of exposure to the deadly H.I.V. virus. Again, due to confidentiality reasoning, officers were not supposed to know an inmate's medical issues. During one afternoon briefing, the team talked about their fears. Robby started, "It's like playing Russian roulette with each fight responded to, especially where there's blood involved. There's always a chance of becoming infected!" Robby felt this was probably the scariest element of the profession. Rubber gloves would not prevent fresh blood entering an open cut, or eyes and so on. When breaking up those fights, many times Robby would find himself rolling around and wrestling on the ground with the violent inmates. The close contact was there and the fear of contracting the disease existed as well. AIDS was a major and quickly spreading problem in prison. Keith knew, only too well, that it was also spread throughout the facility through the use of dirty needles.

Keith said, "I was working the property room one evening, admitting a detox patient. I started a thorough search of the junkie's clothing when a dirty set of works fell out of the inmate's jacket pocket, which just missed pricking me. I was so pissed off, I had to go for a quick walk. It was scary to think of how extremely close I had just come to being stuck with a diseased needle. I was lucky, but the next time it could take my life and the lives of my innocent, unsuspecting family."

AIDS was just another occupational hazard, which any officer might be unfortunate enough to contract. If this disease should befall an officer, there was no turning back. The chances of this happening were increasing. There had been verbal confrontations between infected inmates and staff, but those situations were handled with kid gloves, not only rubber gloves.

As Keith complained about the close-call, Robby told his friend that he was not alone. "There had been a detoxing inmate with full-blown AIDS and open soars which oozed with puss. He was refusing to move. In any other similar case, the inmate would be ordered to move and if still non-compliant, extracted from the room by a move team. In this case, however, I took over an hour of negotiating before the dying man was talked into moving into a single cell. I knew that all efforts to avoid conflict or physical contact were needed. Diplomacy was essential because even the smallest of altercations could spell out death to all staff involved."

Frank laughed, saying, "That's nothing. A few years ago, I remember stupidity almost costing an officer his life. He thought he could disrespect an inmate who was dying of AIDS. The inmate had showered and used the officer's chair to place his clean clothes on. The officer, upon discovering this, threw the man's clothing onto the wet, dirty floor. After finishing his shower, the inmate found his clothes lying in a pool of dirty water and became infuriated. The inmate wanted to fight him. He made it clear that although he had nothing to lose, he refused to be disrespected. The officer, who was at a loss for words, stood back in fear, as I talked the angry inmate down from his fury. I'll be honest, I was scared shit the entire time, hoping the infected inmate did not lunge for my brother officer. That would have left me no choice, but to physically restrain the dying man."

Conflicts and confrontations between staff and inmates were merely another accepted factor within the correctional business. There was animosity felt on both sides. Officers disliked the criminals they got paid to interact with everyday and the inmates hated the officers who held the keys to their freedom. Not all hated each other, but friendships were certainly not formed between the two sides. Exchanging insults was commonplace with the officers being called Screws (years ago the doors did not possess keys, but were screwed shut), Turn-keys, Bulls and Guards. Even the term Prison Guard was considered an insult by Robby. It implied a person watching over a fixed object. Robby, like most officers, interacted with criminals on a daily basis while striving for professionalism. Robby returned the insults by stereotyping an inmate into a group which he did not belong. Being called a skinner or diddler drove many of the inmates crazy. Words by themselves meant nothing and it was important for Robby to become thick-skinned, trying not to let any type of verbalization get to him. It was the nature of the business. Robby thought, "If a person did not want to get their feet wet, they didn't become a lifeguard. If they cannot tolerate, or are bothered by swears and insults, then corrections is the wrong business. Sticks and stones..," as the childhood rhyme went. Frank had always said, "A person either owns a piece of your mind or you own a piece of his." Innocent verbalization was acceptable, however, officers did not get paid to be abused. Whether there were threats or assaults, those actions were dealt with accordingly, from disciplinary action to the use of reasonable force when necessary.

Some threats were not put into the form of words. John, who was securing the Muslim chapel one morning, was surrounded by a large group of Muslims who demanded he open their temple. The threat was taken the moment they had circled him in an aggressive fashion. For that simple act of attempted intimidation, the Bravo Team swooped down to assist their partner. Most were transferred to higher security the following day.

Unlike assaults, most threats were just shrugged off by staff. It would certainly be easy enough to walk around in complete paranoia every time the team was threatened. Many of those threats were empty. However, there was always that one inmate who made the boys wonder. Frank Gagne, known to be assertive and quite tough with the cons, started to have a personality conflict with an old-timer who was allegedly connected to organized crime. With each day that would pass, the two would exchanged bitter words. Frank was slightly more disrespectful about the whole situation. On Easter morning, Frank walked past the inmate's cell and called the man a derogatory name. The inmate stopped Frank and asked, "Can we talk?" Without a reply, the inmate continued, "Let me tell you my friend, you have a beautiful wife and your two young daughters are as cute as their mother. From what I understand, your house is in fairly good shape, but it's about time you paint the white fence out front." He then told Frank even more about his life. Suddenly, in a angry voice, he warned him, "We do not have to like each other, but if you continue to disrespect me, you're gonna face more problems than you can ever handle!" The inmate was transferred from the facility that same day, but not before Frank had been taught a terrifying lesson. Those inmates were not cut off from the world. It was always a possibility that Frank's family could pay for his actions. Frank had definitely played with a man who possessed outside connections. Robby wondered if, perhaps, he was only trying to redeem himself for fearing old Dom years ago. Shaken up for a short while, Frank still chose the style of a hard-ass, though he was more respectful about his comments and actions. Frank, or any of them, could not fear an inmate to the point where it interfered with his duties. However, it was wise for every man to know his enemies.

Probably the biggest question Robby was asked by people living outside of the prison was, "Do inmates get beaten?" His honest response each time was, "No." Living in a world full of informants, administrators, video cameras and other electronic surveillance, not to mention civil liability and hordes of personal law suits, those days had passed. Granted, there were personal conflicts and if an inmate was searching for trouble, he need not look far. An inmate, whether he chose to acknowledge it or not, was at the mercy of the correctional staff. Their lives could be altered through their visits, disturbed by searches, loss of sleep, the list went on. If an inmate pushed an officer in a figurative sense, other officers felt as though they too were being pushed and eventually something would give. If an inmate physically assaulted an officer, then that man was considered open game until the restraints were applied. Officers would fight if such situations arose and for good reason. There was, of course, the self-defense factor, but more importantly, if the assault went unanswered, all inmates would take the lack of response as the wrong message. When officers retaliated fiercely, it became a preventive measure for future assaultive inmates. Most would think twice, knowing the possibilities of getting hurt were really good if a staff person was struck. The quiet and compliant would not experience any problems with staff, but those that chose to test the limits of an officer would be tested as well. History had proven that most inmates would lose the game sooner or later.

Random or subjective beatings did not occur. However, in this environment, spontaneous uses of force and extractions seemed to be a daily event. The bottom line was that physical confrontations between inmates and staff had to be initiated by the inmate, whether it be because he was being assaultive, aggressively threatening or non-compliant with the orders of staff.

There had been blatant attacks on staff resulting in serious injuries and the need for force. One inmate, a completely psychotic man, had been informed by his correctional counselor that he did not receive a transfer to lower security, Minimum. The inmate, who was filled with rage, stood up and punched the tiny woman in the face, knocking her to the floor. She got back on her feet and the crazed inmate hit her again, this time breaking her nose. Finally, the Bravo Team arrived and subdued the man, but not before he had caused her traumatic injury. The lady left work on industrial accident status (equivalent to workman's compensation). She bravely returned to work a short time later.

Another staff person, this man a hated sergeant, had peered into the cell of a hispanic inmate. The inmate threw a full pot of scalding water into the sergeant's face, causing serious burns. Again, Frank and the boys responded like lightning. Keith and John had to subdue the sergeant, preventing him from entering his attacker's room. If not for the two investigators, that sergeant probably would have ended up incarcerated for murder.

Several months later, a sergeant who was assigned to a segregation unit, entered the cell of an inmate who began calling him down for everything. The sergeant ordered a strip search and the inmate refused by punching the man in the face, which dazed him. A wrestling match ensued. The inmate, who was attempting to rip an eye out of the sergeant's head, had the man screaming for dear life. The Bravo Team entered the cell and tossed the inmate off of their brother officer, only to find him bleeding profusely from his eye socket. Each one of them wanted to kill that inmate. The shift commander arrived on scene and ordered that the inmate be transferred to another prison, adding that the entire move would be videotaped. This had angered the vengeful staff. However, had he not made that decision, the team may have actually killed the piece of shit. That captain had, in essence, saved the inmate's life, but more importantly to him, the jobs and futures of his staff. However, as an important ingredient of surviving in this abnormal environment was the ability to possess spite, Robby felt the need to react. That vicious inmate may not have gotten beaten, but his property was sent in slightly different condition than what he would have remembered. Robby, unable to control his bladder, had accidentally urinated in the rear of the man's television set. He was sure that the reception would be different.

A female officer, admitting a drunk man into the detox program, was thrown through a glass window. Sustaining serious injuries, requiring multiple surgeries, her life was forever changed as a result of the inmates attack. Another female officer, from a sister-institution, was abducted on the graveyard shift. By jamming the electronically controlled cell door, the inmate was able to abuse the female officer at will. She was beaten severely and raped for hours, all the while, begging to be freed. The inmate, after approximately five hours of tormenting the woman, let her go. The physical pain would eventually subside, it always did, but the emotional burden of that horrific experience will be with her for the rest of her life.

There had been other responses by the team, finding inmates on drugs assaulting staff. However, that same staff had returned the punches, because again, everybody had the right to defend themselves. There had been many, many other assaults on staff, while most occurred without warning and ended the promising careers of some outstanding officers. An officer never knew when it would be his, or her time to fight for their life. Within this isolated world, the chances of having to do so, more than once within a normal twenty year career, were very likely.

Some inmates chose to try their luck at fighting with staff. John laughed at a large, white inmate, who was summoned from the yard, but refused to move, calling John and Keith out to come and get him. The confident partners approached the inmate and gave him one last chance to comply. The inmate only smiled, grabbing for the throat of John. A struggle took place from which the inmate sustained injury. Handcuffs were applied and as he was escorted off, he started to spit at Frank. It was not a wise move. Due to the hatred felt by the team toward this inmate, he was immediately transferred out. He had been fortunate for that gifted move.

That same day, another incredibly large inmate had been searched by Keith. The inmate was uncooperative and was ordered to place his hands behind his back to be cuffed, to which he refused. Keith, quite smaller in size, attempted to force the inmate's hands, but there was no give. At that time, a call for assistance was transmitted and within seconds, Frank, Robby and John were on top of the monster trying to cuff him. Other officers also rushed in. The inmate, who was not throwing any punches, was still not complying. Instead, he laid on the floor and laughed at how weak all of the officers were. The giant had a man on each limb, with Robby holding his head. As they said in the academy, "You control the head... you control the body," but it wasn't working. It was amazing, as the inmate moved any part of his body he wished. Finally, Lieutenant Redman arrived on scene and began to calmly talk to the moose, asking him to cooperate. During this conversation, the boys continued to try applying handcuffs on the inmate, but to no avail. Eventually, the monster said, "Enough's enough. I'll go peacefully." Surprisingly, he did. It was found at that time that regular handcuffs would not fit the wrists of this inmate, so leg irons were used to restrain him.

When the inmate had been strip searched, it became instantly clear why there had been a problem. The inmate had the body of a professional wrestler, with shoulders as big as volley balls. He was huge, muscular and possessed the strength and intelligence of an ox. A lesson had been learned that day which was more of a good, hard slap of reality. This man had been underestimated by Keith and could have hurt any one of them badly, had that been his intent. However, besides a lot of laughter, some good did come out of the episode. John quit smoking while Keith and Robby returned to the gym. Frank joked, "It has to be the food because they're getting bigger every year."

Many times officers would get injured while breaking up a fight because an inmate felt he could get a cheap shot in. John, who was a tough bastard and trained in martial arts, was feared by the inmates. Separating two combatants who had been fighting, another inmate looked to make a name for himself. This inmate ran up behind John and broke a pool stick over his neck and back. The inmate was immediately taken down by Keith. In serious pain, John returned to work the following day. He was too proud to take an I.A.. Besides, he did not want the inmate to think that he had taken him out of the picture. John possessed a strong moral and ethical conscience, but felt differently than many other officers. Like John, there were officers who refused to have an inmate beat them, even if it was only their own mental reasoning.

On the other side of that same coin and right around that same time period, a fight involving two incredibly small inmates had put two power lifters out of work for years. The inmates were probably the combined weight of two hundred pounds, while the officers possessed the physical capabilities of bench pressing V.W. bugs. Those officers, who had been looking for their ticket out, had a different view about what the right thing to do was. They were always searching for the easiest way out and had finally found it. Officers' opinions on Industrial Accidents(workman's compensation) varied greatly. They were easy enough to get. Though, John proved that there were still some officers who possessed the integrity to return to the prison, even though things could get really hairy inside at times. Men, like John, were the officers who could be most counted on when the shit really hit the fan and everybody knew it.

Then there were the formal, ordered uses of force, the extractions. In those situations, normally an inmate had burned out, flooded out or refused to move from his cell. If an inmate was still adamant about resisting the move, after several generous opportunities to change his outlook on the bleak situation, an area lieutenant would give a direct order. If refused, chemical agents were very often administered, but there had been seasoned inmates who would easily combat this tactic with their own. By saturating a wool blanket with water and completely covering themselves, they were protected from the gas, as the wet blanket would absorb much of it. Those inmates, who refused to go down without a fight, were usually greased up and in possession of some type of weapon, even though they knew it was a losing battle.

An inmate, called Clyde, was admitted to a segregation unit. He decided he did not like the view, so he demanded that he be returned to higher custody. The administration, who had a difficult time allowing inmates to call the shots, flatly refused his demand. For the following two weeks, this inmate assaulted officers by throwing food, urine and feces at them. Each time, he would be moved by the Bravo Team to a different cell. The unappreciative team did not handle this inmate with care. Two-to-three times per day, Clyde was moved, until he finally stopped throwing things. He had learned that the transfers from one cell to another were, at the very least, uncomfortable and progressively getting worst. His spirit, finally broken, left him to ponder his awful ways in an empty cell, consisting of a toilet and bed.

During Clyde's rebellious bouts with staff, another inmate was admitted into segregation. He, too, wanted to go back to the Hill. This inmate was allowed to fill his water pitcher one night and after doing so, he placed the container on the floor. He then proceeded to wrap his large arms around the water fountain and with one quick grunt, ripped the fountain completely out of the concrete floor. Returning to his cell, he told the officers that he did not want to hurt any of them, but he was not at all happy with his current living conditions. He added that if things did not change immediately, he would become uncontrollable. The following day, both Clyde and the strong man were transferred back to Max. Security, leaving the unit peaceful for a few short days.

Behavior such as Clyde's produced very normal feelings and actions from abused staff. Though the department stressed professionalism, when urine or feces were thrown into the faces of Frank and his crew, some had returned the kind gesture. It sometimes seemed necessary, if only for self-respect and peace of mind, to get 'down and dirty' and right in the gutter with those types of animals. Robby learned that showing an inmate that you were just as crazy as he, had stopped the surety of future, similar confrontations.

In a trade off, another bad-ass was sent down from the Hill and though he could care less about the living arrangements, he thought he was going to call the shots within the tightly secured unit. Requesting to take a shower, the inmate was informed that he was last on the list and when his time came, he would be allowed access to the facility. Hours had passed and without so much as a peep, the man was escorted into the shower room, where he bathed. He then tore every fixture, pipe and tile clean off of the walls. The place was completely destroyed, forcing the Bravo Team to go in and remove the vandal. Though he fought, he went down quick and had nothing to say, except, "I told you that I wanted a shower hours ago. You should have listened!"

Robby reported to assist in another shower incident. Upon arrival, he found a distraught hispanic inmate covered in his own feces, refusing to exit the area. The team was assembled and several orders given by a translator, because the man claimed he could not speak, or understand English. This problematic inmate began throwing water at the boys, claiming that he was blessing them because they would need God's help. Without further delay, the team entered the small shower area. The inmate, who was waiting for the exact moment, spun around, turned the cold water off and the hot water up. He then placed his body flush against the back wall. Standing directly under the shower head, the inmate was not touched by the scalding water. However, Frank and his team, who were all burned, scrambled over each other to turn off the hot water handle. The inmate was then taken to the floor and forcefully removed. Restraints were applied, but he continued to struggle like an animal anticipating death. Screaming in Spanish and attempting to bite whoever came within reach, the man was placed into a van and transported over one hundred miles to a court house. The presiding judge only signed off that the unstable man be committed to the State Hospital, located directly across the street from the originating prison, which was now over one hundred miles away.

During the transport, the crazed inmate bucked, fought and tried to bite through the soles of Robby and Keith's boots. He was definitely a high spirited young man with his energies focused in the wrong direction. Eventually, the long journey ended up back at the Bug House where this inmate, who had been refusing to take his behavior-altering medication, started to speak fluent English. Within a matter of minutes, he was strapped to a bed in four point restraints, then injected with a sedative which made him drop off to sleep almost instantly.

This was a strange experience, but as in all extractions, anything and everything was possible, with a strong possibility of an officer getting injured. This one had been a little more bizarre than most because it was a prolonged experience. Most uses of force were dangerous and fierce, but over in a flash. Robby thought, "Thank God for small favors."

Many inmates would claim excessive force was used on them, file internal grievances which had to be investigated by I.P.S.. They would file law suits, claiming brutality, as well as other civil rights violations. Force and the amount used was often difficult to determine. Being either excessive or reasonable, it was a judgment call. Many of the internal investigations proved inconclusive because the inmate, in question, had given staff no choice but to physically restrain, or subdue him. Hoping to get moved, receiving false compensation, or costing a hated officer his job were some of the motives for many of those fraudulent claims.

Frank and Robby were assigned one of those extremely extensive investigations. An inmate, who was known to be mentally-ill, alleged that officers had entered his room in the early morning. He said they placed a pillow case over his head and led him down several corridors before he was ordered onto his knees. The inmate claimed that his hands were bound together with rope and that he was beaten for over an hour. Thrown back into his cell, he waited until sunrise before reporting the incident to the day shift staff. A medical evaluation was conducted which found that the man had sustained injuries. However, those injuries were old and inconsistent with his story. After weeks of intense interviews and reviewing the alleged crime scene, Frank and Robby concluded that this particular inmate was being strong-armed for all of his canteen, as well as his psychotropic medication. It was very likely that the inmate never lied to Frank or Robby, but truly believed that the incident had taken place. Transferred into protective custody, the case was later reviewed by federal agents who had suspected a cover-up. Due to his extensive mental health issues, they too found that all of the disabled man's allegations had been fabricated.

With law suits being filed every day, officers needed to cover their asses. However, Robby knew of a limited amount of documented cases where an officer overstepped the boundaries and actually struck an inmate. There had been one incident where an officer had been displaying black tape across his badge, the sign of respect for a fallen brother officer. An inmate, who was trying to be funny, asked the officer, "What's the black tape for?" The officer reluctantly explained, "A brother correction officer has recently died and the covered badge is symbolic of the loss." The inmate laughed cynically, replying, "Actually, it's too bad more officers don't die, but at least it makes me happy that one did!" Without delay, that officer jumped the inmate and gave him a 'facial,' slapping him open-handed across the face which not only stung, but was a display of the utmost disrespect. He had not given the inmate the respect of punching him like a man. Three officers, standing-by, stopped the angry officer before he attempted to strike the inmate again. Though all witnesses tried to sweep the incident under the carpet, it was no use. The Bravo Team investigated the case and had no choice, but to disclose their findings. The officer was suspended and later sued by the compassionate inmate who had been hit. Of all involved, Frank and his crew had probably felt the worst.

Other excessive uses of force had found frustrated officers getting carried away. With months of hatred brewing between a certain officer and an inmate, the day had come where the inmate refused to strip search. A spontaneous use of force took place. However, the officer, venting on the inmate, had used too much force. When an inmate showed up at the H.S.U. with cut wrists, that injury could be considered consistent with his resistance of being restrained, but when his face showed fresh bruises, somebody had to answer for it. It was rare, but it did happen. Again, the team had to look into it. Officers took some type of abuse day-in and day-out, so when a legitimate use of force transpired, some officers did not know when to quit. On occasion, other officers had to intervene, as the incidents occurred in the heat of passion. There were officers who had to be reminded that when it was over, it was over.

One practice that the Bravo Team detested was when those few officers attempted to hit the inmate once he had been restrained. Once the inmate was handcuffed, it was definitely over and there was no excuse for striking the helpless person, regardless of the reason for his being locked up. Robby thought, "Why sink to the inmate's level?" There was no honor in striking an infant, no respect given to a person who hit an elderly woman. The same was true in stomping a man who had been restrained. If an officer felt so strongly that he needed to hit an inmate for any reason, then it better be done when the man's hands were free. Justified or not, only a coward would take the cheap shot. There had been a few, but fortunately very few.

Besides the assaults and fights, the team had to continually monitor the inmate population to detect the possibility of other major disturbances or disorders, nipping them in the bud. There had been inmates who had written petitions, inciting others to rebel against the established administration and its officers. Those documents were taken out of circulation and the author disciplined with a usual transfer.

Robby had witnessed different situations where one or more inmates had initiated food boycotts, or work stoppages. One inmate placed the claw of a dead pigeon into a large pan of soup. The word spread like wild-fire and the inmate population became outraged, refusing to eat. Another inmate started a fire in the laundry for the simple fact that his co-workers would not strike along with him. Yet another, wielding a steel butter knife, stood on top of one of the tables in the I.D.R., attempting to invoke the same response from his co-workers. Lieutenant Redman eventually talked that inmate down, but the man had bought himself a one-way ticket to Maximum security. Those types of incidents were always considered dangerous and the loud-mouths were quickly removed. Any legitimate problem got a fair amount of attention from the administration. If a problem was determined to be genuine, it would be corrected. As far as an inmate controlling the opinions of hundreds of aggressive men, well, that could only turn ugly. Every man had his say, but unity was potentially dangerous. Therefore, the old divide and conquer method was utilized. Normally, it was only the renegades who initiated those attempts at controlling the general consensus. It was never a rational man who would deal with a complaint peacefully.

With all of those realities of prison life set aside, every once in a while, Robby and his friends would witness a very vicious, atrocious crime. Those crimes committed were namely rape or murder. If unprevented by staff, each one was committed with the utmost cruelty, thus leaving the need for damage control. The boys always walked in to sweep up the remains, as life had to go on.

There were rapes which were committed within prison walls, just as Robby had always pictured them. Usually occurring at higher security, a young, naive and almost defenseless inmate would be admitted into the system. Immediately, some older deviant would take a real liking to the boy. Through intimidation or brute force, the inmate was figuratively seduced into performing unwanted homosexual favors. With this fresh, young stuff, it definitely, "did not count in prison," as some even took pride in it all.

The other way rapes occurred was through teamwork, or gang-style. The victim was held down by several, allowing each to take their turn sodomizing the newly admitted inmate. This was more or less a welcome, or initiation, into the system. On the other hand, it didn't happen to them all. The strong or well-connected would avoid this torture. Some of the predators claimed that they would protect their new "kid," or love slave, but normally once they were tired of the free sex, they would toss the prey back into the pack of wolves. Eventually, some inmates would approach the Bravo Team for help, for which they did receive, but they then became P.C. issues and were locked up for a good part of the day. Others would just take their own lives.

Rape in prison was exactly like rape on the streets. It was a crime of violent control, of humiliating the victim and taking all that he had inside of him. Sex was plentiful in the 'Big House,' with pimps, prostitutes and some homosexual inmates just giving their goods away. Yes, even in prison, rape was a crime of gruesome control.

The team received a couple of cases where inmates had claimed rape. Those men were immediately transported to a rape crises center in one of the best hospitals in the state. During one trip, the inmate, a professed homosexual, who enjoyed publicly washing the genitals of an older, crippled inmate, claimed he had been brutally raped. The medical evaluation diagnosed that the inmate indeed had been recently sodomized, but during Robby's interrogation which followed, the gay inmate admitted that he had been lying. According to him, he had allowed a friend to penetrate him from behind, but the friend became rough and later forced the alleged victim to perform oral sex on him which made him both angry and emotionally hurt.

Shortly thereafter, an extremely weak homosexual inmate reported to the I.P.S. office. The man's reputation was that he adamantly just hated to say no. Finding a new lover, he had agreed to oral sex, however he did not want to engage in anal sex. He believed that a man could only contract AIDS in that manner. The two started with oral sex, but as the gay inmate put it, "That sneaky, little bastard tricked me." Caught up in the moment, the new lover had placed the man's penis into his rectum which caused him to ejaculate immediately. The inmate claimed, "Believe me, it felt good, but I know I was not in control of the situation, so I'm not sure that I consented!" He wasn't sure whether he was raped, so he had brought his concerns to Frank and Robby. The two sat in disbelief, as the inmate explained his situation. Frank sternly informed the inmate, "You will be disciplined for being a whore and I'm not sure that date rape is an issue which has yet been addressed in prison."

Keith and John picked up another case involving an inmate with mental illnesses, who claimed that he had been raped in the middle of the night. This meant if the allegation was true, it would have had to be a staff person with a set of keys who committed the dirty deed. The medical evaluation noted no signs of penetration. Evidently, the inmate was suffering from a stomach virus. Unable to separate reality from fantasy, this inmate was experiencing rectal and stomach pains, assuming he must have been raped. Keith submitted his findings, with a strong recommendation that the inmate be shipped to the Bug House.

There had also been numerous unsuccessful murder attempts which always shook the population of the institution. The team investigated a situation involving an inmate beating another in a fair fight which went unreported. That night the victor went to sleep while the friend of the loser sharpened his shank. While he was sleeping in a dormitory, the assailant slashed him in the lower torso, waking him from a dead sleep. A quick fight took place and the assailant was disarmed with ease. Only suffering from a superficial cut, the inmate went back to sleep, apparently very confident in his abilities to fight, or his enemies inability's to hurt him.

Others had not been so lucky, dying from stabbings and strangulations. In one grotesque murder, an inmate was thrown from a third story tier where he smashed his head on the railing of the second tier, eventually snapping his neck on the flats below. The boys responded to another who was beaten to death with the leg of a chair. It was rumored that the killing transpired because the man's television was too loud which disturbed the lifer, who had nothing to lose by exterminating another human being. Each murder was investigated by I.A.D. and the state police. The defendants were charged and prosecuted. If found guilty, they were sentenced to serve more time. Ironically, this entire process had only been a waste of tax money, as many of those murderers were already serving multiple life sentences. For many, there really was nothing to lose.

Robby found that with all of this violence and living in fear constantly, many would leave the institution earlier than mandated. Besides wrapping up a bid, or being paroled, there were only two other ways that inmates exited this world of monsters. One was through escape and the other suicide. At times, one road or the other was taken.

Those that wanted out alive had made countless escape attempts. In three of them, the theory that some inmates cannot do anything right had been proven. The first was a parole violator, returned to prison to detox. He was also facing murder charges which he was unlikely to beat. Living in an old dorm, he started to work on one of the grilled windows leading to the roof. However, the attempt was discovered by Keith when the man began stockpiling ace bandages, tying them together and concealing them in his own locker. He was not a truly bright inmate, but a lucky one. He would have surely fallen to his death had he tried to climb down from the roof on that weak rope. Shipped to higher security, he never thanked Keith for saving his life.

Another had actually made it to the perimeter fence, but once he reached the top, he was unable to climb over the coiled razor wire and got all tangled up in it. Frank and Robby responded to the scene, only to find the inmate hanging upside down, screeching and flopping around like one of the seagulls that occasionally met the same fate. A comical sight, Frank, Robby and inmates alike got a hearty laugh out of that one, but the inmate, once taken down, was found to be cut bad. He was hurt so bad that it would be impossible for him to forget.

Almost one month later, John was patrolling through the sections when he came upon a big find. An inmate, residing on the fourth floor, had removed the wooden floor planks in his cell. He had replaced them with colored cardboard, as he was tunneling into the room below him. Not a completely intelligent move, but it was good for another laugh.

Then there were the successful escapes which caused the public to curse the department. Three inmates had escaped from the Treatment Center from the third floor. A small window was punched out and the first rapist out had gotten stuck. His two buddies pushed him to his death, as he had cracked open his head on the concrete below. From then on, he was used as a cushion for the landing of the other two who did make it out. Both rapists ran to the fence with a pair of wire cutters. It was only minutes before they were free men. Then, it was probably only days until they had taken more victims.

An even wiser inmate had escaped from a medium security facility. He had lost a lot of weight. Then, night after night, he cut out the window's steel grill with a hacksaw blade, while braiding an incredibly strong rope capable of towing an automobile. Fastened to the end of the woven rope was a steel grappling hook, fashioned from a stolen piece of flatstock. Gaining access to the roof one evening, this inmate easily lowered himself down a four story wall, where he ran to freedom. He was never captured.

Escapes, of course, only brought about bad public relations and vicious media coverage, but Lieutenant Redman had his own theory. "Those communities which will fight to the end to insure that no prisons are erected in their backyards should investigate the issue further. It's a fact that the state has been extremely generous in granting tax revenues to towns allowing a correctional institution within its borders. This money creates better police and fire services, benefiting education as well. Those communities also enjoy the equal safety of any other because most escaping inmates will never stay in the area longer than needed, especially when they know the area is being flooded with fugitive hunters. I know that many people feel differently about this very issue, but if they were to give it serious thought...?"

Shooting the bull in the office one morning, Robby explained his own awful experience regarding an escape. "From the Minimum visiting room, two homosexual lovers had gotten drunk and decided to elope. Picked up by a get-away car, they fled with ease, leaving me to explain how this could have happened. It was considered more of a walk-away than an actual escape. Of course, the inmates at minimum level had free access to the grounds, with buses, taxis and pizza deliveries always passing by. As usual, the two were captured and returned to prison. Two years later, one of them was returned here, but was assigned to the medium side. He claimed enemy situations with an established Hispanic group and requested help. I requested the assignment in order to assist the poor lad." Robby shook his head, laughing, "And they say there's no justice in prison! I helped the boy by sending him completely across the state. This caused his family difficulties visiting him, but at least he was safe."

There were other inmates who wanted out, however, they chose a path completely out...suicide. No matter how it happened, death was never peaceful when it occurred in prison. Normally, the team, who was unlucky enough to find the bodies, were left with an eerie feeling which was hard to describe. Always a negative environment, suicides were just a reminder of how negative it could become for some. Surprisingly enough, as in the real world, suicide notes were usually left behind and very rarely would an inmate take his own life due to the heavy guilt, or remorse felt for the victim of his crime. Holiday seasons were a popular time. Actually, any time that despair was felt. The methods used, differed greatly.

There was an inmate who had felt that his time had come. With a loud scream, he took a swan dive off of a balcony which had to be at least fifty feet high. Dead upon impact, other inmates had walked around him, as though he was not even there. As always, the Bravo Team secured the body until a doctor pronounced him dead.

Another had written a long letter to his sister telling her that it was all over and that he had become a burden. Tying a short piece of braided bed sheet around his neck, he tied the other end to a light fixture. The inmate had to sit down in order to successfully hang himself. That was exactly what he did. Frank, finding the 'hanger' administered C.P.R., but he had been too late.

Then there were those who fabricated a suicide attempt for the attention. One inmate would start at the rear of his cell and run full steam, head down, smashing his head into the thick oak door. After several runs, he was still alive, but his head was split wide open and Robby believed that he may have lost a few more brain cells, which of course, he could not really afford to lose.

Robby knew, all joking aside, men like this one were only asking for help, though their means were a bit indirect and quite brutal. Some would attempt suicide, others self-inflict serious wounds and mutilate their own bodies. Then, there were those who would declare a hunger strike which could last for days. Most would eat only after they had received the help that they needed, or were satisfied that their requests were being met. Regardless of their means of asking, each was treated by both medical and mental health personnel.

Sergeant Frank Gagne was eventually nicknamed "Sgt. Death" because he always seemed to find the corpses. He would always attempt to revive the inmate, but the public would never read about his efforts, or the efforts of men like him. Frank received the Humanitarian Award one year. Little did he know, the following year would be filled with even more death.

In one incident, a young inmate was working on the outside grounds. He was on Minimum status. Located out of bounds, his supervisor requested that he be sent back behind the wall to be urine tested for drug use. Robby handcuffed the young man who appeared extremely nervous, then locked him up, so that he could provide a urine sample. The inmate, overly concerned with his status, was informed by Robby that if he was clean, he would be returned to Minimum. The inmate seemed relieved, as he swore that he was clean.

Approximately two hours had passed, when a code 99, medical emergency was called for the Fort, cell #16. It was the young inmate's cell. Both Robby and Frank arrived on scene to find the inmate hanging. His eyes were wide-open, his fists clenched so tight that his knuckles were white as snow and his neck had stretched enough, so that his toes were touching the floor. The most startling part of the scene was that the inmate's opened eyes were facing a note which he had left in spaghetti sauce on the wall. It read, "To the man that locked me in here for no reason, you better hope there's an afterlife." It was a last act of terrorism which was working on Robby. Paramedics arrived on scene, but refused to touch him, so Robby climbed onto the toilet with a pair of shears. With Sgt. Death holding the dead inmate around the waist, Robby began to cut, joking, "Watch out, this is all dead weight coming at you." It was a perfect example of the dark humor needed to cope with those situations. The room filled with laughter, though most officers did not find it that funny. The doctor pronounced the man dead. The state police conducted an investigation and it was later found that this inmate was getting ready to escape. As his destiny would hold, he ended up leaving another way. His neighboring cellmates swore they did not hear anything. One added, "That had to be one cold son-of-a-bitch, but there's no doubt he knew what he wanted." The written warning, left by the inmate, haunted Robby for months.

The following winter, another bizarre suicide occurred, which had all staff searching for an escapee. A sex offender, who was incarcerated for raping his own daughter, was apparently having domestic problems with his girlfriend. She had told him that she could wait no longer and that she was done with him. Unaccounted for during a major count, the skinner was considered a possible escapee. Keith and John rushed to the man's cell to find all of his property bagged up. This was a big indication that he had intentions of going somewhere. The sheets were missing from his bed which may have been used to fabricate a rope. However, the search shifted once the inmate's locker was opened. On his calendar, each day was colored out in blue ink, with the exception of this particular day. On this day, the date was scratched out in black ink. From then on, Keith advised via radio to look for a 'swinger' (hanging inmate), due to the absence of the sheets. For over an hour, a search of the entire prison was conducted. Then, sure enough, Sgt. Death called it over the radio. The inmate had killed himself in his workplace, the industries darkroom. Frank had found the corpse, but there were no sheets involved. The inmate had placed a plastic bag over his head, wrapped the ends around his neck, then slid under a shelf not more than three feet off the floor. Knowing he would be difficult to find and that the shelf would not allow him to rip the bag off of his face in a last minute panic, it became apparent that this inmate really wanted to die. Again, C.P.R. was administered, but to no avail. Many jokes had been made about this suicide because of the method and the inmate's crime. Regardless of the fact that he was a skinner, Frank and Robby still attempted to save the man's life. Though, they were left sick to their stomachs because the inmate had been frothing at the mouth. His glass eye stared blindly at them and once again, the distinct feeling of death filled the air. A feeling that Robby would never get used to.

8

Besides dealing with the deceptive games, the violence and daily life inside the walls, every once in a while, Robby would take a step back to observe the unbelievable. Just when he thought he had experienced it all, something totally bizarre would happen, leaving him scratching his head in disbelief.

According to officers' standards, by far the most devious game played in prison, involved the weakest of correctional personnel and the most cunning of inmates. This game was forewarned by the academy in a class referred to as 'the Anatomy of a Setup.' However, the prison terms were 'taking down a duck,' or 'setting up a pigeon.' Attempting to invoke sympathy, or compassion from an officer was how it all began, but if unsuccessful, the process took much time and effort on behalf of the inmate.

The typical set-up was when a naive, overfriendly or just plain weak officer was manipulated into lugging in contraband. Normally, it began with a new officer who did not appear as though he fit into the realm of corrections. He may have been shunned by other staff and was usually uneasy around his supervisors. He was probably sloppily dressed and not capable of 'taking care of business,' by giving firm orders, saying "no," or controlling the inmates in his custody. The shrewd inmate sat back and patiently watched while the officer started to get himself into trouble for not maintaining a clean and controlled unit. After some time, this inmate, who came across as a nice guy, started to help the officer by controlling his rowdy friends and assisting in the cleanliness of the unit. The officer, grateful for the inmate's kind efforts, began to get on a first name basis. This type of friendliness made it that much harder to say "no" to the man. While continually building up the officer's ego, other inmates were intentionally breaking small rules for which the officer overlooked. Careful planning on the part of the inmate would produce small busts, such as old homebrew, in order to make the officer look good. Other times, fights would be staged and that same shrewd inmate would assist in breaking them up. In the meantime, the officer did not forget those good deeds and both trust and friendship were being developed between the two.

As time went on, the inmate started slowly, by bumming cigarettes, then asking for extra privileges not normally allowed him. If denied, which was unlikely, the inmate played hurt, as if a friend had betrayed him. This alone could completely turn the tables in the inmate's favor. Before a couple of months had elapsed, both the inmate and officer were confiding in each other. It was imperative, however, that the inmate continued to play the part of the student, while the officer believed he was the teacher and always in control. As the relationship developed, the inmate began asking that his new friend, the officer, to bring him in magazines, cigars, food and other petty items. Sometimes he would receive them. When the inmate felt that he had outfoxed the poor slob, to the point where he could blackmail the man, his true intentions would be revealed. As a result of all of the rules which had been broken by the officer, he was now at the mercy of the inmate. Bigger, more illegal items would be demanded for which the duck delivered. In a feverish attempt to save his job and even his own freedom, before long, the officer could be smuggling in drugs, money and any other contraband demanded by the con-man. With no other options, the pigeon was now owned by the inmate, until the Bravo Team caught on and broke the connection between the dirty officer and the con-artist.

The academy's example had indicated that during one of those dangerous games, an inmate had controlled his pigeon to such an extent that he was able to coerce the officer into bringing in a uniform, for the purpose of the convict's escape. Whether this scenario was true or not was irrelevant. What was important was that Frank and his team were well-aware that such possibilities did exist.

Robby had first-hand knowledge that those inappropriate relationships did exist. He had investigated a sergeant assigned to the Minimum Unit, who was having extreme difficulties at home and had turned to an inmate for support. That inmate had used religion, converting the sergeant into a Born Again Christian, while receiving special privileges not permitted to other inmates. Before long, all of the inmates residing in the unit became furious and started to complain loud enough so that the Bravo Team would hear. Once discovered, the sergeant was re-assigned to a post where he could be closely supervised. The inmate was transferred to another institution. Prior to the transfer, Robby found a small amount of marijuana in the inmate's pocket. The inmate claimed he had been set-up and betrayed by his brother-in-the-Lord. In turn, the sergeant stated that he had always had a hunch that the religious fanatic was dirty. Robby told Frank, "Some truths will never be known!"

This very dangerous and deceptive game could lead to officers lugging in drugs. This was considered to be the number one act of betrayal by the team. Any staff person who introduced illicit narcotics into the hands of an inmate was, at the very least, a traitor, as the personal safety of all staff was placed in serious risk. There was no one act more despised by honest correctional personnel. There were other reasons besides blackmail for this unforgivable deed. There could be unknown outside street, or family connections. Perhaps the drug dealer was fortunate enough to pose as a correction officer, collecting a state check while supplementing his income with drug sales from an enormous open market.

Working with one of their many informants, Keith and John discovered that an officer had recently introduced seventy bags of heroine and a one-eighth gram of cocaine into the hands of several inmates. His supplier was the brother of an inmate. This bundle had been snorted up instantly by the hungry addicts who waited to pay dearly for more. The informant produced a few bags to prove that the officer was no good. A second shipment was scheduled to be brought in, but it was believed that the drug pusher, disguised as a correction officer, was tipped off and the deal never went down. The officer was terminated and his hat was swiped off of his head by an enraged Officer Petrie.

A similar case involving the team eventually required the assistance of the state police. A correction officer had been dealing small amounts of marijuana for a healthy profit, but being paranoid, he was nearly impossible to track. An informant agreed to make a buy with marked money. The bust was made. Removed from the institution, the dirty officer was arrested, prosecuted and convicted, but it had taken the assistance of an inmate to take the maggot down. Frank tore the officer's shirt from his body, as he was a disgrace to his uniform and did not deserve to wear it. In all related cases, shirts and hats would be ripped off of offending officers by other staff. With the proper prosecution, a different outfit would be issued to those criminals who hid behind their badges.

Shamefully, there had been other cases with informants providing the product, putting the drug peddling staff out of business. Catching an officer lugging was no easy task, but occasionally they got their just desserts outside of the institution. Each night, Robby read the police logs within the local newspaper. At times, a correction officer would get arrested in drug related cases, while others had been taken down for different crimes ranging from robberies to the rape of their own children. They were an embarrassment to the profession, but basically, they were no different than other people. Every profession had to carry this burden, though Robby could never understand the logic. Strangely, these people had seen the other side, yet still decided to risk their freedom, destined to become another number in a system for which they had sworn their loyalty. Robby despised every one of them.

The second worst act of betrayal in the department was when a female officer engaged in sexual relations with an inmate who had been placed in her custody. At that point, she had become a sympathizer. She was not to be trusted and was considered a walking breach of security. Immediate removal was eminent, as it was unknown if the female would introduce contraband to her lover, putting other staff in danger. There were many females who had been caught in the act because they could no longer contain their feelings for the inmate they had fallen in love with. From engagement notices in the newspaper to correspondence between the two, some just didn't care anymore. Others even attempted to visit. Termination was sure to follow. Many had abandoned successful careers for the love of a man who had done nothing with his life, but serve time. Robby and his friends had a difficult time understanding how their sister officers could fall for an inmate who they would battle with every day.

One ingenious inmate was having an ongoing affair with a female staff person. Lieutenant Redman quickly discovered it through institution telephone bills. The team was sent out and found that the man had stolen a telephone and placed the mouth piece into one side of his radio's headset, with the ear piece being placed on the other side. The internal parts of the phone were placed inside of his radio and a paper clip was used to punch in the numbers through the tiny holes in the speaker's cover. This inmate had gained access to the housing unit's telephone room and had actually run wire through conduit directly into his room. The lengthy conversations transpired during the late hours of the evening. Once caught, the inmate swore that he had been set up. Before being shipped off to federal custody, this inmate swore he would exact revenge on Lt. Redman and his I.P.S. unit, who had done him in. Fortunately, that man was sent away for a long time because not only was he known to be a genius, he was also known to be a man of his word, every cruel one of them.

John busted a different Romeo who had literally charmed the pants off of at least three female staff members, costing each of them their jobs. He was incarcerated for sex related crimes, which all staff were aware of. This fact did not stop the silver-tongued devil from getting as much sex as he wished. Considered to be an ass-kisser by male officers, John caught him kissing more than that at night.

Those incidents placed all female staff in a bad light. It was a controversial issue to begin with, females in corrections. Many officers felt strongly that a females' presence in a male dominated environment was no more than a dangerous distraction. Some inmates would act differently. Some refused to 'lose face' in front of a woman, while others acted violently, almost in the fashion of a show-off.

However, there had been other situations where female officers displayed a calming, somewhat maternal affect. Though those women got paid equal salaries as male officers, many would never have to work the tougher, more stressful areas of the prison, such as the dormitories. Most did not get involved in breaking up fights, nor did they conduct strip searches. Therefore, the basis for the constant complaints on behalf of the men. However, there were female officers, employed within the department, who were worth their weight in gold, contributing equally to the collective goals of the institution.

If the temptation to engage in sex with inmates could be blamed on human nature, then in all fairness, male officers assigned to the Medium Security facility for female inmates had been found just as guilty. Placing their jobs in jeopardy, the percentages were comparable. Though these men were also terminated for their intolerable behavior, it seemed that their forbidden acts were not frowned as much upon. This proved that the old double standard existed within this sub-society as well.

In prison, male officers did not recognize gender. While in uniform, an officer was an officer and not a lady. Chivalry and even common courtesy did not exist within this working environment. Therefore, crude and vulgar language often led to sexual harassment claims. This was also a major cause of animosity, although many of the claims were warranted. Inmates masturbated and spoke in similarly graphic terms in front of these women, therefore some male officers did not comprehend the complaints from their sister officers. No matter, hours upon hours had been spent with female officers trying to justify their usefulness within the institution, while the male officers refused to hear it.

The entire I.P.S. unit was brought together in order to investigate an extremely odd case which had surfaced. Per Lieutenant Redman's orders, an old maintenance worker, Mr. Grogs, was being closely monitored. The surveillance, though brief, proved both unbelievable and disgusting. Mr. Grogs had been warned in the past for being a bit too friendly with his inmate workers. Every morning, he would bring them doughnuts and coffee. He stopped and all other staff felt that the old-timer was harmless. Lieutenant Redman had a different feeling.

At one point, the maintenance man hired two homosexual inmates, Lucy and Larry, who where known to be lovers. Larry, the bigger of the two, had become so engulfed in his own jealousy that he informed Redman that Grogs was lugging in everything under the sun, to include marijuana. During an interview, Larry produced the pot, then disclosed, "That dirty old Grogs has paid me generously with cigarettes and pot to protect

Lucy. Grogs doesn't want to see my small, fragile friend getting hurt out in population. It's gone on for weeks, but I figured there was something going on between Grogs and Lucy."

Lucy was brought in and interrogated by Frank and Robby. She knew right away that her golden goose was about to be cooked, so she told all. Lucy revealed, "Grogs hired both me and Larry, but I could tell right away that he really took a liking to me. He was trying to get Larry out of the way and wanted nothing more than to have sex with me. Believe me, we haven't had sex, only kissing and heavy petting, but he is a good kisser for an old man. The problem is...I've seen him naked, he could never satisfy me. He's just too small!" Robby looked at Frank, but his older partner could only shrug his shoulders. Lucy continued, "He's showered me with gifts and money, so I'm not happy with my real man, Larry. If he hadn't been so jealous, we would have continued to live like kings amongst peasants!"

Lucy's property was inventoried and some of the presents she had received included radios, a pair of ladies leather gloves, and lingerie from a well-known retailer. Apparently, Mr. Grogs would enjoy sneaking up to Lucy's room to watch her perform a strip-tease. She really did have the old man conned. Also found, was Grogs telephone number and a Valentine's Day card, later confirmed as being signed in his handwriting, "Love, your Sweetheart." Robby couldn't believe it, but when he retrieved twenty-two money order receipts which added up to over twenty-five hundred dollars, he knew it was all true. Mr. Grogs had deposited the money into Lucy's account. Lucy laughed, saying, "Believe me boys, this wasn't my first sugar daddy, nor will it be my last." The obsessed man wanted sex bad. Lucy kept stalling him while collecting something every day. Both her and Larry were transferred to different institutions, but before leaving, the young lovers had gotten into quite a spat.

Mr. Grogs was questioned. He adamantly denied all allegations. Lieutenant Redman produced the evidence against him and the man, not three years from retirement, was forced to resign in shame. He would then have to concoct a believable story for his wife, assuming he could contain his embarrassment. Strangely, it was not only the female staff who had been swept off of their feet by sweet talking, well-built inmates.

Thankfully those immoral personnel made up only a very, very small percentage of the staff who had worked behind the walls. Most officers would never think of lugging drugs or having sex with criminals. Inmates who were looking for just that. Like Robby, most officers would turn in those traitors in a minute.

Unfortunately, some of those episodes had involved outside law enforcement agencies, which did not help with the already poor public relations that the department suffered. The community only read about the scandals and negative aspects of the profession, such as inmate deaths, alleged beatings and staff improprieties. They never learned about the valiant efforts of the real and true officers who had fought fires, broken up huge brawls and saved the lives of hundreds of inmates. Police departments, however, had been assisted by correctional personnel in anything from outside drug busts, to tracking down dangerous criminals.

A court ordered wire tap which lasted over a month involved the Bravo Team working with the state police. Before the case was closed, nine inmates and eighteen civilians were convicted on drug charges and conspiracy to violate the Controlled Substance Act. Months later, a different case involved an informant incarcerated for raping and killing his own mother. In assisting local undercover narcotics officers, Keith utilized the informant to set up an outside drug buy, intended for delivery into the prison. Four subjects were arrested during this bust and one hundred bags of heroine, along with a small package of marijuana was confiscated. It was a good pinch on such short notice. The informant had done his homework. However, good or not, that same informant would receive a Mother's Day card every year from someone who refused to let him forget his terrible crime. Keith believed the sender to be an officer, but each year that passed, the inmate appeared less bothered by the expected correspondence. Frank and the boys always enjoyed reaching out and lending a hand in the fight against drugs. Several times, they reached out farther for other reasons.

One inmate, rightfully released from prison, took no time before he abducted two girls, who he raped and killed. With prison intelligence provided by the team, he was captured within a matter of days and returned to his rightful home, prison.

Soon after, another demented creature had been released. Being obsessed with a state nurse, he decided to stalk the woman. His intentions were squashed by Frank and Robby, who apprehended him in the parking lot of his old home, the Treatment Center. Most of these busts happened because of good informant information. The prison was a wealth of knowledge, as most inmates kept in contact with the streets and knew what was happening out there. Informants had even assisted in murder cases. While most people would think the last place to look for clues to a crime would be prison, sometimes it was the first place that should have been tapped into. Assisting the police could be positive, yet limited when attempting to touch the public.

One place that always touched the public was the visiting room and outer control. This was where officers, who were assigned to these areas, interacted with the public through the citizens who came in to visit. Most of those experiences had not been positive either. When an inmate was caught with both pockets ripped out of his jeans and his visitor was vigorously moving her hand inside of his pants in a piston-like fashion, the visit was then terminated and the visitor was barred. Therefore, the family, friends and loved ones of the inmates, who made up a small percentage of the community, were not truly appreciative of the authority the officers had to sometimes flex.

There had been requests from good people who absolutely feared the criminals who had victimized them. In one such incident, a child molester, incarcerated for sexually abusing his two young children, was continually trying to correspond with them through letters and collect phone calls. These were refused. The mother of the children did not know where else to turn when she informed Robby that her demented ex-husband was interfering in the children's therapy. He had been confusing them with excuses for his acts of love. She asked if someone could speak to the inmate. Robby insured her that he would be more than happy to be of service. Robby and John interviewed the sick son-of-bitch who proudly admitted his crime. He stated, "My father did it to me, so I see nothing wrong with it. Besides, it's none of your business, anyway." Before the partners acted upon their emotions, they ordered that the man cease and desist in any attempts to contact his kids. They warned that if he did not stop, he would become the hobby of all staff. Robby and John left the inmate with only these words. They never laid a finger on him, though he was bawling like a baby because he knew what his future held if he continued. The man did stop for fear of being harassed, but in his own mind, he could not understand the trauma which his twisted acts had caused.

Two days later, a woman contacted the institution and spoke to Robby. She convincingly explained that she was receiving threatening telephone calls from her ex-boyfriend who was in prison, through a three-way party line. The inmate was ordered to stop, but he denied ever talking to the "crazy bitch." That same afternoon, the woman called again, claiming that she had just received another call and was afraid for her life. At that time, the inmate, still in denial, was secured in a segregation unit where his every action would be monitored. Early the next morning, the same woman claimed that the calls were continuing, only this time she was insolent in her speech, demanding that her ex-boyfriend be stopped, or Officer Robby Cabral, who was handling the case, would face a civil suit. Robby proceeded to the segregation unit and due to all telephone calls being logged in, he verified that not only did the inmate not make any calls, but he had never even left his cell since being admitted. The inmate was immediately released and the "crazy bitch" had to call only one last time for Robby to explain, "I know that you have been less than honest with me, so your credibility is at an all time low. Trust me, any future contact would be futile!"

Several months later, the case was brought to court and the inmate was charged with stalking. Robby was summoned in on behalf of the defense and did testify for the inmate. This was not a normal occurrence. With his testimony, the case began to smell of shear perjury and was blown right out of the water. The inmate, who was found innocent of the charges, could not believe that Robby had gone to bat so strongly for him. What he failed to understand was that if he had been guilty, Robby would have surely helped convict him. The man was being set-up and justice had been served. However, the public witnessing the proceedings had felt the man was guilty before he ever entered the room. Robby could only walk away shaking his head. He knew that another kick for P.R. was accomplished that day.

Throughout all the staff working in the prison, Robby found that Frank Gagne was most concerned with good public relations. Frank was "Mr. P.R." himself, who began a one man quest to clear the good name of the correctional profession. His efforts began when a program called Project Outreach, based on the old scared straight program, was started. The program consisted of inmates who were hand-picked to speak to groups of school children on life in prison. It had become evident that these inmates were more interested in the good time, rather than the important message which was intended to be put across. After each session, the students were polled and it was found that most were sympathetic for the poor men who were apparently just victims of society, now forced to spend years behind bars. Frank then stepped in and taking the entire burden upon his own shoulders, spoke in school after school. Setting up tours, many of the students experienced the rare opportunity of seeing inmates acting in their normal, disrespectful manner. In conjunction with the existing drug programs, Frank gave the 'real deal' on prison life while being open, honest and answering any of the graphic questions that the students had asked. His teachings left a lasting impression on the nations' future, its children. He once told Robby, "It's refreshing to possibly make a young kid think about his future. To think about the consequences, if the wrong path in life is chosen." Explaining reality, he sincerely hoped that his fearsome stories were a crime deterrent for these youths, who, according to Frank, "Are much more receptive than the hopeless inmates we are used to dealing with on a daily basis." The Bravo Team agreed that there should have been a hundred more Sergeant Gagne's. It would have definitely boosted public relations, informed the community about the profession and above all else, maybe made the difference in a life or two. In essence, it was correcting the problem before it even got started, rather than having to deal with it years later.

Unfortunately, with the direction society was heading in, Frank knew that many of America's youths would eventually help to overcrowd the system even more. But, as he pointed out to Robby, "Prison life can't be all that bad. Most convicts seem to enjoy the free ride within this very structured environment." It was true, without a responsibility in the world, or a decision to make, each moment of their existence was regulated by prison staff from the time they were waken, to the time they ate, to the time they retired for the evening. Inmates lived better than many of the working poor in society, not to mention the homeless and disabled. They had warm clothing issued to them. They ate nutritious food, which was of better quality than that fed to America's servicemen. The comfortable and cozy bed was the clincher. Frank and Robby talked for hours about the liberal life afforded the inmates. They agreed it was probably the biggest reason for the high return rates.

Robby was always astonished at the long list of activities, or programs offered to keep each inmate busy and out of trouble. There were sporting events from football to basketball which were acceptable. Though, the sports banquets and awards issued at the end of the season was a hard one for him to swallow. Outside civilian teams were even allowed to enter the institution to compete with the convicts. At one time, administrators even permitted inmates from different facilities to compete against each other. This stopped, when during a soccer game, some heated words almost turned into a riotous situation. Robby laughed when he heard that one. He thought, "Boys will be boys..."

There was A.A. and N.A., with outside volunteers coming in to share their problems and possible solutions. One such recovering alcoholic began encouraging the inmates to revolt against their oppression and bondage. The team removed him from state property and he was never seen again.

Religious programs also offered outside assistance, but their instruction seemed to be somewhat more peaceful. Then there were the educational opportunities which allowed each inmate the chance to attain a college degree, free of charge. Most inmates found it easier to receive federal grants for continued education which was much harder for ordinary college students to attain. Robby snickered, "Not a bad deal for men who could not afford the classes on the street. By ruining a few lives, they've found doors opened to them. Opportunities they have never had before!" Frank nodded in agreement.

The holidays, though depressing behind bars, provided the inmates with Thanksgiving dinners trimmed with all the fixins', finished off with a healthy portion of pumpkin pie. Shortly thereafter, the Christmas Season rolled around. The visiting room was decorated with a Christmas tree while some inmate pranced around dressed as Santa Claus. The Salvation Army gave each inmate a generous care package and the state deposited five dollars into each and every inmate's personal account, to be spent later at the canteen. Each deposit was tax money, of course. Robby laughed again, "And a Merry Christmas to one and all!" However, the strangest of holiday festivities to date had to be the Halloween party which was held at the Minimum Visiting Room. A haunted house had been set up for the kids to walk through, with the unit manager's only concern being, "Because of the kids, I don't want any sex offenders allowed to join in the fun." It was still not a very bright idea. Then again, what else could be expected from a unit that allowed Nintendo video games and both pizza and Chinese food to be delivered right to the inmates' front door.

The friends ridiculed another program which had been set up at Maximum security. Some administrator decided that the inmates might enjoy a weekly game of bingo. The final prize was a twenty five dollar canteen order and a one pound chocolate bar per week. After two weeks of playing, the cons got together and decided to beat the system. On that third week, the first inmate to get bingo just sat tight and said nothing. A few more letters were called, allowing several more inmates to have bingo. Finally, when all thirty inmates in the room were sure that each man had his card covered, they simultaneously yelled out, "Bingo." The recreation officer, running the program, checked all cards, as each inmate claimed, "I didn't realize that I had won earlier." All thirty inmates received the grand prize and the program was aborted due to the lack of funds.

They continued to laugh, though it was anything but funny. The closest thing resembling a chain gang was the D.P.W. crew. This was considered to be one of the best jobs. Trash which was littering the state's highways was not the only thing these inmates picked up. Drugs and money had been introduced into the prison through these workers who saved the state thousands of dollars each year, insuring that the detail would remain intact. Other inmates had enhanced their criminal skills through prison employment. One inmate, who was incarcerated for welding steel boxes under drug transporting vehicles, found a job in the prison's welding shop. Even he had found the irony slightly hilarious. Other inmates convicted for fraud were working as office runners. Drug dealers found employment in the health service unit. The list went on.

The health care the inmates received was the best that money could buy, allowing that a person was lucky enough to have that much money. There were inmates who could never afford the medication which was prescribed to them if they still lived on the street, especially those with AIDS, or in need of psychotropic meds. One inmate, who was in desperate need of back surgery, explained to Robby, "I had no money or insurance, so I committed a few small felonies to grab myself a couple of years." Once incarcerated, this man received extensive and very expensive surgery, with therapy to follow. Before he was fully recovered, he was back on the streets and the state had footed the bill.

Robby remembered those outside hospital trips and court trips as being very dangerous. He always hoped that the inmate had no previous knowledge of the transport, so they were not met by any unwelcomed guests while en-route. Court trips could find the transporting officers in contempt of court, if they arrived late. This all depended upon the mood of the presiding judge. Hospital trips were just as bad, with the inmates being escorted in full restraints. The hospital staff never comprehended the reason why the poor inmate could not be unshackled while being examined or treated. Robby, who looked like the bad guy, had to bite his tongue because it would have been much easier to say, "I'll uncuff him, but if he rapes you, it's not my fault." Robby had to stay with the inmate, who was within his custody at all times, unless the inmate was knocked out cold. In most circumstances, Robby was right in the room while the medical procedure was being performed.

During one trip, an inmate who was numbed up, but completely awake, was having surgery done on his eye. The officer, Keith Petrie, however, had passed out at the first sign of blood. From then on, Robby kidded Keith, "At least one of you stood awake."

By far, the worst outside details were the funeral trips. With special permission granted from the Superintendent, an inmate could go in full restraints to pay his last respects to a deceased loved one. The ideal situation was when the visit occurred during off hours. Frequently, Robby and his partner found themselves escorting the hobbling inmate, secured in waistchains and leg irons, into a room of grieving family members. Those situations could get hairy because that inmate could very well be the brother, or father of a person who was not in their right state of mind to begin with. Confrontations were always a possibility and, at the very least, it was an embarrassing ordeal for all involved.

Lastly, there were the midnight runs where an inmate was transported out of the prison in a flash to be transferred to another. As usual, during one run, Robby and Keith were not made aware of the whole picture. The inmate was an influential drug dealer who was ordered to be sent back to Maximum Security. It was well-known that his connections were so vast that the possibility for an escape attempt was good. While driving north, the inmate explained, "I've gotta tell you guys. I'm facing some serious charges, but I'm confident my attorney will overturn the cases against me." Smiling, he added, "But, if I had any doubt in my lawyer's abilities, this trip would have been one for the history books." Robby knew in his heart that the man was not bluffing. As fate had it, he never overturned his cases and was sentenced to serve big, big numbers. Robby later told Keith, "Fortunately, he was only a drug dealer and not a fortune teller!"

Besides the occasional trip here and there, many inmates did not see the outside world for years, especially the lifers. This was not true so long ago when a furlough system was very active, but the system had since been, more or less, aborted. This program had allowed inmates, more specifically the lifers, to leave the prison unescorted to spend time with their families. These excursions lasted anywhere from four hours to periods of a whole weekend. It was designed to alleviate the frustration of the inmate's depressing existence.

Then along came a murderer named Willie Horton. While Willie was serving life without parole, he had completed nine successful furloughs. On his tenth, he had escaped and approximately one year later, had entered the home of a Maryland couple. He terrorized the occupants for twelve hours before stabbing the male and raping his fiancee twice. He was captured and convicted. The sentencing judge stated, "Due to the man's lack of conscience, he should die in prison," and so he will.

An embarrassment to the state and its liberal programs, all lifers, who had resided at Minimum, were brought back behind the wall. The program

was brought to a screeching halt and the governor at the time may have
even lost his shot at the Presidency partially due to this exact incident. Inmate Horton was a hated man by the lifer's and that ex-governor. It was
better that he remained in Maryland for his own well-being.

Without question, Robby thought that the funniest inmate liberty was
the special requests by inmates who wished to get married. Most were
even granted. Those weddings, though not very traditional, were always
entertaining to the officer, assuming he had a sense of humor. The groom,
at one such wedding, was a cop killer who had also taken the lives of inmates while being incarcerated. His other credentials included putting officers into retirement, taking hostages and engaging in sexual intercourse
with his own mother in the Maximum Security Visiting Room. With all
that aside, on this happy day, even his mother, an ex-felon herself, was
allowed to observe her only son's marriage vows. The ceremony did not
take long, as the justice of the peace wanted out. The best man, a muscle-
bound black inmate, was actually just the groom's weightlifting partner.
After the ceremony, the murderer's mother started to dance with her little
boy, singing, "You are the apple of my eye..." Frank Gagne, the officer in
charge, looked on in disbelief. He later recalled, "The best man was wiping tears from his eyes. It was incredible. He was emotionally moved from
all of the love that filled the room. Suddenly, the old lady became furious
over something said and screamed out, 'They should've fried you when
they had the fucking chance!' She then stormed out of the room. It makes
me wonder. Whatever happened to that traditional mother and son favorite, 'Sunrise, Sunset?'"

Robby took part in a very different wedding over at the Minimum Unit.
The bride and groom exchanged vows under the shade of an old willow
tree. Before long, the entire wedding party was drunk because bottles were
allowed. These bottles could not be opened by Robby due to board of
health regulations. Caught up in the moment, the blissful couple made a
bee-line for one of the bathrooms to consummate their marriage, but were
intercepted by young Officer Cabral. While they pleaded for mercy, Robby
terminated the festivities. He threw the wedding party out, keeping the
groom behind. Handling the incident informally, as many officers did,
Robby ordered that the inmate paint the entire Visiting Room. This took

two weeks. The inmate was grateful because he knew that he could have been lugged back to Medium. He was happy to do the extra work. It was a wedding present of a sort given by Robby, though the infuriated bride could never see it that way.

Taking a walk through the prison, it was obvious to Robby that the Minimum Unit would always be a security nightmare. The detox. unit, filled with diseased vagrants, was only a holding pen for thirty days, or until that monthly Welfare or Disability check arrived. Once that was gone, many returned, some with drugs tucked up the vault. Due to the lice, crabs and blood diseases, this area could be one of the worst stops in the house.

Continuing the tour, Robby decided that many inmates lived better than they deserved to. It was also evident that many positive changes had taken place over the past few years, with one privilege being taken away at a time. Many federally trained and experienced administrators had come on board and had tightened security, resulting in a safer working environment. It was incredible to think of what was allowed not so long ago. There was a medium visiting yard with an old swingset. This area had been shut down, forcing inmates to find other reasons for litigation. Their unsupervised children no longer had the opportunity to hurt themselves by running around and falling off of the rusty swings.

The auditorium, which used to hold Valentine's Day dances, no longer did. At one time, wives, girlfriends or both, could come in and dance the night away. It was mind- boggling to think of how many children were conceived during those dances.

Family day was a yearly summer festivity. Families would enter the institution with packed coolers to barbecue and play games for the day. This popular event was ended when an inmate, high on L.S.D., knocked a sergeant out cold. Acting like a crazed dog with rabies, this inmate started to bite on a drain pipe until he was restrained. Then, it was farewell to family day.

The Avocations were also gone. This program, designed for lifers, had close to fifty inmates making furniture, leather goods, and other products which were sold at a gift shop located in the front of the institution. Due to the use of power tools and the fact that many inmates were clearing more income than the superintendent, tax free, the program was stopped. There had been other privileges affected, as well. For instance, the many pool tables which were scattered throughout the prison had been removed, with the exception being the Minimum, of course. Somebody finally figured out that the pool balls and sticks, were used more as weapons, than for their true intents and purposes.

However, Robby looked disgustedly, as he passed hundreds of steel weapons located in the weight pits. This program remained because administrators believed that this activity alleviated, or helped to vent anger and frustration. Whether or not that was the case, the inmates were getting stronger and the desire for steroids existed because of it. Robby knew from experience that many of those weightlifters had been a challenge when a confrontation took place. Perhaps, it was another way to keep staff on their toes.

The changes had been good. This was evident even in the working styles of the officers. At one time, years ago, officers relied on the stronger, more influential inmates to control their units. This, however, bred corruption, because eventually that inmate controlled all the illicit activities, as well as the officer. The mighty beatings that had taken place no longer did, but as explained by Lieutenant Redman, "In those days, only pain was understood by the tougher inmate population." It had been normal for officers to accept favors from inmates, including shoe shines, haircuts and art work. Fortunately, it was later determined that if you took nothing from an inmate, then you owed nothing. That was, without question, a better position to be in. Yes, many changes had transpired, but Robby still felt the weight of the challenges he was faced with each day.

⑨

After almost eight years of battling with inmates, investigating deceitful con-artists and chasing down dirty staff, Officer Robby Cabral was burnt out and he knew it. Walking into the local bar, Robby felt frustrated with all of the negativity and confused about his future. He was searching for answers, but he didn't have to look too far. Seated at the bar was Lieutenant Stephen Redman. With a concerned look on his face, he gestured for Robby to take the stool near him. Robby didn't have to say a word, his boss already knew what was on his mind. Redman ordered a pitcher of beer, then poured out two glasses. He put his arm around Robby, saying, "I think I've seen that look before. Except last time, it was in a mirror. Don't sweat it Robby, you're not alone. We all feel like shit sometimes. The job will do that."

Lieutenant Redman had better than twenty five years in the business and most of his time had been spent at the Hill. Robby knew that if anyone had a clue about what they were talking about, it was Redman. For the next three hours, the two men sat at the bar, drinking one beer after another. Throughout that entire time, Robby was lucky if he had said three words. He didn't care. In fact, he became engulfed in Redman's reminiscent stories. The older man was one of the best in corrections, so for those three hours, Robby hung on his every word.

Redman started, "Robby, prisons are not the easiest or most relaxing environments to work in, nor was that their design. When housing criminals inside of tight quarters, problems are inevitable. Yet, not so long ago, maybe two decades, the job of a correction officer was unbelievably more difficult. Greater risks of injury, even death were almost accepted as a job hazard. Most people remember the past with warm sentiment, but those who endured that era in corrections, would sooner forget it ever existed.

It all started in the early 1970's when Attica, a state penitentiary located in New York, experienced the bloodiest prison riot in American history. This violent uprising caused forty three deaths. Thirty two of these deaths were inmates, the remaining eleven correctional personnel. The mass of death and destruction had occurred because inmates complained they suffered poor living conditions. It was an issue of civil rights. The ultimate demand had been for prison reform, but the means of negotiating had been beyond insane.

This atrocity triggered a chain reaction nationwide. Many of the states' systems functioned in turmoil. The country had been leading into the postwar era. Inmates were entering the system younger, while the state government was considered ultra-liberal at the time. Times were changing and many of the state's prisons were literally out of control. But as change always brings conflict, we all knew that the years ahead would not be untroubled. The dire need for stiffer rules and regulations governing inmate's behavior would be implemented. Certain privileges would be taken away and a more rigid and disciplined environment enforced. The 'Decade of Leniency' was coming to a close and the men and women charged with enforcing the new laws of those concrete jungles were the officers on the line, the grunts, just like you are now.

In corrections, the department's objectives could instantly change from rehabilitating inmates to strictly confining them as punishment. Those goals were dictated by the political views of the time. The early 70's was not a time when inmates were being rehabilitated. The struggles to regain control began.

Believe me buddy, it was a time spent in constant fear and horrible anticipation. I didn't know in the morning if I would return in the same condition that afternoon. The inner societies of the prisons were out of control. They were being run by the inmates. Those were times that the realization, of that lack of control, would become so paralyzingly fearsome that some officers had even contemplated vacating the facilities.

Those were the days when inmates walked freely within prison blocks. They flaunted shanks which were tucked into their waistbands, as though they were pirates. The physically strong and the most evil, lacking any conscience, controlled the environment. Most inmates feared each waking hour, even more than the officers who were locked inside the walls with them. Brute force was the only understood communication which put many officers into hospitals, or out collecting early pensions. Eventually, it would be that force, as well as the changes in management, which would return control to where it belonged, into the hands of the officers.

It's funny, people my age, the officers who had worked while those changes led to constant confrontation, are now referred to as 'Dinosaurs,' a breed on the brink of extinction...and you think you've got problems!" laughed Redman. Robby thought, "He's right. The younger staff have a completely ignorant thought process." Redman continued, "Those 'Dinosaurs,' well, it was through their physical, mental and emotional sacrifices, as well as shear determination and unquestionable courage that officers currently enjoy today's well-running institutions. The conditions will never be perfect inside, but that cannot be expected."

Redman then carefully explained the extreme situations faced by those brave men and women of the past. For Robby, it was like listening to a history teacher. Redman constantly stressed that those same situations could happen again, if the same circumstances were to occur. It had taken two long decades before control was regained by the security staff. It was genuine war during that period of time. Redman's 'war stories' detailed each battle fought, one after another. Robby knew that if anyone overheard their conversation, they would just think it was an old man rambling about his days of glory, but Robby didn't care. He needed to hear that things weren't so bad in his own career.

Lieutenant Redman said, "I remember witnessing those nightmares, but the worst were always the hostage takings. There was one hostage situation where one of the state's most feared inmates, Lafferty, had made his move. Already serving multiple life sentences for killing police officers, he had also taken the lives of weaker inmates while incarcerated. The incident occurred in the segregation unit at the Hill. Lafferty had broken free from being restrained by officers, instantaneously smashing the unit sergeant's skull in with a mop ringer. The keys to the unit were then taken and eight inmates were released from their singular cells. As the sergeant laid on the corridor floor, bleeding profusely from a terrible head wound, all the unit officers were secured into the opened cells, with the exception of one, who was allowed to freely walk around the unit.

There were a total of five hostages, one seriously injured. Inmate Lafferty, who was protesting the conditions of the prison, began to make serious threats. His first threat was that he was going to start cutting the fingers off of an officer, who was known as a loud mouth. One finger would be removed at a time. That officer pled for mercy, which he did receive. At one point, the superintendent, while negotiating for the release of his officers, had selflessly offered himself as a hostage, in trade for the dying sergeant. This unusual request was denied. Almost seven hours into the negotiations, the superintendent was permitted entrance into the block to check on the condition of his men. Giving each a supportive word, he was curiously allowed to leave unharmed. With snipers and Special Reaction Teams in position, the green light was never given to storm the block and seize the hostages. The waiting continued and after ten long hours of anxious talk, Lafferty had given up on his demands. He released the officers and turned himself over to awaiting staff. The sergeant, who was dragged from the blood covered floor, miraculously survived the incident.

During this crises, the father of one of the hostages, who was also a correction officer, was removed from the institution, as he waited for his son's release. He was anticipating the worst. The reunion was quite emotional. So was the release of each hostage. The officer allowed to roam free within the block was later strongly criticized by us all, as he had not suffered the same trauma as the others.

A short time later, a different hostage situation, involved a female supervisor. She was taken at knife-point by an enraged hispanic inmate, who was expecting to be released to lower security, but did not receive the classification move. The woman was tied to a chair and a homemade knife was unrelentingly held at her throat. There had been non-stop negotiations which lasted better than twenty hours, but the crazed inmate wanted only to speak to the news media.

A sniper, who was lying behind a podium between the negotiators legs, could not get a positive aim. He never fired upon the prisoner. The petrified woman was denied food or water, and was humiliated further by being forced to urinate into a coffee can. Finally, with weapons teams, who were located both in the ceiling above the inmate and in an abandoned closet located to the left side, the inmate was rushed with sniper rifles and automatic pistols. The inmate, without delay, dropped his knife. He was then escorted to a segregation unit by I.P.S.. The Superintendent ordered he be left unharmed. The escort was filmed to insure this order was carried out.

Ironically, years later, that same hispanic inmate, who had been locked up for an extensive period of time, successfully committed suicide. He jammed his door and food slot with paper, which he had been accumulating, then set his cell ablaze. As we responded, we could not open the door and reach the burning inmate. Access to the cell was finally gained and the charred remains of a cold-hearted man was discovered. As a result, the state police conducted a formal homicide investigation due to the man's involvement in the hostage taking, years earlier. After some time, all officers were cleared of any wrong doing. But, believe me, my friend, there were no tears shed for that death."

Redman informed Robby that in one year, there had been eleven brutal murders committed within the maximum security prison. It was a stinging reminder of how inmates could interact with each other when they took control of their own world. Redman added, "It was considered a blessing to be off duty when these incidents occurred."

He continued, "These murders were committed for a variety of inhumane, often meaningless reasons. Men were killed over simple arguments. Gambling debts which were not paid, or so much as a disrespectful comment, could get an inmate stabbed to death, or thrown off an upper tier causing him to snap his neck, or crush his skull on the floor below. Inmates covered in blood, with a weapon clinched in their fist, was true reality then. For example, imagine entering a cell and finding a decapitated head lying in the toilet with the torso draped over the bed. With panic surging through my body, my thoughts were spiraling, as I left the gruesome scene. As I attempted to exit the block, I knew that the killer's weapon was between me and the door leading out. It was one of the scariest days of my life."

Specific murders were also described, "The infamous Boston Strangler, or the man believed to be the serial killer, was stabbed to death. Many believed there had been an identity switch prior to the trial, so the actual notorious madman may have lived for years after his own assassination. The real strangler or not, the old-timer laid on a gurney in the corridor of the hospital ward while two younger inmates, deciding to possibly make a name for themselves, jammed a shank several times into the inmate's chest. A blanket was then placed over him, completely covering the body. It took us close to sixteen hours to find the corpse.

In another case, two inmates believed another to be an informant. They entered his cell, removed the man's eyes with a shank, then commenced cutting the inmate's penis and testicles off, shoving them into his mouth. The block officer, who was doing his security rounds, discovered the body sitting up on the bed. At least two inches of already coagulating blood covered the cell floor, creating footprints of personnel entering and exiting the crime scene. The body was removed and an autopsy ordered which subsequently indicated that the inmate had died of asphyxiation. The man had actually choked to death on his own penis and was probably aware of it the whole time. The ridiculous ingredient in this wicked killing was that the man killed was not at all an informant. It had been his neighboring cell-mate who these killers had been seeking out. Poor information and a case of mistaken identity allowed the real informant the comforts of years of protective custody."

Robby ordered another pitcher of beer while Redman came up for air. Staring off into space, the older man said, "I worked the blocks when the inmates lived by the real 'code.' They were the days when inmates did not speak to officers, the prison hierarchy was well-defined and informants were few. The ones identified were killed. Literally, only the strong did survive. For example, two inmates entered the room of another and began beating him to a pulp until the guy started to scream for help. At that time, a cloth wrap was tied around his neck which caused his windpipe to be crushed, killing him. The killers dragged the body to the back stairwell where it was found later that afternoon. In the meantime, both killers took showers. They tore up and then flushed their blood-covered clothing down the toilet. The victim's room was then mopped up and cleaned.

Once the body was found, the block was sealed off and locked down. I was sent in, as part of a search team. We found blood on both killers sneakers, as well as blood which had splattered under the victim's bed. It had been a sloppy, incomplete cover-up and both were tried in court for the crime. The first pled guilty receiving manslaughter, sentenced 12-15 years on and after. The other pled not guilty. He was convicted of second degree murder, a life sentence on and after. According to one of the killers, 'They were both on drugs and beat the victim because he was skimming marijuana for himself. It got out of hand when he began to yell, so he got what he deserved, death.'

A different slaying occurred only two weeks later over another drug deal gone bad. Evidently, the victim had been a young inmate who was being forced to lug various drugs into the institution through a visiting friend. One summer's afternoon, the visitor could not produce, causing the distraught inmate to return to his housing unit, empty handed.

There had been two cunning, more dominant inmates who awaited his arrival with the pills. Both became angry and suspicious, thinking the young man was holding out on them. They were absolutely enraged because neither was going to get high as expected. One of the older inmates attempted to toss the young inmate off of the third tier, but he held on for dear life. As hindsight is twenty-twenty, he probably should have taken his chances with the fall because the other inmate proceeded into his own cell and shortly returned with a shank. As one prisoner held the young inmate, the other began stabbing him countless times in the back and shoulder areas. The dying inmate slipped off of the railing. His clothing somehow got caught up, causing him to just dangle there like a motionless puppet. The two killers, who had not completed their brutal act, ran down to the second tier where they could reach the boy. They stabbed him several more times in the chest area, eventually causing him to fall to the flats below.

The block officer, undoubtedly terrified, watched this murder in disbelief, as he was unable to help the young inmate. After the killing was com-

pleted, both subjects dropped the weapon near the blood covered body and
turned themselves in, showing no emotion at any time.

Then, I remember responding to an emergency where a lone inmate
was swarmed by a number of other prisoners. When the assault was finally
broken up, the victim was found on the bottom of the pile, dead. The state
autopsy revealed that one hundred and ten puncture wounds in the inmates
upper torso had caused the death."

Robby's lieutenant shook his head, saying, "Homosexual rapes were
also a big factor in those days. There are horror stories of young men entering prison only to find themselves being immediately assaulted and
violated sexually. This prison crime became dominant, as we had little
resources to stop it at the time."

Redman looked into the bloodshot eyes of his young audience. He said,
"You have to remember that these murders, rapes and violent assaults were
being committed by inmates who were incarcerated for committing similar
crimes on the street. Many had little or nothing to lose, as they were serving extraordinary sentences to include natural life.

It was the time of riots, with amateur arsonists burning out their cell-
blocks, while others flooded the institutions with water. Costing the state
millions, it was decided more force would be needed to quell these intolerable acts of aggression. From boycotts to work stoppages and non-passive
protests of living conditions, the problems continued. Leaders were identified and removed from the prisons. They were shuffled around, causing
havoc wherever they ended up. We fought harder to enforce stricter rules,
but it was to be an upward battle all the way."

Redman snickered, "One day, a few of the lifer's told me, 'You never
give up anything without a fight, no matter how small or meaningless.
Once gone, you can never get it back.'

Oddly, one of those same lifers enjoyed any violence directly involving
staff. On one particular day, an officer who had been calling for assistance,
was found locked in his cellblock, wrestling with the convicted murderer.
When we responded, we had to wait for the emergency keys to gain access
into the unit, so we could only standby and watch our brother officer get
stabbed fourteen times before we could enter through that steel barred
door. The assault occurred because of a personality conflict and the in-

mate's angry resentment toward authority. The officer, a good friend of mine, lived. The inmate, already serving two life sentences, was shipped out to federal custody."

Redman, gazing off in deep thought, shook his head in disgust. Finally, he continued, " Around that same time, we strongly suggested that a walk-through metal detector be installed inside the prison's entrance trap. This had not been done for fiscal reasons.

The wife of a lifetime member entered the institution wearing a long coat. Hassling the staff, who were searching her, she was quickly permit-ted to enter the institution in order to visit with her husband, Inmate Jones. With two pistols strapped to her inner-thighs, the woman entered the vis-iting room, kissed her husband and handed him the firearms. Jones imme-diately approached the visiting room officer and frantically demanded his freedom out of the institution. The heroic officer dryly answered, 'No.' He was shot once in the head, resulting in instant death. As we began to re-spond to the scene, Jones shot another officer who fell to the floor, but lived to tell about it. Inmate Jones, now knowing escape was impossible, grabbed his wife and ran from the visiting room into the court yard. Inside the yard, Jones killed another man. This person was one of the prison's shop instructors. As he entered his housing unit, Jones searched for the officer, but could not find him. Turning to an inmate worker, Jones asked where the officer was. The inmate responded he hadn't seen him. The madman replied, 'I'm out killing Screws and if I find out you're lying, I'll kill you too.'

Inmate Jones began destroying the living quarters, until finally bedding down with his wife. After having sex with her, he placed the muzzle of the pistol to her forehead and fired once, killing her instantly. Jones then turned the handgun on himself and shot one bullet into his own chest at point blank range. State police arrived on scene and began bombarding the housing unit with inconceivable amounts of tear gas. After a long while, they stormed the unit, only to find Jones and his wife had been dead for over an hour. No matter, this had been a dark day in corrections history. The staff, my friends, who lost their lives will not be forgotten." Redman's eyes swelled with tears. Robby excused himself and headed for the bathroom. After relieving himself, Robby waited a few more minutes before returning to the bar. He figured that his boss could use the time alone.

Eventually sitting back down, Robby poured himself another cold beer while Lieutenant Redman added, "Oh, by the way, as it turned out, the inmate worker had been lying. He helped conceal the unit officer who had been hiding in a closet nearby. Saving the officer's life, the inmate worker later received a commutation from the governor, pardoning him from the remainder of his life sentence. It's strange, but he was not the only inmate to have ever saved an officer's neck.

Same year, several months later, there was a librarian who had transferred to the position of correction officer. Entering the facility for the first night of the new duty, a confused and distraught inmate, high on drugs, shot this officer in the head three times with a zip-gun. The officer's partner, who responded to the scene, ended up trading himself, so that medical attention could be administered. This officer was then stripped naked and the remaining bullets in the zip-gun were emptied into his belly. Strangely and miraculously enough, both officers lived.

Exactly one year later, a female staff member was taken hostage and continuously raped for twelve hours. Again, snipers didn't have a good shot at the rapist and it had become extremely difficult to gain access into the barricaded area. Finally, we got inside and took the inmate into custody. The female staff member, evidently suffering from the Stockholm Syndrome, had requested to marry the rapist. That one made me sick, until I learned what the Stockholm Syndrome meant. She had become a sympathizer due to the trauma she had experienced."

Redman took a long swallow of beer, then continued, "There was even a conspiracy to assassinate the superintendent at the Hill. This scheme was intercepted just in time. The plan was that the superintendent was expected to be standing in the main corridor during the lunch meal 'Happy Hour.' A battle ax, with the head measuring over three feet in length, was fashioned in the industries shop. It definitely resembled a weapon carried by a knight of the Middle Ages. This weapon had been smuggled in and out of the institution twice. The first time to be sharpened, the last to be hidden.

At least two perpetrators from four different blocks were intending to 'take out' the officers assigned to the chow hall corridor. In other words, five officers were to be murdered simultaneously. A group was then going to walk past the Superintendent, while the inmate located in the center, was to swing the ax with hopes of beheading the 'Boss-Man' with one blow. The inmates involved in this conspiracy had just received a drug shipment and were planning to be high when the slaying was to be carried out. Two days before the murder was to transpire, informant information assisted in transferring all conspirators out of the institution. Some of them ended up in federal custody. It's funny, but I've often wondered if it was so good that the conspiracy was discovered...that superintendent was a real asshole."

Robby laughed, saying, "It sounds like those days were a good time." Redman chuckled, "They weren't all that big. On a smaller level, there were also fights between inmates and staff. On occasion, some officers ultimately fed up with an antagonizing inmate, would remove his shirt, symbolic of removing his status, and call the inmate on, to fight right inside of the block. These fist-fights would take place on the flats, or bottom floor. Other inmates looked on and often respect was only gained in this fashion.

One incident, where an emergency alarm was activated from the shop area, had thirty of us saturating the shops, but we couldn't find the officer in need of assistance. Eventually, the officer was discovered, with his shirt off, bravely fighting an inmate who was wielding a large shank. Though the officer had received several stab wounds and deep lacerations, he continued to fight for his life."

Redman ordered another pitcher, then returned to his memories. "Fights amongst inmates were a daily occurrence, with most getting way out of hand. In one situation, a fight broke out in the main yard involving one white combatant and one black combatant. In no time, the prison seemed to empty into the yard, filling with four to five hundred excited inmates. The blacks looking on from one side, the whites from the other. These inmates began demanding that four responding officers and myself, not dare attempt to break up the fight. Suddenly, a group of these yelling inmates started to push us, so we started pushing back. A sergeant then got struck over the head with a rock causing him to collapse to the ground. Just as a major melee started to occur, the tower officer fired several shots into the ground located near the disturbance. These flying bullets instilled reality back into the minds of the inmates, causing them to disperse.

The white inmate had been beaten severely. The fight was finally broken up by a couple of black inmates who had felt the man had taken enough. The white inmate was dragged from the yard, leaving us all shaken up as well.

Because of escalating tensions such as these, fights turning into mini-riots were not uncommon. Whether for racially motivated reasons or revenge, the list went on. The major fights occurred in the chow hall, blocks, yards, wherever. Many of these fights resulted in staff injuries. Most happened at night when there were less staff on duty and when almost all illicit activities were taking place.

It was a time when the pecking order, or prison hierarchy would fight for the top seat. As the old inmate code called for, an inmate's status was fought for and only the toughest and meanest would survive, or control these populations. The weak were left continually victimized, in protective custody or dead.

As the unrest continued, the extraction of inmates from their burnt out, flooded out cells was being practiced often and perfected. In one extraction, an inmate possessing a shank, refused to move from his cell to another. Tear gas was administered on the inmate, but to no avail. Apparently, he had become immune to the point where he could breathe, without so much as a cough. The move team was then sent into the small room and the inmate plunged his homemade knife right through the plexi-glass shield. The shield, no longer of any use, was sent out of the cell, striking the team leader, a lieutenant who was standing in the threshold of the room. The shank, which was buried in the shield, cut open the lieutenants leg, causing the old-timer to limp off of the tier, cursing the whole time. That same lieutenant shortly returned with another canister of tear gas to spray on the still non-compliant inmate. That lieutenant was a tough old bastard. Actually, most of the old-timers were.

Extraction teams were always suited up, always ready and seemingly always used.

However, these murders, rapes, violent fights or riots, assaults and hostage-takings, all vile in their own sense, are just a fraction of the horrors which occurred during that era."

Obviously intoxicated, Redman excused himself, then stumbled toward the bathroom. He returned within minutes, ordered another pitcher of beer, then grinning from ear-to-ear, he said, "There were also several ingenious escapes in those days. The most dramatic was when an inmate, called Hoppy, approached the block officer with several lacerations on his back. He claimed he had just been assaulted. The man then complained of chest pains, trying to convince the officer he was suffering from a heart attack. The inmate was immediately transported by ambulance to a nearby hospital for medical treatment. One officer was in the room, his partner carrying the firearm, was located in the hallway. That second officer was conducting a phone check with the institution. The inmate, lying on the examining table, was grunting in pain. He was just waiting for the big moment. It had been a short wait. A nurse entered the room, later identified as Hoppy's girlfriend in disguise, and handed the inmate an automatic pistol. Without delay, Hoppy sat up, pulled the I.V. out of his arm and wearing leg irons, he raced out of the room and down the corridor. The stunned officers took chase. They finally began firing at the escaping felon, as he jumped into the getaway vehicle. The officer had emptied all bullets into the speeding vehicle, but Hoppy had successfully escaped, unharmed.

Several years later, Hoppy, who was surprisingly not living the life of a productive citizen, got himself killed in a shootout with a Colorado Police Department. Hoppy's girlfriend, the merciful nurse, is still serving time for aiding in the well-planned escape.

Another escape occurred from the automotive shop located behind the massive walls of the Hill. The institution's priest had his vehicle brought in for minor repairs. This turned out to be the last element of an inmate's plan. The back seat had been removed and the inmate concealed himself behind it, returning the seat to its original position. The unsuspecting priest was then bid farewell by the other inmates in the shop, as he drove the stowaway out of the confines of the prison and into freedom. That inmate has not been captured to date."

Robby's head was spinning. Between the alcohol and the amount of information he had been absorbing, he started to forget why he had even entered the bar. Redman wrapped his arm around Robby, saying, "I hope I'm not boring you." Robby snapped, "Absolutely not!" The older man chuckled, asking, "Well then, where were we?" Robby shrugged his shoulders. Redman said, "Oh, I remember! Drugs were also a big factor adding to the problems of that era. There were thousands of drug related incidents, all leading to trouble. In one case, an inmate named Walton was a friendly prison junkie. He was caught by I.P.S. shooting up heroine into the foot of another inmate. As we rushed in, Walton went straight for his pants to 'tuck' the drugs and set of works. Both inmates were escorted to the prison's hospital unit where strip searches were conducted. Reluctant to remove the drug paraphernalia from his 'vault,' Walton was convinced that if he did not, then I would. Without further delay and knowing there were no other options, he removed a full set of works. The needle was bent over, with no cap covering the tip. There had not been enough time. Walton bled internally as a result.

A separate incident involving drugs happened several weeks later. While processing visitors into the institution from the outer control center, a female officer sensed trouble. She had already arrested better than a hundred visiting people for active warrants, attempts to smuggle in drugs...you know the deal. She was no stranger to this trouble.

Waiting in the lobby of the institution was a large woman, without doubt, as high as a kite, on some type of drugs. Approximately fifteen minutes had elapsed before a prison nurse exited the trap and left to go home. Without warning, the large visitor leaped up and assaulted the nurse. A struggle ensued involving our I.P.S. unit. State police were summoned to transport. The state trooper arrived on scene and assisted in subduing the crazed woman. During the struggle, the woman attempted to free the trooper's handgun from its holster. Eventually she was restrained, but not before every person involved realized that this 'drugged up' woman had the strength and endurance of many, with the intent to kill. Not all of the violence occurred behind the wall.

Without doubt, drugs attributed to many of the fights, assaults, extortions and even deaths back in those days. I don't know Robby, it's strange how some things don't change."

Robby agreed, but kept his comments brief because Redman was still on a roll. The lieutenant added, "There were also the inmates who enjoyed dabbling in pyrotechnics. One in particular was making a pipe bomb by packing match heads as tightly as possible into an ordinary hollow pipe. Without ever knowing it, the inmate packed just a bit too hard, blowing his face completely off. His intent had been to attempt to blow down the steel, exit door to the prison. Although this was an improbable scheme, the man had worked diligently for weeks.

Another, more ingenious inmate, sent out his television set for repairs. Concealed inside was a book bomb intended to take revenge upon the receiver who was a trial witness. The testifying witness did open the packaged book which exploded shrapnel into his face. The man did not die, but was scarred for life. It was another reminder that inmates were not cut off from the outside world. Some would strike out fiercely, even from behind those giant walls.

My favorite, the con-artists, were also in abundance as the department was evolving. At one time, there was a naive superintendent who had been clearly fooled by an inmate named O'Leary and his pack of thugs. This tough crew consisted of eight inmates. They devised an 'Inmate Committee' which used to meet with the big boss twice a week, for the purpose of identifying and solving problems within the prison. This committee had been more powerful than the officer's union at the time. During one meeting, O'Leary informed the gullible superintendent that there were many dangerous inmates within his population, who always carried weapons, namely shanks. The superintendent, with a head full of steam, ordered his staff to conduct a major shakedown during the early morning lock-down. Surprisingly, the information had been correct and all of the weapons were confiscated.

The following day, that same clique, or committee who had 'ratted out' the armed inmates, systematically beat each one until they could not be recognized. The committee members then took over the jobs of the beaten inmates who had been set up from the start. The jobs included work in the kitchen and canteen, as well as the property room. The plan had worked flawlessly and O'Leary and his merry band of hoodlums had used staff to get rid of their competition. They controlled the population for some time."

Redman finished his beer, then turned to Robby. He slurred, "Well, my drunken friend, I think that I've taken up enough of your time." Robby shook his head, "Are you kidding me, I could listen to these stories for hours!" Redman laughed. He stood up, placed his hand on his young friend's shoulder and concluded, "The examples of the extreme or normal situations of the past are endless. There are hundreds, no thousands of similar stories, experienced and observed by all of the officers of that time. Each staff member from that era has a piece of history that many people will never know or understand. In those years, on the best of days, you could cut the tension in the air with a dull butter knife. Just remember Robby, I know it can get tough sometimes, but I'm always here for you. And, I know that your crazy friends on the Bravo Team are there for you too!" As they paid the tab, Robby thanked his compassionate boss for the talk. He realized why Lieutenant Redman had shared his most painful experiences. The older man merely wanted Robby to know that things could always be worst, and at one time, they had been.

Like an intoxicated idiot, Robby jumped behind the wheel of his truck and started home. Driving slowly, he realized, "Corrections today is the result of the powerful struggles, sacrifices and changes of not so long ago. It was the officers on the line, like Redman, who steadily forged ahead to create an easier path for other staff to follow. Mistakes had been made, but were learned from. Control now lies in the hands of its rightful owners, the officers and administrators. It has been proven that the inmates couldn't handle the control when they possessed it. In major disturbances, which often become tragedies, the administration of today, must rely on its most valuable asset, its personnel. It will be the officer in 'the trenches' who will possess the information and instincts to prevent these crises, or at the very least, de-escalate them once they begin. May corrections never revert back to its old ways, but learn from the brutal lessons of the past and strive to better the working environment while maintaining complete control at all times, if only for safety sake."

Robby returned to work the following day. His head banged with every noise he heard, but he felt at peace. In a strange way, Lt. Redman's long-winded pep talk had given him a second wind. Not every doubt had been wiped away, but he decided to stay with Frank, Keith and John to meet the inmates head-on. Like always, each day was busier than the one before it.

Three short weeks after the talk, Robby responded to a 10-33, "Officer needs assistance." As he rushed up a flight of stairs, Robby saw the officer wrestling with a crazed inmate. Immediately, he attempted to restrain the assaultive bug. Before he knew it, Robby was tumbling down the granite stairs with the inmate in tow. He could feel each step pounding into his body. Within seconds, they landed at the bottom, with the inmate on top. Robby could feel a piercing pain in his lower back while the right side of his body throbbed. Looking up, he saw the boys of the Bravo Team pulling the lunatic off of him. That was the last thing he remembered...everything went black.

⑩

Robby Cabral woke up to the wails of a siren. As he opened his eyes, he saw Frank Gagne's tortured eyes staring down at him. Strapped to a stretcher, Robby finally realized that he was the occupant of a speeding ambulance. Frank asked, "How do you feel partner?" Robby winced in pain, but replied, "I feel better than you look, that's for sure." Frank laughed nervously. He said, "You took a pretty good fall buddy, but the paramedics say you're gonna be alright." Robby smiled, then closed his eyes again. The pain in his back and legs was almost unbearable. Before long, he was carried into the emergency room. It had taken hours before all the tests and x-rays were completed. Frank stood by his side the entire time.

The test results showed various sprains on the right side of his body. However, there were two discs which had dislodged in his lower back. It was those discs which were causing the intense pain. To the point of sedation, Robby was medicated, then released from the emergency room. Frank drove him home. On the ride, Frank said, "Well pal, it looks like you'll be out of commission for awhile. Take your time, but not too long, hah? In the meantime, we'll pick up the slack!" As always, Frank Gagne had been right. One week later, Robby limped into the office of a neurologist. The doctor quickly discovered a pinched nerve in Robby's lower back which radiated pain down his right leg. No doubt, he was going to be out of commission for awhile. Other than doctor's appointments and physical therapy sessions, Robby found plenty of time to do some soul-searching. Even after the encouraging talk with Lieutenant Redman, Robby still knew that he had his doubts about corrections. After nearly eight years, he finally had the time to realize the effects of the job. It was time well-spent.

Week after week, Robby mulled around the house, thinking about his chosen profession and his future within it. He knew that working conditions had changed dramatically for the better. However, problems still existed even amongst the rank and file. There was the issue of racism, where black and hispanic officers complained of discrimination based on bigotry and prejudice concerning promotions, job assignments, etc. White officers complained of reverse discrimination based on affirmative action regarding the identical issues. It was an age-old problem which seemed to diminish when an officer of any race was on the losing end of a fierce altercation, or found himself at the bottom of a pile of inmates. Suddenly, skin color seemed meaningless and all staff placed their ignorance aside, somehow becoming color blind, while seeing only one color, blue. Robby felt that it would be in the best interest of the entire brotherhood, if officers would remember those times of need. The times the assistance they so gratefully received from staff, who were that different skin color.

Turmoil had also been caused by the union which had been established for years. They had recently converted over by majority vote to a newly-formed union, run solely by and negotiating for, correction officers. This new union was adopted by a slim margin, therefore, officers' opinions were split and greatly differed. From parking lot brawls to the most bitter of feelings, those conflicts later subsided. Officers finally realized that their greatest chances for monetary and benefit increases in contract negotiations would be granted only if all officers unified. After years of working without a plan, a reasonably fair contract was ratified, proving again that strength could be found in numbers, on both sides. Robby had been more than pleased with the new contract.

Another huge trouble-maker for staff behind the wall was that the prison was a huge rumor factory. Referred to as the grapevine, much of the gossip was passed on from one officer to the next. Thirsty for information of any kind, staff eventually found that rumors were either so completely exaggerated or just not true. Normally everybody's name got thrown into the boiling pot, with stories from love affairs to inmate beatings. Due to this twisted grapevine, heated arguments had turned into nasty feuds.

Robby recalled an incident where two female officers, who were in full uniform, stood toe-to-toe in the parking lot and exchanged punches. It had occurred because one was discovered 'talking shit' about the other. The Bravo Team was dispatched to break it up. Another more volatile confrontation found two male officers drawing their own personal firearms on each other because of gossip which had completed its vicious circle and gotten back to each of the men. Unfortunately, interacting with criminals everyday, five days per week, some of their violent behavior was bound to rub off.

Surprisingly enough, of all the problems faced by Robby and the team, they agreed that the administration, with its daily inconsistencies and constant changing priorities, was the cause of the majority of the internal problems. Those problems included stress on staff and poor morale, which was generally felt by all. With politicians and correctional administrations here today and gone tomorrow, the very cornerstone or foundation of the profession were the officers who would tow the line for twenty or thirty years of their careers, their lives. Becoming creatures of habit themselves, officers found difficulty with changes, especially when a valid or rational reason could not be found. There had been fantastic administrations formed who had concentrated on security and the safety and well-being of its staff, while many others were determined to deal with less pressing issues. For instance, when security took a back seat to the cleanliness of a prison, staff felt as though their hands were tied and morale would drop through the floor. There had been administrators who had never had the pleasurable experience of dealing with potentially aggressive inmates. Yet, they began to change policies and procedures at will, implementing rules and regulations which were extremely difficult to enforce and for the most part, created chaos within the daily running of the population. Worst yet, those administrators could be replaced every few months by others with even brighter ideas, people who were less willing to listen to the line staff's strong suggestions. Most managers, attempting to make their mark for upward mobility, did not stop to think of the negative and long-lasting effects that they imposed on both inmates and staff. A smart administration would surround itself with competent and professional personnel, trusting those people to get the job done, while maintaining law and order.

Strictly concerning staff, some administrators focused all of their attentions on the behavior, appearance, attendance and promptness of their work force, while totally overlooking issues pertaining to inmates. This was considered harassment and managing through fear and intimidation by the Bravo Team, who claimed that problems dealing with convicted criminals were expected and would always exist. However, unjustified pressure from above only caused less effective line staff and animosity felt on both sides. Working in an uncivilized environment with criminals of every capability, negative pressures from management was recognized by the team to be the number one stress creator in the business. John Donovan had once said, "The inmates I can deal with, but it's the administration which is causing me the most heartache." Improvements in management were slowly making their way into the system with ex-federally employed administrators being aware of the abnormally negative experiences each officer had to endure. Therefore, although they continued to keep staff honest and 'on their jobs,' priorities fell upon the safe-working conditions and the all-around well-being of the officers who walked the line. Robby had served under both different styles.

As Lieutenant Miles forewarned years earlier, each officer was affected by working in such a hostile environment. It was unavoidable. The extent of the changes in an officer's life depended largely upon his own beliefs, attitude, goals and support which he might have received. However, Robby knew, only too well, that fate had sometimes played a part as well. Within the very best of circumstances, he would view the world differently. Any innocence once possessed had been wiped away, almost from the start.

Beginning his career in the correctional profession, Robby found it crystal clear that he was faced with difficult challenges that he had never dreamed possible. Getting through those hardships with the help of brother officers was good. They would form tightly knitted friendships, but if not balanced properly, this 'bonding' could easily ruin what used to be a normal, healthy home life. Working strange hours and holidays, with odd days off, Robby found himself associating with the team members while losing contact with friends outside the profession. Out partying until late with the 'boys' became habitual, a rut, and his family life began to suffer. Lieutenant Redman always said, "The only thing louder and more rowdy than a room of inmates is a room full of correction officers." Robby had sometimes forgotten that the most basic reason for being employed within the department was to put food on the table and provide his family with life's other essentials. The job was not who he was, it was what he did. It paid the bills. It was easy, however, to become engulfed, with his heart and soul being swallowed up by the job, losing a piece or all of his true identity. Dedication and pride within the profession was admirable, but it had to be kept in check. Robby learned that family had to come first.

Communication, or the lack of it, was a huge dilemma for the team and their families. They had experienced situations which were frightening, possibly traumatic. Rather than share or vent those experiences and the feelings that went with them, with their true partner, they kept it bottled up. Whether they believed their spouse was incapable of understanding, or felt they were protecting them from the horrors of the job, what they were actually accomplishing was shutting their families out. They put up barriers and carried the burden of their difficult responsibilities solely upon their own shoulders. Communication shut down and the boys turned to and confided with brother and sister officers, who they were sure would understand. Many extra-marital affairs were started because of those exact factors.

At one point, Robby even stopped listening to his family because he felt that their daily life experiences could not possibly match the trying times of his own. What he failed to realize was that whatever message, large or small, that his family was trying to convey, was very important to them and without any apparent interest on his behalf, the communication cycle had become completely severed.

Frank Gagne, who was both extremely competent and professional at work, admitted, "When I'm on the job I feel in control, but at home where there is less organization, I become frustrated." Apparently, acting upon his frustrations, his own children had told him, "Don't treat us like inmates." With that said, he had to take a step back to realize he was not leaving his job where it belonged, at the prison. Fortunately with counseling, he saved his marriage and family, but he was one of the lucky ones.

Other officers in the prison had emotionally or physically abused their families, taking the pressures of the job out on them. Those officers became no better than the inmates within their custody. The divorce rate in corrections was incredibly high due to lack of communication and infidelity. According to most, the stress of the job caused alcohol and drug problems. Another unfortunate truth was that spouses and family members of correctional staff were never credited for their support, though they were equally affected by the stresses of the profession. Robby realized, more often than not, it was those people who held it all together on the home front. He knew they should not have been overlooked. It would never happen again.

Stress, or more precisely distress, was among the highest percentage in this occupational group. Few would argue, however, that it could be controlled. The first step was to recognize whether an emotional wear and tear problem existed. If so, it had to be faced head on. Entering the academy, Robby was told that he may retire after twenty years of faithful service and immediately begin collecting a pension. However, statistically he would not receive many checks because the majority of officers died from heart-related diseases in their early fifties. This had been true, but for a variety of reasons, statistics could change. Not a physical job whatsoever, many officers sat, or stood around, eight hours per day. They performed routine duties which were occasionally broken up by an emergency of many types. Going from zero to one hundred miles per hour was not healthy for anybody's physiology, however, that was the nature of the business. What had been on the rise was that officers, like Robby and John, were entering the department younger and were forbidden to smoke due to the Heart Bill. Being better educated on good health, physical exercise and better dietary habits were also on the rise. There was a positive attitude which most fought to retain. Good mental health was critical while working in a world full of hopelessness and despair. Stress was a factor in all walks of life. The key was to control it by learning ways of coping. One of Robby's goals had always been to collect retirement checks way past the young age of fifty.

There was a stress unit set up within the department which was run by one man, a virtual God-send, but even he could only handle so much. Providing classes on proper stress management, this ex-officer in the strictest of confidence, had referred officers to psychiatrists and psychologists. Professionals who had provided hours of therapy for the stress-related problems suffered by many correctional personnel. From depression to anxiety disorders, some officers experiencing trauma had even been diagnosed with Post Traumatic Stress Disorder (P.T.S.D). Often meditation and other coping techniques were taught. There were those who were in undeniable need of sedatives and anti-depressants to get through each working day. On a smaller scale, the department's stress unit provided counseling as well, with a support group which met at different times.

The most difficult element of the job for Robby was letting go, relaxing and releasing what was bothering him. On the other hand, he had known that the smartest and strongest of men would cry privately, yet laughed in the face of a dangerous criminal. It was all about turning it on when needed and more importantly, turning it off and being yourself while at home. If not dealt with in that sense, even physical problems could arise to include ulcers, migraines and similar problems.

While on the job, training had taught Robby to remain objective, not to take anything personal. But, with even more years of training in being a human being, it was difficult to merely cast feelings aside, so that duties might be performed while staying unbothered, unaffected. A survival trait was to become hardened like the inmates for which he controlled and some officers were successful at this. However, in reality, Robby knew this was also sacrificing a piece of his inner-self. Looking at situations from two different extremes, it became evident why the job created such strong emotions which had to be suppressed.

Dealing with child molesters and sex offenders on a daily basis, Robby or his brother officers might have personally known a victim of one of those deranged men. Not only was he expected to, but he was required to treat that inmate without bias while providing anything that the sick man was allowed. Feelings of seething anger and hatred began to build, but the department had determined that a professional officer should handle those situations, as though no emotional factor was present. On the other side of the warped spectrum were two unrelated, but very similar cases involving Vietnam Veterans. Serving his country during Operation Desert Storm,

Robby had also experienced the horrors of War. It was those experiences which made him sympathetic to both veterans.

Records indicated both inmates had started life out on the right foot, but were drafted into the military where they were broken down and re-built as killing machines. Sent into a jungle to fight a hidden enemy in one of history's largest atrocities to date, those monsters returned after one year of combat. Unable to re-adjust normally into society, they both suffered from P.T.S.D.. Two of the U.S. government's killing machines had broken down and rather than become fixed or treated, one had slain his girlfriend during a drunken state. The other served time for a drug addiction which he also happened to pick up during his tour of duty.

The first of these veterans was found one afternoon, stark naked in an abandoned cell. He held a jagged shard of broken window pane to his own throat. Threatening to end his miserable life for the unforgivable crime he had committed, he began to convulse and froth at the mouth. He was suf-fering a seizure. While still coherent, Robby Cabral, an assertive officer with a military background, took charge of the shaky situation. He began screaming out basic military commands to include: Attention, Right Face, etc. and to the Bravo Team's amazement, the inmate complied with each barking order. The inmate's soldiering skills and training had been so deeply branded into his memory that during this time of crises, a few sim-ple orders had saved his life. It was later discovered that the ex-soldier had stopped taking his required medication. The Bravo Team foursome, who witnessed the unusual incident, felt only sympathy for the man, who was himself the victim of horrible circumstances.

The other veteran had been a P.O.W. during the Vietnam War and suf-fered severely from claustrophobia. Unfortunately, he was also prone to violent outbursts which he claimed he could not prevent, nor remember. After one of his vicious assaults, he was secured into a cramped cell. Sounding very much like a small child, the man begged each passing offi-cer to release him, swearing that he would not strike out again. Mental Health staff were not convinced of his promises, so he remained in the Hole. Walking by the ex-P.O.W.'s small cell, Robby found it difficult not to open the thick wooden door and free the man who was sure to suffer mentally for the rest of his life.

Justice had been very difficult to recognize in both of the veteran's situations. There was a widely used saying in the Big House that most inmates used. They would say, "Do not mistake kindness for weakness," so Robby closely watched his expressions of compassion which were rarely felt to begin with. Prison was not a place for the weak at heart and there was no room for feelings there, only duty. After such a tour of duty, all officers were released from the rat race and sent back into the human race. For some, the transfer was quite difficult. For others, it had proven to become impossible.

Robby had witnessed times when officers would just mentally snap. They lost it without any real warning signs. In one such case, an officer assigned to one of the gun towers, began to call out that he could see God. Telephone calls were made and snipers, brother officers of the man who had obviously lost touch with reality, were strategically placed in a nearby wooded area. With expert riflemen sighted in on a brother correction officer, a priest was sent out to the tower to counsel the sobbing man. Leaving the arsenal of weapons alone which were close at hand, the tower officer chose to speak with the priest. The men spoke extensively about God and the devil before the officer was talked down. Escorted out of the institution by the team, that officer, who was once known as "an Officer's officer", was forced into retirement. Prison work had taken its toll, leaving Robby and the others with a terrifying lesson.

Robby thought, "God and the devil. In prison, the inmates worshipped both and seemingly the works of the devil were all around. However, for the believers, God walked the line as well." For many Christian officers, like Robby, comfort was found believing in the Lord Jesus. He knew in his heart that he never walked alone. He felt that at the most trying times, he was carried on the shoulders of the Divine One. Without this strong faith, Robby believed he would not return safely to his home each night, because only God could get him out of the most terrifying situations he had encountered. Though, it was that very faith which often made his duties conflict with his peaceful spirit. For Robby, it was never easy.

Some officers, finding tremendous hardship handling the harsh realities of the job, attempted to leave with dignity. For some strange reason, perhaps that five year curse, staff did not normally just quit the profession.

Some were smart enough to leave when they had taken enough and never looked back. Others would begin to use up accumulated sick time, only facing more problems from the administration. There had been officers who had left on stress-related industrial accidents. This was not recognized as an honorable way out and most never returned. False industrial accident claims were filed and the officer hoped that the time off would place problems and the future into perspective. Some officers would reach the edge, but be able to pull back on the reigns and regain control of their lives. Others would take that final step over the edge and feeling despair, believing there was no other option, no other way out, they would commit suicide. Those were the officers who had hung it up or swallowed a bullet. Some of them had been Robby's friends.

With three years experience working behind the wall, one of those friends parked his car near the local pond. It was an incredibly serene location, where he had hooked flex hose from his vehicle's exhaust into the interior of the vehicle. The carbon monoxide fumes eventually caused him to sleep for eternity. Many people considered the suicide a cowardly act, but not Robby. As Lieutenant Redman explained, "If you have ever seriously contemplated suicide, the last thing that should enter your mind and body should be fear." No, this was not the act of a coward, it took nerve and may very well have been the last act of a desperate person who was not in his right state of mind. Each one of those deaths were no less than a tragedy. Robby felt there were always other options.

Countless other officers committed suicide over a prolonged period of time by poisoning their bodies with excessive amounts of alcohol and narcotics. Trying to cope with the job and its related problems, those self-destructive people abused themselves to the point where living to the age of fifty would be a modern-day miracle.

Those that were able to cope with the intense stress and frequent trials of spirit and courage still found that their lives had not been left untouched. The dangers of working in a prison did not remain behind the walls. Dealing with thousands of inmates coming and going, most who were unappreciative of the officer's responsibilities, unknown enemies were released and waited for the day when they could get back at an officer, any officer. While wearing the uniform which displayed the departments patch on one shoulder and the American flag on the other, each officer was a walking target while dressed in the attire.

Keith Petrie, who was leaving a late-night breakfast stop, was approached by a masked man. The masked man, who was never identified, yelled to Keith, "Hey, Screw!" The next thing he could remember were the lights from the emergency room shining into his eyes. He believed that his unidentified attacker, presumably an ex-inmate, had used a pipe to split his forehead open enough to require ten stitches. Another officer, confused about his jurisdiction, attempted to break up a bar fight by displaying his correctional badge. Not knowing it, one of the combatants had been an ex-con and immediately turned his violent aggression onto the unprepared officer. That officer was beaten so badly that reconstructive surgery of his face was needed. Unable to return to work and face other inmates, he too retired early in his career. Although traumatically victimized, he was lucky to be alive. There was no doubt that the hatred felt for all officers by that ex-inmate was taken out on that man, who was only looking to make peace during a brutal fight. Robby found that in any public place, at any time, contact could be made with an ex-inmate. Those meetings were usually uneventful, but he never knew. It was better that Robby stayed on his guard against an enemy he might not even know he had.

Survival techniques or traits learned and practiced inside often overlapped into Robby's personal life. At times, he found himself becoming cynical, almost sadistic in his thinking because of the hostility dealt with each day. Even within safe places within the community, Robby became just shy of being paranoid of all people. He became non-trusting and forever suspicious of being conned. Always on his guard, even while eating at restaurants, he would place his back to the wall because, in prison, blackouts occasionally occurred when all staff had to place their back to the wall in order to remain uninjured. It was difficult to turn those survival skills off after eight hours. Perhaps they were sunk too deeply into the mind. Inside prison, to anticipate a hostage situation or a unit arsonist at work was unreasonable. To be aware such incidents could occur, now that was a survival skill. In the real world, that level of awareness or anticipation was not needed, nor was it healthy. It had taken many years for Robby to learn to adjust.

Robby remembered a practical joke played on his balding, yet fun-loving lieutenant. The Bravo Team, working under Lt. Redman, had sent him an envelope via mail. It was full of long hair which had been confiscated from an inmate (possible escape tool). Enclosed within the package was a hilarious form letter allegedly sent by a fictitious hair replacement company. The letter read that this company had received a sample of the man's few remaining hair follicles and with extensive lab testing, they had closely matched it to the hair of a female baboon. Lieutenant Redman was advised to wear the hair weave for a couple of weeks before making his decision. The letter ended with a warning that he not "sport" the weave at any zoos or places which housed male primates because the company could not guarantee his safety. It had been a funny joke and although Redman laughed about it later, it initially caused him some serious anxiety.

Apparently years ago, he had been threatened by a fruitcake who swore vengeance upon him. When he opened his mailbox, he knew right away the package was a hoax. He automatically assumed that the old threat was being carried out. The job had some very unusual effects, though Robby knew that it was better that Lieutenant Redman remain on his guard because someday it might not be a practical joke.

The boys of the Bravo Team claimed to have a love-hate relationship with their jobs. Maintaining a positive outlook in a completely negative setting was a gift, which some of them possessed. They enjoyed the camaraderie the profession offered and the exhilaration the fight or flight response produced while reacting to an unknown emergency. They had all found self-satisfaction through their own merit and hard work. Courage, nobility, loyalty and that strong call to duty were the basis of their job performance. Those men were the true spirit of a correction officer. There were very few positive attributes offered by the job, with the exception of a weekly paycheck and good benefits. Therefore, the remainder had to be found within and shared with others through friendship, humor and most importantly, the knowledge that each man was there for the other, come hell or high water. Only very recently were officers recognized for twenty or more years of faithful service and this was established by a few correction officers through a retirement club.

From this largely thankless profession, there were very few pats on the back, though this too was slowly evolving. Administrators were attempting to recognize their staff with written commendations for a job well-done and a yearly awards ceremony for those who had performed above and beyond. One year, the entire I.P.S. unit had been the recipients of that award for shutting down the tax and mail fraud, as well as the telephone scam. There was also a Memorial Service held each year for officers who had given their lives in the line of duty. There was the Honor Guard which performed all funeral details. When an officer was laid to rest, he would receive full honors. Security was provided at the casket, with a twenty-one gun salute and "Taps" being played at the cemetery. Robby was always emotionally moved when watching officers stand shoulder-to-shoulder while they saluted their fallen comrade, as the Honor Guard folded the draped American flag into a perfect triangle. That flag was then handed over to the officer's spouse. It had taken one funeral before Robby fully understood the sacrifices of correctional service. His eyes filled with tears and a lump choked his throat, as he watched the fallen officer's spouse cling tightly to the flag, shedding tears of both pain and pride. Every correction officer's funeral proved to be just as emotional.

Lieutenant Redman had said, "An effective correction officer has to be able to adapt, adjust, improvise and overcome any obstacle placed in his way. Thinking quickly on your feet could make the difference between life or death." Yet, the profession was described as tedious, frustrating and monotonous work. Compared to a firefighter, sitting and waiting to go to work, correction officers might be sent into a unit set ablaze, save the lives of one hundred inmates, then not an hour later, find themselves in a riotous situation with a group of criminally insane inmates. Versatility was imperative, as officers drudged along within the same routine for months, but within a ten minute period of time, earn their money for the year. As a result, they probably lost time off of their lives for the stress experienced. Robby knew that correction officers got paid well for the dangerous potentials which lied within the tons of concrete and steel. However, he also knew that many of those potentials became realities which had to be dealt with.

Inmates residing in overcrowded, undermanned units, some temporarily sleeping in corridors or gyms only aggravated or magnified the many negative problems inside. With a concentration of potentially violent men, those convicted felons were not known for possessing well- developed impulse control or obedience to authority. Their behavior, both individually and collectively, was impossible to predict at most times. Their explosive behavior made them each a walking powder keg. Nevertheless, correction officers would not sway, as they continued to walk the line, maintaining control of those men who had been deemed unfit for society.

There was a theory, though cynical, believed by the boys of the Bravo Team. In an officer's twenty year career, it was probable that he sees the same faces come through the system five or six times. Basically, crime had to be big business. It employed millions, from the police officers, to court personnel, to the lawyers who eventually became legislators who created the laws, to the final dumping ground of the entire system, corrections. With those same members of society committing the greatest majority of the crimes, the boys wondered why stiffer penalties and longer sentences were not imposed. It was a good idea. However, if the judge placed a career criminal behind bars and insured that he remained there for thirty or forty years, then nobody could make any money off of that man for a very long time. Watching inmates leave, only to return months later was common. Release of the criminal would create revenue through his intolerable acts, but in the meantime, more innocent people were victimized. Perhaps even more changes were needed. With the economy down, crime rates up, business was booming in corrections, sometimes referred to as the cesspool of humanity. Lieutenant Redman had warned that his team keep their theory to themselves, though Robby was sure that he silently agreed.

After four months of analyzing the negative aspects and brutal effects of the job, the answer finally hit Robby with two rings of the telephone. He picked up the receiver and heard the long-lost voice of his police partner, Mike Ferreira. Mike asked, "How you doing buddy? I heard you were hurt at work."

"Yeah, some nut took me down a flight of stairs, but I feel better. I'm almost ready to go back," replied Robby, feeling curious about the call.

"That's too bad," said Mike, sarcastically, "I thought you would have wised up by now. To hell with hiding in that prison. Why don't you come back on the police force and deal with some real danger!"

Robby waited to hear some laughter, but there was none. His old friend was serious. Instinctively, Robby got pissed. He snapped, "Real danger? You've got to be kidding me. I've already done that police thing and it wasn't so hard! Why don't you come inside of the prison, tough-guy. We don't just arrest one or two, then drop them off. We actually deal with hundreds of them year after year!"

There was silence. Finally, Mike said, "Easy Robby, I don't know shit about corrections and I didn't mean to insult you."

Robby dropped his defenses. "That's the problem Mike, everybody in the world knows about your job, but even cops like you, don't know a thing about mine! I only wish you could see the prison through my eyes, or the eyes of any correction officer. I'm sure there would be a little more re-spect!"

Mike agreed and the two said their good-byes.

Robby hung up the receiver, then walked into his bedroom. Sliding open the closet door, he noticed his faded blue uniform hanging alone. Smiling from ear-to-ear, he removed it, knowing that it was time to go back inside.

Robby knew that he had made personal sacrifices and suffered job related problems, but he also knew that it was a public service which he helped provide. His job was to keep all inmates under lock and key regardless of the price to be paid inside. Though he was hidden from most people, Robby Cabral was making a difference. Of course, he wanted nothing more than better public relations which, in turn, would bring both recognition and respect to a job which many preferred others perform. There had been rumors through the grapevine that everyone expected a "Hot Summer." This did not refer to the weather or climate of the season, but meant that the inmate population would be heating up inside. It meant that together, Robby and the Bravo Team would be earning their pay, no matter the circumstances.

Robby reported directly to Lieutenant Redman's office the following morning. The old-timer stood up from behind his desk and extended his hand. Smiling, he asked, "How does your back feel?" Robby replied, "Better than ever!" Redman's smile grew wider. He asked, "How does your mind feel?" Robby chuckled. Redman was a smart man, but it was his concern that Robby appreciated most. Robby responded with confidence, "Better than ever! Though, it took some outsider to open my eyes and show me the truth. For one reason or another, the negative reality of this place has always clouded the reasons for which I work behind these walls."

Lieutenant Redman nodded his head with understanding, then as always, he offered his advice, "I believe that reality is only a person's perceptions of the world. In this world, an officer requires good vision to understand that reality can change from one minute to the next. Fortunately, you have re-discovered that reality behind prison walls, differs tremendously from reality of the outside world, that which is known to most people."

Robby thanked his boss, then headed for the door. As he turned back, he noticed Lieutenant Redman still standing. The older man asked, "Robby, why did you really come back?"

With the greatest sense of pride he had ever felt, Robby replied, "Because the men and women who work behind these prison walls are not guards, they are correction officers. I know that there will always be problems in this profession, but I've finally figured out that there is one constant. Most officers, like myself, would lay their own lives on the line for their brother officers, if only for one very simple reason...we all wear that same 'different shade of blue.'"

The End.